USING SOCIOLOGY

USING SOCIOLOGY

AN INTRODUCTION FROM THE CLINICAL PERSPECTIVE

Roger A. Straus

Alfred University

GENERAL HALL, INC.

Publishers

23–45 Corporal Kennedy Street
Bayside, New York 11360

USING SOCIOLOGY
An Introduction From The Clinical Perspective

GENERAL HALL, INC.
23–45 Corporal Kennedy Street
Bayside, New York 11360

Publisher: Ravi Mehra
Editor: Eileen Ostermann
Composition: *Graphics Division,* General Hall, Inc.

LIBRARY OF CONGRESS CATALOG CARD NUMBER: **84–081428**

ISBN: 0-930390-57-1 [paper]
     0-930390-58-X [cloth]

Manufactured in the United States of America

Contents

and Prisons 128, Sociological Intervention and Social Control 130, Concluding Remarks 132, Review Questions and Exercises 133, Readings and References 133

ABOUT THIS BOOK

The authors feel that the sociological perspective is eminently practical, that it has the power to change people and to change the world. This book will not only tell you about sociology but will show you how sociologists are using science to analyze social life and then bring their knowledge back into the world.

We hope that you will learn from this book how our perspectives, methods, and knowledge apply to the real world, and how *you* can make practical use of sociology in your own life, career, and field of study. This text is therefore meant to fulfill a variety of purposes to meet the needs and interests of different students.

Instructors will want to know that this volume has been designed for several possible applications. The basic material covered by conventional textbooks has been integrated within its ten, theme-oriented chapters. This book can thus serve as a basic introductory text or as a companion to other textbooks in general sociology and social problems courses. It can also serve as an introductory text in clinical or applied sociology. Each chapter is followed by thought-provoking review questions and an exercise, which is generally designed for small-group discussion. Our goal has been to provide a text that is at once accessible and interesting to the lower-division student, conveying the excitement and materials of contemporary sociology without sacrificing rigor or intellectual depth.

Using Sociology has been several years in the making. Initiated as a project of the Executive Board of the Clinical Sociology Association in 1980, it could not have been completed without the continuing help and support of the clinical sociology network. In particular, the editor would like to acknowledge the untiring efforts of former CSA president Jan Fritz and the faith that our publisher, Ravi Mehra, has placed in this first volume to be sponsored by the Clinical Sociology Association.

SOCIOLOGY AND THE QUEST FOR
PRACTICAL UNDERSTANDING

I might as well confess something right off: I've got the sociology habit and I've got it *bad*. Looking back over my life, I suspect that I have always been a sociologist in my heart and mind, although I never suspected it until a few years ago.

Maybe it was growing up in the "Sputnik era" that did it to me. From earliest childhood, I wanted to be a scientist. But in high school I had the chance to study with some "real scientists" and discovered that they were not supermen. I was disenchanted, began writing poetry, and looked for something else to do with my life.

At least from the time I entered college, I found myself on a quest, a quest for practical understanding of the world in which we live. By the mid-1960s, I definitely got the idea that something was wrong, that the things I had been told about people and the world just didn't add up.

Furthermore, I have always been a snoop. I have always wanted to know the rest of the story, to find out what lies behind and beneath the surface of things we see. I have always been constitutionally unable to mind my own business.

My first college career ended in 1968 when I finally walked out of college to explore life on my own. During this period, I learned a great many things that school could never teach me. About five years later, I was ready to go back.

I stumbled into an interdisciplinary social science program at Humboldt State University, up in the California redwood country. There I acquired the one true mentor I have ever known: T. Lane Skelton. I would like, in very partial acknowledgment of my debt to him, to dedicate my work on this book to Professor Skelton. He "turned me on" to sociology. That did it. I was hooked.

I found in sociology what I was looking for, a way of making practical sense out of the world. This discipline proved a perfect meeting ground of science, philosophy, and creativity. As a sociologist, I have professional license to indulge my passions, to probe behind the facades of life's drama, to follow my quest for a systematic understanding of what human life is all about.

Much about life is so obvious to us that we just don't see it. What we *do* see is generally seen only through the peephole of our isolated, individual perspective; we rarely glimpse the rest of the picture, we rarely see the pattern of the whole. Even when we do, the problem still exists that things are not always what they seem. That is where the challenge of social science comes in: how to make systematic, practical sense out of the whole.

Why bother? Of what value is "science for science's sake"? While there is certainly value in pure learning and the pursuit of scholarly knowledge, the role of clinical sociologist offers the opportunity to take science one step further and feed back that knowledge into the world, to make it a better place in which to live. In this way, I can feed my sociology habit and also do what I can do to make my life *count* for something.

That is why I am a sociologist, and, specifically, a clinical sociologist.

This is also, more or less, the vision of sociology shared by my coauthors in this textbook. Each of us has come to sociology in a different way, but each of us is dedicated to this *humanist* (people-centered, people-serving) ideal of sociology as a tool for practical understanding. We are all "turned on" by sociology. We all hope to share this passion with you.

Get ready to have your eyes opened, your mind exercised with startling new ideas. But, be forewarned: once you get the idea of the sociological perspective, you may find yourself hooked just as we have been!

Roger A. Straus
Alfred, N.Y.

January, 1985

Chapter 1   USING SOCIAL THEORY TO MAKE SENSE OUT OF LIFE

Roger A. Straus

The first and most basic fact of life is that each of us is aware of being alive in an ongoing world that we share with other people. Everything else is supposition.

As the American philosopher and psychologist William James (1842-1910) put it, the raw sensory environment is a "big blooming, buzzing confusion." Human beings transform the ceaseless torrent of experience into something that *makes sense* to us. We are compulsive about this. It is almost as if we were born "programmed" to make things make sense, to force reality into bits and pieces we can deal with — words, images, categories, and ideas. What is more, we have a need to organize these elements into some kind of picture or story to which we can relate; otherwise, they just don't make sense to us (Pepper 1942).

These "pictures" and "stories" are essentially what we mean by *theory*. We cannot act without theory. It is through theorizing that we make sense out of things.

Most of the time, most people operate on the basis of a kind of theory we know as *common sense*. Common sense is a potpourri of what we have learned from experience, intuited for ourselves, gleaned from others, or borrowed from the "conventional wisdom" (i.e., what most people concerned with a matter believe to be the truth). The problem with common sense is that it often betrays us — all too often, things are *not* the way they seem.

Our entire modern world is built on the idea that there is a better way to go about understanding the world than common sense. This "better way" is called *science*. Science is really a method for generating practical theory — practical in the sense that it fits the workings of the objective world. A scientific theory must always be derived from, restricted to, and tested against the external reality we directly or indirectly observe or experience. Rather than a set of *beliefs* about the world, science is actually a *method* for systematically building up a number of trustworthy theories about the world that we can use to understand what is going on around us, to predict and control the pattern of things and events.

The point I am making here is that theories are only stories we fit to the facts as we know them in order to help us make sense out of the patterns we perceive around us and within us. Theory is nothing to be frightened of: in

4

fact, it is something you already rely on in everyday life. The only difference between common-sense theories and those we call scientific is that the latter are usually phrased in a technical language and style and follow certain rules designed to keep them tied to the available facts (Handel 1982).

The Origins of Sociology

Another of these "programs" with which humans seem to be born is the need to have other people in our lives. We are domesticated animals; as children and as adults, we cannot live long without our fellow humans. We make our lives in society. We are, in the most literal sense, *social* creatures.

Sociology is the scientific study of the relationships between people and the patterns of social life. Thoughtful men and women have always sought to understand the workings of society and its effects on people, but it was not until the Industrial Age that the organization of society became an object of study in its own right or that the scientific method existed to permit the systematic investigation of sociological questions.

For most of history, human beings subsisted mainly through labor-intensive agriculture. They lived in harmony with the cycle of the seasons. Generation after generation, people followed the ways of their ancestors. Life might not have been too pleasant for most people most of the time, but the way things were could pretty much be taken for granted: Tomorrow would be pretty much the same as today, next year pretty much the same as this year. You could bet on it.

The Industrial Revolution shattered that traditional world. In just a few generations, mechanical technology broke down almost every aspect of the traditional order. The authority of the church; the divine right of kings; the ways things were done; even the sense of what was right, proper, and desirable—all were swept away by the values of the marketplace. Money became the sole measure of power; factories and mass production replaced ownership of land as the source of wealth.

People began to view themselves as individuals, demanding their individual rights. More and more, they left their homes and flocked to the new industrial cities in the hope of finding employment so that they could feed themselves and their families. Just as in the Third World today, this wave of industrialization brought with it previously unimagined population concentrations living in previously unimaginable conditions of poverty.

The great problem facing thinkers and institutions alike during the early nineteenth century was to find some way to cope with, and to understand, this suddenly changing world in which the very underpinnings of society had begun to come apart. At the same time, a new constructive force was at work in the Western world—the First Scientific Revolution.

The development of the scientific method first led to the theory and then to the technology required to build steam engines capable of driving industry. The physics of Sir Isaac Newton (1642-1727) triggered a breakthrough in humankind's ability to predict, control, and manipulate the forces of nature. As the Scientific Revolution gained momentum, it became apparent that enormous benefits could result from applying the scientific method to society itself.

Methods easily become ways of thinking and then come to be accepted as matters of faith. This happened with science; the First Scientific Revolution not only reshaped our material world but reshaped the way in which we viewed that world. Behind all the theories and controversies of the Machine Age lay an image of the "real world" as a kind of machine governed by mechanical laws of cause and effect, which scientists could harness to further human progress (Pepper 1942).

Put the last two paragraphs together, and you will see that it was almost inevitable that someone like Auguste Comte (1798-1857) would come along and invent sociology. Originally an engineering student in France, Comte became caught up in the social-reform movement of his time. Eventually he retired to a Parisian garret where he eked out a living as a tutor while pursuing his true passion, the creation of a science of society.

Comte envisioned *sociologie* to be an extension of physical science, to be based on material facts alone. He believed that scientific analysis of past and present societies would yield up the laws governing social life, just as it was yielding up the laws of nature. Initially he expected that progress to a scientifically based form of society was inevitable. Eventually, disenchanted with the course of events, he called for the establishment of a sociological church whose priesthood — sociologists — would guide this transformation of the social order.

Scientific progress soon came to be dominated by advances in biology. By the mid-nineteenth century, biological metaphors were replacing the older mechanical imagery, even in Comte's writings. This trend reached its culmination in the work of an Englishman, Herbert Spencer (1820-1903), with his analogy that *society is like a biological organism.* The "organismic" analogy both likens society to a self-regulating biological system and holds that societies evolve much like biological species do.

In fact, Spencer's immediate influence stemmed from his conceptualization of Social Darwinism, tying the ideas of biological evolution together with free-enterprise capitalism, which, as a good Englishman, he considered to be the pinnacle of human progress. Spencer's phrase "survival of the fittest" neatly captures his theme that those who win at the game of industrial life are the best adapted and so deserve the right to their wealth and power, while the losers deserve to lose. Needless to say, this theory was accepted by the "right kind" of people and strongly influenced the thinking of intellectuals in the United States and everywhere else wealth ruled.

There was, however, one social science, that had already undergone considerable development: economics. With the Industrial Revolution came the theory to guide and understand the economic form that went with it: capitalism. Accepted theories, however, presumed that people would be ruled by reason and would therefore make rational choices to the common good of society.

This was pretty hard to accept in light of how the capitalist system developed in Europe. Trained in law and economics, Karl Marx (1818-1883) became disenchanted with German society when he saw the terrible life conditions of industrial workers; he turned to radical politics as a strategy for resolving social injustice. Forced into exile, Marx went to England, where he developed a sociological perspective to account for these vast problems.

A valid theory of history and society, Marx argued, must be based on the material facts of life, not philosophical speculations. The specific forms that social relations in a society will take, he held, will be determined by (and only by) how work and production are organized in that society.

Marx proposed that the capitalist system is based on the fact that workers must sell their labor to factory owners in exchange for wages on which to live. As owners make their living off the profits they squeeze from the factories, they have every incentive to exploit the masses by keeping wages low and prices high, while ignoring the plight of workers and their families.

Marx contended that every aspect of social life is patterned on these economic relationships — a theory known as *economic determinism*. Marx's theory directly contradicts the "social systems" approach of Spencer and others, who held that the normal state of a "healthy" society is one of harmony. Social conflict, said Marx, is universal.

Once again, it all boils down to economics. With capitalism, you need money to obtain the necessities of life for yourself and your family, yet there is only so much money to go around. Everyone, therefore, is forced to compete for a share of the pie. Economic relationships place groups of people in the same position in this contest, creating *social classes* and pitting them against one another — owners versus workers, for example.

History, to Marx, was the story of class struggle. One economic system might replace another, but the same old conflict between the haves and the have nots remained. One group comes to power, takes over the means of economic production, and becomes the ruling class of society, living off the sweat, toil, and suffering of the rest. Marx believed that the capitalist system would be the last straw, that it would finally drive the lower classes to rise up and take control of the factories for themselves. Then there would be no more classes and no more struggle, and humanity would at last be free. For Marx, as for Comte, sociology was a *clinical* science whose purpose was to find solutions to social ills (Lee 1979).

The Establishment of Sociology

Toward the end of the nineteenth century, the Industrial Revolution was pretty much complete in Europe. Things began settling down, and so did sociology. During this period sociology was firmly established as an academic discipline and began taking on the form and style we know today. As social conditions became less tumultuous, sociologists turned their attention to more abstract questions concerning the nature of society and its institutions.

Perhaps more than anyone else, Emile Durkheim (1858-1917), a Frenchman, can be credited with establishing sociology as a formal social science. In addition to his ground-breaking methodological contributions, Durkheim established the principle that *the social order exists as a reality in its own right,* not merely as a by-product of economic, biological, or psychological causes.

For Durkheim, society's existence was external to its component human beings in the same way that an organism consisted of the relationships between cells and not the cells themselves. This led to a *macrosociological* approach, meaning that concrete social phenomena came to be viewed from the perspective of their relationship to the whole society.

The basic unit of sociological analysis, in Durkheim's view, was the *social fact,* an element of the overall pattern that shapes human behavior. Social facts, in this original sense of the word, include laws, customs, beliefs, rituals, and all the social rules governing life in a society. Such things can be explained only by reference to the society and their relationship to the social order: *Social facts must be explained by social causes.*

This led Durkheim to propose *functional analysis* as the main explanatory principle in sociology. If society is indeed like a biological organism, then its parts are linked together by the exchange of functions necessary to the survival of the whole. In explaining any social fact, the main thing you want to know is, What function does it serve? What role does it play in the total scheme of things?

Why do we bother with sociology, then? Because it offers a scientific alternative to the vagaries of common sense. It provides a way of making "uncommon sense," which in turn enables us—individually and collectively—to understand and do something about the way things are. (This paragraph is, of course, an example of functional analysis.)

The other towering figure in the establishment of sociology was Max Weber (1864-1920). In effect, much of Weber's work involved a critical reexamination of his countryman Marx's thought. Weber rejected economic determinism as too simplistic, favoring a multidimensional analysis of the social order in which the basic focus is *social action.*

For Weber, the individual and his or her social acts are the building blocks of society; the individual is the sole carrier of meaningful conduct, so the forms and structures of the social order must be dealt with as categories of human interactions rather than as functions of society or effects of "more real" causes. An adequate theory of society, he argued, must reflect the complexity of social life and social causation in a systematic way.

In contrast with both Durkheim's functional view and Marx's economic determinism, Weber brings into social theory the role of ideas, meanings, and motives. In order to understand social action, he held that one has to consider both the objective facts and also how the human beings concerned understand what they are doing and why. One must have *Verstehen,* a German word combining connotations of our English "understanding" and "empathy."

For Weber, capitalism is not a natural development spurred on by the forces of history, as Marx would have it, or a response to the "needs of society," as Durkheim or Spencer might put it. Rather, capitalism is a specific social form whose origins lie in a combination of social, economic, and religious factors. Weber ascribes the emergence of this particular system to the "Protestant ethic" of Northern Europe; given similar historical conditions, the Catholic Mediterranean societies underwent no such transition. Beliefs, since they affect what people do, can sometimes change history.

The Second Scientific Revolution

The nineteenth-century sociologist was a child of his time; his "science of society" was necessarily modeled after the natural sciences of the First Scientific Revolution. By the end of the century, however, the leading edge of the physical sciences was moving far beyond the Newtonian model of the universe as a predictable cause-and-effect machine.

A Second Scientific Revolution was in the making, one in which the theme (even of physics) became not "predictability" but "relativity." The key figure in this shift was Albert Einstein (1879-1955), who showed that the fixed and objective reality central to "empirical science" is little more than a veneer overlaying a mysterious *space-time continuum* in which even solid matter proves to be a dance of energies, in which "the facts" prove relative to both the observer and the act of observation. Thus the natural order on which the First Scientific Revolution was premised now rested on a larger, fluid reality characterized by novelty and change. While patterned, this reality is never still; webs of chance and causation lead to a complexity beyond comprehension.

A second building block of the "new science" was the principle of *complementarity* worked out by physicist Niels Bohr (1885-1962), who recognized that *seemingly contradictory descriptions of the same thing may all be valid.* For example, photons, units of light energy, are shown by one set of experiments to be waves; another set of experiments shows that photons are "actually" particles. Bohr concluded that both statements are true.

How can this be? Bohr proposed that there can be more than one valid description of the same phenomenon, depending on the mode of observation: What seem to be contradictory findings may really be *complementary.* Each way of looking at the phenomenon is valid insofar as it goes, but remains essentially incomplete; the complete picture requires one to adopt an expanded frame of reference that includes both models as *alternative truths.*

Again and again, the existence of competing theories of society is held to be evidence that sociology is "not yet a real science." This is ironic in view of the fact that physics — the usual role model for "real science" — now accepts the possibility of alternative truths. These different social theories, therefore, may represent another case of complementarity; rather than haggle over which theory is "true," we might be better advised to inquire about the complementary insights contributed by the different perspectives in sociology.

In the spirit of the Second Scientific Revolution, let us now turn to the four major *paradigms,* or theoretical perspectives, dominating contemporary American sociology.

The Empirical Paradigm

Classical sociology combined three basic elements: a macro-sociological focus on the problems and concerns of whole societies; a belief in progress as the natural outcome of applying the scientific method to the social order; and an acceptance of the First Scientific Revolution's conception of a machinelike universe governed by material forces following natural laws of cause and effect. All three elements seemed to go together.

So-called empirical sociologists (e.g., Lazarsfeld 1955) have sought to make sociology "more scientific" by, once again, borrowing from the "hard" sciences. They have employed sophisticated mathematical analyses with their data as if "the facts" could speak for themselves. Actually, what they have done is simply to adopt the nineteenth-century scientist's paradigm of an objective external universe driven by material forces as the *only* reality. This underlies their contention that scientists should consider only those phenomena that can be counted, measured, or otherwise treated mathematically.

Their assumptions are questionable, to say the least. Not everything can or should be quantified. "Number crunching" for the sake of "number crunching" might give the appearance of "real science," but it tends to produce little or no information of value. Nevertheless, it is essential to acknowledge the value of quantitative (mathematical) methods in social science. The power of these methods has been enormously enhanced by the development of computers; now computations that once were all but impossible are available to anyone who takes even an introductory course in computer methods.

Used with discretion, quantitative techniques are invaluable; sociologists simply could not do without them. Moreover, empiricists such as Lazarsfeld have been instrumental in bringing sociologists' attention to the fact that since a theory in science is a statement claiming a certain kind of relationship between two or more things, we must take great care to be both clear and precise in conceptualizing *what* it is we are talking about and in identifying the objective *relationships* between these things.

Theoretically, perhaps the single most important contribution of the empirical paradigm is its insistence that *one cannot ignore the material elements of social situations.* Some contemporary empiricists, calling themselves *sociobiologists,* argue that social patterns and social behavior are nothing but the effects of genetic "programming" (Wilson 1975). This seems to be an overly extreme position, but it may serve to correct the opposite tendency of many social theorists to discount entirely the role of our biological "hardware" along with such other objective factors as environment, economics, and material technology.

This paradigm also contributes a tool of enormous practical value, *functional analysis,* which is one of the most generally applicable explanatory principles in social science. As Durkheim suggested, in explaining a social fact, the main thing you need and want to know is, *What function does this serve?*

This is a question of common sense. If I were to tell you about a friend of mine (I really do have such a friend) who runs the Quattwunkery, I bet your first question would be, "But what does he *do*?" The sociologist asks the same kinds of questions about sociological things: What need does this serve? What role does this play in the total scheme of things? (My friend, by the way, does research, design, and contract manufacturing for the electronics industry—so now you know.)

The empirical attitude, then, is central to a sociological perspective. One needs to know, in concrete detail, how things actually happen to be and how they work if one is to have any practical control over events and their outcomes. Nevertheless, one can maintain this essential discipline yet accept neither the self-styled empiricist's beliefs about the universe, nor his or her blind faith in quantification.

As a student, you will find it well worth your while to acquire a familiarity with at least elementary statistics. But you can already use the practical insights of this paradigm. All you need do is to apply an empirical attitude, asking four basic questions of any social scenes or situations that puzzle you or that you are curious about:

1.   What are the *material facts* of the case?
2.   What are the *objective conditions* here?
3.   What *functional relationships* are involved?
4.   What can be *predicted, changed,* or *controlled?*

The Conduct Paradigm

Most classical European social theorists shared a belief in *social determinism,* the idea that social forces cause and control our beliefs and behaviors. This premise did not sit well with Americans, given our cultural tradition of rugged individualism. Out of this conflict between liberty and determinism, an alternative paradigm was synthesized by American social theorists associated, for the most part, with the University of Chicago in the first decades of the twentieth century.

The core of this paradigm is the premise that *conduct* distinguishes the behavior of people from that of the rest of the animal world. Conduct is self-conscious, voluntary yet conventional behavior oriented toward goals that are not immediately present (Wirth 1931). That is, conduct represents a sort of balancing act in which the individual strives to satisfy his or her personal needs and desires while following rules learned in lifelong exchanges with other people. Conduct, in effect, lies at the interface of the individual human organism and society; it emerges from that confrontation. The *conduct paradigm,* then, stresses the working out of social order in the exchanges between discrete human beings.

Although foreshadowed in the writings of Weber and others, this paradigm was first brought together by George Herbert Mead (1863-1931) in his graduate seminars on social psychology. For Mead, humans do not just react to empirical stimuli as the lower animals do; we act according to *how we interpret things to be*—according to the *meanings* we have learned to ascribe to objects, others, and events. By representing and then communicating meanings to one another in the form of *symbols* (words, gestures, or things standing for the qualities of something else), we become able to share understandings with our fellow humans. This, then, is the basis of social cooperation and, hence, society; according to Mead, it is also the origin of our sense of self, who and what we are in the real world.

This is a model of liberty in that, while symbolic exchanges shape our perceptions of reality, through our social interactions we simultaneously shape the world. Not the raw empirical nature of things but their meaning to human beings is what matters from the perspective of this paradigm. The atomic units of sociology are neither "the data" nor "social facts"; rather, they are the *social acts* by which meanings are created, expressed, and impressed on others and the world. Conduct is the stream of these social acts.

Such flowing, process-oriented language is characteristic of this paradigm's many contemporary variations, or "schools," of theory. All focus on the creation of social reality through meaning-filled acts. All agree that the acts of the actors involved in any situations are what, in effect, define that situation for all concerned. The various theories differ, however, with regard to the weight they give practical, structural, and other nonsubjective elements in the organization of social conduct.

One approach, *symbolic interactionism,* is almost antiempirical in orientation. Developed by one of Mead's students, Herbert Blumer (b. 1900), this school stresses the emergent, ongoing construction of social life. Blumer focuses on the process by which humans interpret and reinterpret one another's meanings as they engage in social interaction, building up their own lines of conduct and fitting together joint lines of action. For Blumer, society *is* symbolic interaction; the center of interest in sociological analysis lies in capturing this fluid process by which meaning emerges in everyday life.

On the other end of the spectrum lies an approach that takes as its theme Shakespeare's analogy that "All the world's a stage/ And all the men and women merely players." This form of conduct theory, known as the *dramaturgical paradigm,* was originated by Erving Goffman (1922-1982). Here, life is seen as a kind of improvisational theater. This analysis, therefore, employs theatrical terms. One looks at actors and their acts and compares their performances "onstage" with their "backstage" conduct. One explores how social actors *strategize* to manage their acts, convey impressions to their audiences, maintain a stable impersonation of "themselves," individually and jointly go about *doing social life.*

The dramaturgical approach, in contrast to Blumer's symbolic interactionism, implies that people and groups need to get certain kinds of things done in order to manage the business of living; it accepts a form of functional reasoning. It also accepts social structure as an emergent element of the actor's *context,* or total situation, along with other physical, symbolic, and interactional factors. It treats context, in other words, much like the fiction writer treats a character's setting. Action is viewed as both directed toward and structured by the situations in which social actors find themselves; thus, *situated action* replaces Blumer's *exchanges of meaning* as the focus of investigation and analysis.

The conduct and empirical paradigms represent polar ends of the scientific spectrum. Where the empiricist asks Why? the conduct theorist asks How? Research and analysis guided by this paradigm, therefore, utilize *qualitative methods* designed to grasp the flowing processes of social life. Where conventional forms of science aim to discover laws underlying observed phenomena, the conduct approach is concerned with generating concrete or *substantive* theory, capturing the ways in which people do social things (Lofland 1976). This paradigm views people as creative subjects actively engaged in living, rather than as objects of external or internal forces making them do what they do.

This paradigm, then, enables us to make sense out of the open-ended processes by which human beings construct the realities of social life. It is essentially *microsociological* in that it builds our understanding of the whole from this concrete level upward, viewing society in terms of the individual conduct of concrete humans.

You can use this paradigm, too, as a student of social life. To make sense out of what's going on, just check out the action with these four basic questions:

1. What is the *script,* or *story,* here?
2. Who are the *actors?*
3. What are their *acts* (strategies or performances)?
4. What *meanings* are being defined or exchanged?

The Systems Paradigm

Conduct theorists disagreed not only with the mechanical imagery of classical sociology but also with its emphasis on the whole society as the starting point of analysis. In the 1930s, however, when the hub of American sociology shifted from Chicago to Harvard and other elite Ivy League schools, the social systems concept was restored to a central position in social thought, largely due to the influence of German-educated Talcott Parsons (1902-1979).

Parsons was concerned with developing a theory of the social system combining the best of classical theory with the insights of the Chicago School. His approach, known as *structural functionalism,* dominated sociology for several decades. Set forth at the highest level of theoretical abstraction, *grand theory,* the approach views society as made up of individuals coordinated into a functional system through the operation of specialized subsystems creating certain "regularities" in social action. These more or less stable patterns of conduct are identified as the structural elements of society: roles, collectivities, values, and norms.

Intellectually, this is a beautiful model. Nevertheless, even Parsons's students found it difficult to relate its abstract considerations to concrete issues and concerns. This led Robert K. Merton (b. 1910) to propose *theories of the middle range* that would relate the structural-functionalist model to areas of substantive concern in such a way that they could be tested empirically. Merton also gave sociology the enormously useful distinction between *manifest* and *latent functions,* that is, what something is supposed to do and seems to do versus its unanticipated, indirect, and often long-term consequences.

Form follows function in Parsons's and Merton's views. Social arrangements are the way they are because that is the way society needs them to be. They are, in short, *functional.* Thus, the explanation for why some people are poor and some are wealthy is that some social roles are worth more to society than others. The only reason conflicts or problems occur is that things may get out of kilter from time to time — the healthy state of society is one of harmonious equilibrium.

Structural functionalism was far ahead of its time in anticipating the modern systems approach, but it remained tied to nineteenth-century empiricism, relying, for example, on Durkheim's functional model of society. In addition, it shared the pro-Establishment bias of many nineteenth-century systems theories. From this perspective, the value of things to society-as-a-whole is what counts; keeping the social system working is treated as of the highest importance.

The basis for a true *systems paradigm* was developed only after structural functionalism came into prominence. First conceptualized as an independent discipline by Ludwig von Bertalanffy (1901-1972), this "science of systems" offers a clear alternative to both the empirical and conduct paradigms. Its central proposition is that all sets of interdependent parts — that is, all *systems* — follow similar "general systems laws" regardless of what *kinds* of parts they are composed.

For example, the properties of a system are held to emerge from the interrelatedness of its parts. They cannot be predicted from knowledge of these parts alone; in fact, the behavior of the part is considered to be very largely shaped by its relation to the whole. This is the principle of *wholeness.* Another systems "law," *equifinality,* states that different systems may arrive at the same place from different starting points by entirely different routes. Thus, for example, one can begin to understand how it is that American and Soviet societies keep becoming more and more alike, despite their enormous substantive differences.

Living systems have several properties not shared with many other kinds of systems. They are dynamic, always in a state of flux. They maintain themselves through processes of mutual adjustment, such as *feedback*, the arrangement by which a change in one element triggers compensatory adjustment in the other parts of the whole so as to maintain the systemic order.

A very important characteristic of living systems is that, like electronic computers, they are coordinated by *information* rather than mechanical linkages. Living systems, additionally, are able to use information about their environment and about the results of their behavior to modify their subsequent behavior. They can learn.

Human systems are a special form of living systems. Often known as social systems, they consist of human actors in identifiable relationships linked together by exchanges of information into an interdependent whole. Each participant in the system plays his or her role as part of a larger acting unit, which can then interact with other systems at a higher level of organization. One can, in other words, identify systemic relationships *between* systems. Thus, society can be viewed as a complex of what my colleague, Thomas Leitko (1984), terms "nested social systems."

In the sociological systems paradigm, then, the center of focus becomes the *configuration* of human systems. The systems thinker wants to know what the patterns are, how the elements of the system are tied together, and how it flows (i.e., how inputs enter the system, how they are processed within the system, and how or what the system outputs). The identical analysis can be applied to a single discrete system, such as a family, or to how one system links into another, such as the complex system formed between families in a community.

Systems theory frees this paradigm from the shackles of the First Scientific Revolution's mechanical reasoning. If *information* can serve as the organizing basis of systems (rather than cause-and-effect relationships), then the question is opened up: What alternative social configurations are not only *possible* but *preferable?* Think about it.

In the meantime, you can begin to apply a systems paradigm on your own. Here are the questions to ask:

1. What *systems* are you looking at here?
2. What *units* are this system composed of?
3. How are they *related*?
4. How does the whole thing *work?*

The Ecological Paradigm

One limitation to the applicability of a systems perspective is the degree to which concrete social phenomena are actually integrated into systems. What if, for example, the whole society cannot legitimately be described as a cohesive system? Even if it is like a system, how can we explain the way in which the social system is arranged (Mayhew 1971)? What if the structure of society was essentially arbitrary, based on the exploitation of one group or population by another?

Precisely Marx's point, this was taken up again by those who questioned the structural-functionalist's pro-Establishment belief that our society is a true system whose social structure flows from necessity and that its normal state would be one of health, harmony, and prosperity for all. Known as *critical theorists,* social scientists (e.g., Darhrendorf 1959) who questioned this belief held that it was nothing more or less than a rationalization for an oppressive social arrangement based on economic inequality—and that there was nothing natural or necessary about it. C. Wright Mills (1916-1962), for example, expressed deep concern that American society was splitting up into a tiny *power elite,* which controlled the nation's wealth and resources, and an essentially powerless *mass public* of consumers whose lives and fortunes were being subtly manipulated from above (Mills 1958).

Conflict, rather than some disease of the social system, is a pervasive fact of social life. It all boils down to the question of power—who gets the goodies, whose interests get advanced over those of others. In the struggle between social groups or classes the party that gets the upper hand seeks to maintain its power by building the arrangement into the social structure. The rest lose out. Thus, for critical theorists, the primary focus of interest becomes these social arrangements and their relationship to the question of power (Mills 1959).

Other approaches also sought to correct aspects of Parsons's grand theory, which by about 1950 had come to be *the* accepted sociological perspective. One was *exchange theory,* in which society was viewed as a series of interpersonal and intergroup transactions, or *exchanges,* where each party seeks to maximize its benefits (Blau 1964; Homans 1973).

However, if any party feels that it has been cheated—more technically, that accepted norms governing *reciprocity* have been violated—then it will act to restore an acceptable balance. The parties to the exchange might, for example, simply work out some kind of deal. Thus this theory suggests that competition need not always lead to conflict. On the contrary, it holds that by protecting their own self-interest, competing groups actively maintain the social equilibrium that Parsons's model sought to explain.

Yet a third perspective, known as *human ecology* (Hawley 1950), emerged in that same period after World War II. This theory emphasizes systematic relationships between human populations and the natural environment. In contrast to structural functionalism, human ecology views technology, population characteristics, and the structure of the physical environment, rather than the needs of society, as the primary determinants of social organization.

These three approaches — critical theory, exchange theory, and human ecology — all seem to be converging toward a true *ecological paradigm,* the groundwork for which had been laid out before the 1930s Depression by members of the Chicago School. Situated as they were in one of the nation's largest cities, these sociologists had come face to face with the massive social problems created in America's rush to become a major industrial power after World War I. Insights from the conduct paradigm were then applied to the problems of the industrial city by a group of researchers led by Robert E. Park (1864–1944).

The work of these researchers resulted in an entirely new approach in which they analyzed the urban community as if they were naturalists studying a complex biological habitat in which distinctively structured populations adopt collective and individual strategies for coping with their social and material circumstances. The focus of interest became the patterns of social relations worked out in this process.

One spinoff from this "urban ecology" perspective was the emergence of *clinical sociology* as a subdiscipline concerned with using sociological method, concept, and perspective to help individuals and groups overcome social problems and gain more active, self-determined control over their lives and circumstances. This seems to be a "danger" of the ecological perspective: Scrutinizing the pattern of social arrangements tends to elicit a desire to do something about the problems and injustices built into the structure of social life.

Building on these foundations, we can now bring together the outlines of an *ecological paradigm.* Viewing society in terms of the patterns of social relations between and within groups and classes, as well as the relationships between these patterns and material factors such as geography, technology, resources, and population density, this ecological paradigm focuses on the *social arrangements* worked out between the constituent groups of society and their consequences for people.

When, from the perspective of this paradigm, one speaks of "the social system," one uses the term in the gambler's sense of *the System,* referring to how the game of society is rigged. The analysis of social reality in terms of group strategies of competition, conflict, or cooperation suggests that life can be described as an never-ending contest whose goal is optimal survival. But for whom?

That is always the big question. If life is a contest, at least so far in history it has been one where the players divide up into teams and then try to beat everyone else to the prize. People align themselves on different sides based on their differing interests or allegiances. They then engage in various *games* involving some combination of conflict and cooperation. These games of social life are peculiar in that the rules must be continually worked out or negotiated as play evolves; life, obviously, does not come with a booklet of instructions.

In analyzing society ecologically, then, one must be extremely sensitive to conflicts between the interests, the stated and unstated goals of the different groups of players. One must always look at the question of power, for built into the structure of the games people play there is always a catch: The winner gets to define a social arrangement in which he or she comes out on top.

Throughout human history, groups have been playing the same games of narrow self-interest, trying to capture the playing board of society to further their own power, privilege, and prestige. Today, however, the stakes have been raised beyond imagination. Given nuclear weapons, biological warfare, over- population, and pollution of the land, water, and air, along with exploitation of natural resources, the old rules simply *must* change. Sociology has become a necessary science whose bottom line is, How can we *all* survive?

Getting back to a more immediate level, you can begin to use this ecological paradigm in your life by asking the following four questions:

1. What are the *social arrangements* here?
2. What are the different *teams* or *sides*?
3. What are their various *games*?
4. What *strategies* and *tactics* are being employed?

Complementarity and You

Taking into account the insights and approaches of these four paradigms, we can now settle upon an inclusive definition of modern sociology: *Sociology is the systematic study of social relations as they emerge within and between human groups, systems, and communities.*

From the perspective of complementarity, we can describe the ecological paradigm as that "expanded frame of reference" within which the others may serve as alternative truths. This ecological approach focuses on the *interplay between acting units* in a manner compatible with each of the other three. However, this "master paradigm" both enables us to see how they all fit together and incorporates additional information to that supplied by the complementary alternatives. In other words, you do not have to pick and choose between them; you can use them alone or in any combination that suits your needs.

What are your needs as a student sociologist? To the degree that you take the role of a scientist, you want to be able to predict, control, or change the patterns of social life. In your role as a college student, you want to be able to gain a better understanding of people as they relate to your particular major field. Finally, as a human being and a student of life, you want to be able to understand, interpret, and (one hopes) finesse what is going on in the world around you. For all these purposes, you can now use sociological theory to sensitize yourself to the patterns of the human world, as well as to help you devise the best way to do the things you want to do and get what you, personally, want out of life.

Why bother with social theory? Because it allows you, as I have been saying from the beginning, to make practical sense out of your life. In the chapters that follow, you learn how these same basic ideas, concepts, and perspectives are used by professional sociologists. But remember, you can use them also!

Review Questions and Exercises

1. Explain how the principle of complementarity helps us understand the special contribution of each of the four paradigms discussed. What does each add to our total understanding of social reality?

2. Write out exactly what you have done today, from the moment you awakened till now. How did you understand why you did each thing you did today? Now analyze your behavior from the perspective of:

   a. conduct

   b. systems

3. This exercise is best done with a group of four students. Select a news article of major regional, national, or international importance. Analyze what is going on from each of the four paradigmatic perspectives, using just the four questions listed at the end of each section in this chapter. If working in a group as suggested, have one student take a single perspective; after doing this, the group members should share how each of them analyzed the situation sociologically and then discuss the differences and similarities between the information each paradigm teases out of the total situation.

Readings and References

Bateson, Gregory. *Mind and Nature: A Necessary Unity.* New York: Dutton, 1979.

Berne, Eric. *Games People Play.* New York: Grove Press, 1964.

Blau, Peter M. *Exchange and Power in Social Life.* New York: Wiley, 1967.

Blumer, Herbert. *Symbolic Interactionism.* Englewood Cliffs, N.J.: Prentice-Hall, 1969.

Bohr, Neils. *Atomic Physics and Human Knowledge.* New York: Wiley, 1958.

Compte, Auguste. *The Positive Philosophy.* Translated and edited by H. Martineau. London: Bell, 1915.

Coser, Lewis. *Masters of Sociological Thought: Ideas in Historical and Social Context.* 2d ed. New York: Harcourt Brace Jovanovich, 1977.

Using Social Theory to Make Sense Out of Life 21

Dahrendorf, Ralf. *Class and Class Conflict in Industrial Society.* Palo Alto, Calif.: Stanford University Press, 1959.

Durkheim, Emile. *The Elementary Forms of the Religious Life.* New York: Free Press, 1948.

_____. *The Division of Labor in Society.* New York: Free Press, 1964.

Einstein, Albert. *Ideas and Opinions.* Translated by S. Bargmann. New York: Crown, 1954.

Goffman, Erving. *The Presentation of Self in Everyday Life.* Garden City, N.Y.: Doubleday/Anchor 1959.

Handel, Warren. *Enthnomethodology: How People Make Sense.* Englewood Cliffs, N.J.: Prentice-Hall, 1982.

Hawley, A. H. *Human Ecology: A Theory of Community Structure.* New York: Ronald Press, 1950.

Homans, G. C. "Fundamental Social Processes." In N. J. Smesler, ed., *Sociology: An Introduction.* 2d ed. New York: Wiley, 1973.

James, William. *The Writings of William James.* Edited by John J. McDermott. Chicago: University of Chicago Press, 1977.

Lazarsfeld, Paul. *Survey Design and Analysis.* New York: Free Press, 1955.

Lee, Alfred McClung. *Sociology for Whom?* New York: Oxford University Press, 1978.

_____. "The Services of Clinical Sociology," *American Behavioral Scientist* 22, 4 (March/April 1979): 487-512.

Leitko, Thomas E. "Applying the Concept of Nested Social Systems." Paper presented at the Annual Meetings of the Eastern Sociological Society, Boston, March 8-11, 1984.

Lofland, John. *Doing Social Life: The Qualitative Study of Human Interaction in Natural Settings.* New York: Wiley-Interscience, 1976.

Marx, Karl. *Selected Writings in Sociology and Social Philosophy.* Translated by T. B. Bottomore. New York: McGraw-Hill, 1964.

Mayhew, Leon. *Societies: Institutions and Activity.* Glenview, Ill.: Scott, Foresman, 1971.

Mead, George Herbert. *Mind, Self, and Society.* Chicago: University of Chicago Press, 1934.

Merton, Robert K. *Social Theory and Social Structure.* Enlarged ed. New York: Free Press, 1968.

Miller, J. G. *Living Systems.* New York: McGraw-Hill, 1978.

Mills, C. W. *The Sociological Imagination.* New York: Oxford University Press, 1959.

_____. *The Power Elite.* New York: Oxford University Press, 1958.

Park, Robert E. *Human Communities.* New York: Free Press, 1952.

Parsons, Talcott. *The Social System.* Glencoe, Ill.: Free Press. 1951.

Pepper, Stephen. *World Hypotheses.* Berkeley, Calif.: University of California Press, 1942.

Spencer, Herbert. *The Principles of Sociology.* New York: Appleton, 1898.

Weber, Max. *From Max Weber.* Edited by H. Gerth and C. W. Mills. New York: Oxford University Press, 1946.

Wilson, E. O. *Sociology.* Cambridge, Mass.: Harvard University Press, 1975.

Wirth, Louis. "Clinical Sociology," *American Journal of Sociology,* 37 (July, 1931): 49-66

Von Bertalanffy, Ludwig. *General Systems Theory.* New York: Braziller, 1968.

Chapter   **2**   DOING SOCIOLOGICAL
RESEARCH THAT COUNTS
Brian Sherman

As you have learned, science is a way of generating accurate, verifiable, and practical knowledge about the world. One task of sociology, as a social science, is to gather factual information about the world of social life. In this chapter we look at some of the basic *methods* by which sociologists go about this process of discovering scientific truths about human life.

Most of the time, sociologists gather their information as an exercise in "pure science"; that is, to gain knowledge for its own sake with little concern for its possible uses or applications. Nevertheless, the identical procedures can also enable us to gather useful insights and information that can serve a practical function of helping to guide, facilitate, or inspire positive changes in human life. In line with the theme of this volume and because I personally have chosen to center my career in this utilization of sociological methods, I discuss these tools of the sociological craftsperson from the perspective of a practitioner.

Research methodology is an entire subfield of sociology in and of itself. In this chapter, therefore, we look at some of the more interesting and more important methods of questioning, methods of noticing, methods of analysis, and methods of explanation employed by sociologists. In this discussion, when I use pronouns such as *we* or *our*, I am referring to the practice of sociologists in general; when I give my own opinion or talk about my own work, I use *I, me, my*, and *mine*.

Methods of Questioning

In order to find things out, you must ask questions. Even when the sociologist works with already gathered information (discussed later), somebody had to have asked questions earlier. We ask most of our questions in direct conversation, so I begin with interviewing. When interviewing is not practical, we use questionnaires and surveys. In discussing these methods, I follow the convention of labeling the person being questioned "R" (for "respondent").

Interviewing

We are interviewing whenever we ask at least one question directly to a person for the purpose of gaining information. We formally arrange some interviews for a specific time and place; other interviews occur when we simply go up to people, introduce ourselves, and start asking questions. We might do this, for example, at agencies, after meetings, and sometimes when we're on the street.

Almost any R can be interviewed about anything if we define the situation appropriately. All people want to make sense out of their lives, both to others and to themselves. Our questions stimulate Rs to put into complete sentences what had been only vague thoughts and feelings. One of the pleasures of sociological interviewing, for me, is the frequency with which Rs say something like, "You know, I never really thought about that before," after I ask my question. Some Rs perceive the sociologist as the first person who will listen to their story open-mindedly, without passing personal judgment.

Questions and answers are the essential mechanics of an interview. If both R and the sociologist are merely mechanical, however, the interview will be less productive and less enjoyable for both. Even with Rs who are suspicious and hostile, a sociologist can develop the situation in a way that both will enjoy the interview and each other, and neither will feel their integrity has been compromised. This requires consciously sensitizing ourselves to R and being genuinely interested in what R has to say.

To avoid the mechanical "me question, you answer" pitfall, I attune myself to the theatrical and rhythmic aspects of an interview. I listen to the rhythms of R's speech so that I know how to keep the momentum steady. I find with some Rs that I have to allow long pauses between their sentences to encourage them to continue in a promising direction; with others I have to cut pauses short with comments or rephrased questions in order to inhibit R from tangents and digressions. I pay continual attention to both R's behavior and my own feelings and energy levels so that I can infer how R is reacting to me and would react to changes I might induce in tension and rhythm.

I give real feedback to R. I acknowledge what R says with a smile or an appropriate response, such as, "I know what you mean," or, "Yeah." When R gives a long answer, I repeat a shorter version of it to show the basic points I got from it. This helps us to know we are making sense to each other. When R speaks confidentially, I acknowledge it by moving closer and talking more softly. I want to reassure my Rs that I take their confidentiality seriously.

Rs are often surprised at the details we ask for. As sociologists, we are trained to see patterns in the seemingly insignificant details of everyday life. This is how we determine the existence, degree, and nature of such problems as discrimination, the extent of R's support network, or the specific value conflicts among groups a community. I overcome R's perplexities by explaining as specifically as I can why I ask particular questions. I tell R what I need the information for, and this helps me get the information I need. It also helps avoid the pitfall of R's telling me what he or she thinks I want to hear.

While I listen to R respond to one question, I formulate the next. As long as I can cover what I set out to cover, I allow the interview to flow in unexpected directions. This allows me to ask follow-up questions about events and situations that R mentioned in response to a previous question.

I begin an interview with questions R can answer easily. These may be social-background questions, such as occupation, age, and current position. By beginning with easy questions, both the interviewer and R can feel out what talking with each other is like. If I see there is a problem in developing momentum, I ask R to elaborate on the answers to the easy questions with such questions as, "What circumstances led you to your current position?"

When R gives vague responses, I probe at the same material until R is more explicit. If I have asked, "Do you receive adequate treatment at that facility?" I can follow up with, "What happened the last time you went there for treatment?"

When I do not follow what R says, I ask for repetition. I say, "I didn't get that," or, "My mind wandered for a moment; could you please repeat what you just said?" Sometimes I convert my own deficits into something we can both laugh at to lighten what may otherwise be a heavy or depressing interview.

I take extensive notes while I interview. Many Rs, I find, sharpen the clarity and detail of their answers when they see me writing. If R asks me what I've written, I always show it, even if it is just some random drawing, to demonstrate that there is nothing covert about my activities. With some Rs I have to maintain a lot of eye contact to keep up the momentum. This means I do a lot of writing without looking at my pad. To learn to do this I made an exercise out of taking notes during movies so I could write without looking and still be able to read what I wrote afterward.

I prefer not to tape most interviews. I pay less attention to R when I know I can hear a tape later. Writing notes while R talks is the best way for me to absorb what R is saying. On the other hand, many sociologists prefer tape recording to taking notes; there is no hard-and-fast rule about this; it is a matter of personal style.

As you can see, a sociological interview is not a cut-and-dried set of questions. It is more like a guided conversation in which the sociologist uses his or her skills to learn about an area or topic of interest, learn how Rs experience and understand things from their own perspective, and gain useful insights into the patterns and processes of social life.

Questionnaires

We use questionnaires when asking the same questions of a lot of different people. It is quicker to distribute questionnaire forms than it is to interview everybody. The main drawback is that we have to think up and word all our questions beforehand. We have to rely on R to interpret the question as we intended, and we also sacrifice the opportunity to ask additional questions stimulated by R's responses to earlier questions.

An *item* is a single question in a *questionnaire,* which is essentially a list of items. A typical questionnaire begins with *demographic items,* which we use to place each R into the various categories that sociologists know affect most people's attitudes, values, and conduct. The most frequently used demographic items are age, sex, race, ethnicity, occupation, education, place of origin, religion, and marital status. These are followed by the *substantive items,* which cover the topics we want to learn more about.

We begin creating a questionnaire by writing a list of questions. We weed out the less useful ones and refine the wording of the remainder. We combine items into groups that make sense to us and put the groups in a reasonable sequence, placing the most important substantive items immediately after the demographic ones. We number the items and print them with enough space between items for R's responses.

The process is easy enough, but any number of pitfalls can produce the flaws that are present in most questionnaires. I spend a lot of energy trying to eliminate as many flaws as I can from the questionnaires I devise. I study each item and imagine how various Rs might respond to it. I rewrite every item until I believe there are no words or phrases that might lead R to misinterpret what I am asking.

Here is an actual example of how ambiguity in an item produced misleading results. A radio station wanted to know what its listeners' favorite albums were. They worded an item, "If you were stuck on a desert island, what albums would you want to have with you?" All but one of the 10 most frequently named albums were double or triple record albums; listeners had taken the desert island setting more seriously than the station had intended! They envisioned being marooned for a long time, and made their choices to maximize the amount of music they would have, rather than pick their favorites. The only single album in the top 10 was the Beatles' "Abbey Road."

Whoever wrote the questionnaire for this radio station made the common mistake of assuming their Rs would interpret items the same way they did. They could have spotted this flaw by *pretesting* their questionnaire. Pretesting means administering a draft of a questionnaire to a few people in order to see how items are being interpreted.

The most important principle here is that *Rs react to every aspect of a questionnaire.* This includes wording of items, the options given for responses, the amount of space provided for responses, the sequence of items, and the overall look of the questionnaire. According to Layne and Thompson (1981), the fewer the pages and the less cramped each page looks, the more likely it is that Rs will fill out the whole questionnaire. Thus the fewer the items, the higher the response rate. As one problem with questionnaires is getting people to respond to them, we cultivate the skill of covering the topic of a questionnaire with as few items as possible.

Painstaking care must be given to the wording of each question. Suppose our clients want to know the religious background of people in their organization. One could ask, "What is your religion?" and put a blank line after it. This could produce misleading information. Some Rs will respond "None" if they are not currently members of a church; some will answer with a theological statement of beliefs; others will leave it blank.

A fixed set of choices is the solution. A standard set is "Catholic, Jew, Protestant, Other." I vary the choices when I know the most likely responses beforehand. In some Georgia cities I use "Baptist, Catholic, Methodist, Presbyterian, Other." I use what I know as a professional sociologist to construct the best possible "instrument" to obtain the information I need from the Rs I will be asking these questions of.

The actual items require proper diction and a careful eye to the physical design of the whole. I care like a poet about the words and like an architect about the spaces between them. I write the introduction to a questionnaire, however, as if I were talking personally to R. I tell my Rs exactly what I want them to do, and I do not assume they already know how to fill out a questionnaire.

Surveys

Surveys involve asking questions of some of the people in a group, category, or area. We survey with questionnaires, interviews, or a combination of the two. We use surveys to get an overview of a particular social condition or situation. As an overview is not the whole picture, we need a reason to believe it is typical, or "representative," of the whole. There are two kinds of surveys, and we deal with this problem differently for each.

When we survey *opinions and attitudes,* we want assurance that the people we question are typical of the whole group. This was the original use of social scientific surveys, by the way. The established principle here is that we feel most confident when those we survey are selected as a *random sample* of the whole. There are statistical procedures for doing this, and we follow them as best we can given our resources — a limiting factor with which every researcher must come to terms.

When doing what we can term an *exploratory survey* to learn the details of a complex social arena, we want to be sure to cover as many as possible of the different groups, activities, and points of view involved. We keep surveying until we have covered the story from every perspective. I tell each R who and where I have already surveyed, and ask if there are any important people, factions, or activities that I have overlooked.

This kind of survey can have great clinical value, as often we want an overview to help us decide on an intervention, or to persuade others of the need for it. For example, in 1981 a client asked me to survey county voting practices in Georgia and how they affect the participation of blacks in the electoral process. He wanted information that would help convince Congress to extend the Voting Rights Act, which was scheduled to expire in 1982.

I designed a questionnaire with 171 items, as my client's organization wanted to collect as much information as possible to document the practices and effects of racial discrimination. To accomplish this, I wrote items about as many aspects of the topic as I could think of. Usually we cannot expect Rs to fill out such lengthy questionnaires. In this case, however, my client knew the Rs were committed civil rights activists who would recognize the importance of the survey.

I presented my findings in testimony at a congressional hearing. I was able to give a comprehensive overview of resistance to fair black participation in the electoral process, the kinds of discriminatory tactics used, how certain legalistic devices prevent the election of blacks, and the negative effects these conditions have on the daily lives of black citizens.

My survey results got wide exposure after my testimony. This included newspaper articles, radio reports, and television and radio interviews. The full report was distributed to civil rights leaders throughout the region, and I wrote it up as an article for the *Civil Rights Research Review*.

I later served as an expert witness in a case regarding discrimination against blacks in jury selection. As my survey provided evidence that blacks were systematically discriminated against in voter registration, it helped convince the appeals judge to decide in my client's favor. I mention all this to show how clinical sociological research, above and beyond contributing to our knowledge about a social problem, can have a direct impact on issues we care about.

Methods of Noticing

"Noticing" means careful observation. It involves bringing more of what goes on around us into our consciousness and then systematically storing what we have observed.

Participant Observation

In *participant observation* we combine watching what is going on with taking part in it ourselves. Normally we notice more as nonparticipants, but sometimes participation is either necessary or superior to detached observation.

As participants, we gain a legitimate right to be in a social arena from which outsiders are excluded. Sometimes, this method gets around the problem that the presence of a detached observer would cause people to act differently and conceal some of their usual activities from us. As an employee of the agency or business, for example, we can observe unwritten rules, how clients are processed, how things work (or don't work) in actual practice.

A participant-observation study may take only a single afternoon, or it may require a total time commitment to a different way of life. It may require joining a community group, taking a paid position in an agency or firm, changing one's life style to participate in a different subculture, or moving to a new neighborhood.

When doing participant observation, we learn the ways of speaking and acting that the observed take for granted. We have to assimilate them quickly so that our behavior and speech do not interfere with the usual flow of action. We get suggestions and clues for acceptable behavior by noticing others' reactions to ourselves. While learning to participate in an arena, we also learn how its people make sense of and justify their actions. As we participate, we come to share some of their meanings and justifications and are more likely to acquire some sympathy for those we observe than if we did not participate.

As participant observers, however, we are not full participants. We may thoroughly enjoy the experience and feel the same intensity as those whose activities we are studying, but there is always a part of us that knows we are there for professional purposes. Our task is to use this opportunity to notice what is going on; for this purpose, we write out detailed "field notes" as soon as we can after each experience, to keep a precise record of our observations.

To illustrate this method, I will relate my experiences in discos at the peak of the disco fad. It began with a call from a reporter who was writing a serious article and wanted to incorporate some sociological analysis. I said that I liked the disco music I heard on the radio but that I had not been to a disco. I told him I would learn about discos through participant observation.

A friend agreed to be my partner. We took a beginner's class with one of Atlanta's better-known disco teachers. We learned enough in the first classes to dance a few steps, so during the next few weeks we sampled a variety of discos including those that were favorites of office workers, the moneyed, gays, and students. Typical disco patrons, we danced a while and between dances watched others dance, commenting on their steps, styles, and outfits.

After I completed my participant observation, the reporter interviewed me for 3 hours. He had a negative perspective on discos, putting down the behavior of participants and saying it reflected some of the worst aspects of contemporary society. Analytically, I agreed with him and had no quarrel with the quote used on the front page of the newspaper — *"An Orgasmic, Sexist, Plastic Response to a Decadent Society,"* says *Local Sociologist* — because it established the phenomena observed as manifestations of fundamental characteristics of society.

Nevertheless, my participant observation taught me something about discos that detached observation would not have. Discos were fun. I enjoyed the dance steps, the sound systems, dancing among the crowds on the floor. Participation enabled me to convey to the reporter an understanding of why people liked discos. I said the feelings dancers had were analogous to the feelings of communality experienced during so-called primitive tribal dances. I saw that discos reflected a need for communal experience without communal obligations. "Tribalism without commitment" is a quote the reporter used from our interview.

I did not prepare a written document for the reporter. Informal presentation of research findings is more common in clinical sociology than in academic practice. Often those who commission our services do not want detailed research reports. They may have some very specific questions, and want from us short answers they can use as a basis for interventions.

Available Data

Available data (also called *archival data*) is a method that uses information already gathered for some other purpose before we use it. Some are organized in data collections such as the U.S. Census, microfilms of newspapers, minutes of committee meetings, and annual reports. Other collections are less systematic, such as the memos, correspondence, accounts, and whatever else is in an organization's files at any particular moment. Some information, such as flyers, brochures, leaflets, maps, posters, signs, and newsletters, is available only briefly or because somebody happened to save a copy. Sociologists make frequent use of all this document accumulation in modern society.

Sometimes our need for the data is specific when we look for it. For example, I use census data in my voting rights work to find out what percentage of a county or city is black. In other instances we acquire readily available data before we have use for them. When I start a case, I ask for copies of all the printed material available. I read and file them. As I became familiar with this information, I begin to see patterns. I also use available data for reference and illustrations when I prepare a presentation or am asked for recommendations.

An example of the value of available data occurred when I was a member of the citizens' advisory council of a community mental health center. The granting agency wanted a self-evaluation, and the center appointed a staff member with no evaluation experience to write it. She asked me to help her design a questionnaire for the staff and an interview procedure for clients. I advised her that it would be more practical to use available data.

I knew the center had a file on every client that contained information on the client's initial contact with the center, referral source, number of contacts with the center's staff, initial diagnosis, disposition or prognosis, etc. I explained how she could use this available information to construct tables and charts to give an accurate account of the volume, type, and resolution of cases.

I also suggested that she use the data with which I was most familiar, the minutes of the meetings of the citizens' advisory council. I said these would give her a good overview of the dilemmas the center had contronted and how they were resolved. These included funding activities the grant did not cover, community relations, and how to reach potential clients who lacked transportation access to the center. She took my suggestions and wrote an evaluation report that the granting agency found satisfactory. The information was all there in the files; no one had looked at it in this way before.

Field Work

A *field* is an arena where social phenomena are occurring. Field work involves placing ourselves in that arena to gather information. Some sociologists spend a lot of time in the field, which may be a neighborhood, an institution, a set of street corners or other places where people "hang out," a hospital ward, a penitentiary, all the waiting rooms in a city's public health facilities, or anywhere else there are social problems or scenes of theoretical or practical interest.

Field work is the method that puts us in closest touch with others' worlds. We experience with them their activities, physical environment, meetings, street life, and special events. We record the details and extract from them the information and generalizations we need.

Field work is a physical activity. Usually we walk a lot and talk a lot. At the same time, we collect sense impressions of everything from billboards and paint jobs on institutional walls to noise levels and graffiti. We try to understand the meanings of what we notice for the people who experience it in their everyday lives. We have to be careful to realize that they may not see it in the same way we do — one person's garishness is another's good taste.

Our understanding of social structure helps us to know when we have covered the most important scenes in a field. Those who are there every day are immersed in their own activities and do not get the firsthand experience that we do with the other people, departments, neighborhoods, or organizations in their vicinity. By covering the field, we find out about people and groups our clients or subjects are not aware of. We rarely have time for complete coverage, so we maximize our minutes and place ourselves where we can make the most useful observations.

In some fields, passive observation is sufficient for our purposes. The information we gather by attending court sessions, taking notes at meetings, or observing who makes what uses of public parks may be all we need. Often, however, field work is combined with other methods discussed in this chapter. We usually interview people and collect available data; sometimes we also conduct surveys or do participant observation.

I can illustrate what I mean by field work with an example that had fruitful results. My voting rights clients in a certain city believed a discriminatory reapportionment plan had been submitted to the Justice Department. After analyzing the statistics in my office, I decided that this social arena was more complex than others I had dealt with and that I needed to make a field trip to find out what was going on.

I had never been to that city and knew nothing about it other than what my clients (local black politicians) had told me on the phone. My work schedule allowed me two days there. I structured my time around interviews with black elected officials and others whom they recommended as knowledgeable. I conducted my interviews in the field, allowing me to observe the flow of social action at the interview sites and to see the parts of the city between them. Interviewees or their associates drove me between sites and remarked how the conditions of roads, housing, and other facilities I saw reflected local political realities.

I conducted interviews in a newspaper office, a funeral home, an insurance agency, two different restaurants, and various spots in the central government building. I saw who talked with whom and who didn't. I became aware of alliances. In person, interviewees were more frank with me. In the restaurants, when I was eating with political figures, others came up for brief chats or greetings. I learned how each person fit into the complex mosaic of the local political structure.

I kept picking up available data including political flyers, reports, maps, and advertising materials. I attended a brief but symbolically important ceremony at a session of a government body, which gave me a clear sense of the self-image the government was trying to project with regard to combating discrimination. Afterward, officials—white and black—came to meet me and make their impressions on me. Others pointedly ignored me. I interviewed and was interviewed by two reporters. All of this provided useful information.

I used two early-morning runs to get a feel for the city. I ran through downtown and adjacent neighborhoods. I saw which facilities were decaying and which commercial interests or the city were funding. I observed the modes of transportation available to early-morning workers, who, as in many cities, are disproportionately minorities and poor. I ran by a tourist display and stopped for the available data, including a most enlightening brochure about fishing.

I used what I learned during my field trip to write a comprehensive analysis of the political relationships among blacks and whites in the city. I ended it with the fishing brochure. I had noticed there were nine separate photos with groups of people enjoying the local fishing—and all were white. This was an official government document, and I remarked that the government was presenting a discriminatory image of itself in the brochure. It substantiated my contention that the reapportionment plan arose from a general context of discrimination against blacks in the city. The U.S. Department of Justice agreed.

Methods of Analysis

We are going to discuss qualitative and quantitive methods of analysis. *Qualitative methods* focus on the emergence of processes, qualities, and patterns in social life. *Quantitative methods* use numbers. With numbers we can express ideas and information too cumbersome to express in words, and we can identify patterns in data that we would otherwise miss. *Variable* is a word used frequently in quantitative methods; a variable is a *characteristic on which cases differ.*

Descriptive Statistics

The first quantitative method we discuss is *descriptive statistics,* used to give an accurate picture of what is going on in one's quantitative data. These are generally taught in your introductory statistics course. We can compute them with pencil, paper, and calculator—or, if we have too many cases, we can use a prepared computer program.

The most frequently used statistics describe the characteristics of a set of cases measured in terms of the frequency in which they are observed or actual scores on some kind of test or scale. I refer to both measures as "scores." A group of scores is called a "distribution." If nothing else, we usually want to know a distribution's *central tendency,* which is a more precise way of saying "average."

One example of a distribution is the number of monthly visits clients make to a county health facility. Let's consider nine clients, to simplify matters. The number of visits for each of the nine clients in one month is

1,2,2,2,3,4,4,5,8: one client visited once, three visited twice, one three times, two four times, one five times, and one eight times.

Three measures describe the central tendency. The *mode* is *the most frequent score;* in this example it is 2. The *median* is *the middle score;* here the median is 3. The *mean* is *the arithmetical average* (found by adding up all the scores and dividing the sum by the number of scores) in this distribution, equals 3 4/9. Each measure has its advantages and disadvantages. For example, when there are very large numbers of cases with unequal proportions at the extremes (as, for example, annual incomes of people in the United States), we normally use medians; most government statistics, for this reason, are reported in terms of this measure of central tendency.

The *percentile* is one of the statistics we use to understand the score of a case on a particular variable; you have, no doubt, run into this measure with respect to standardized tests you have taken, such as the SAT. This measure tells us where a particular score stands in relation to all the other scores in a distribution.

Suppose the Grahams live in County A and the Parkers live in County B. Both earn the same income, $6000 per year. Calculating percentiles, we can learn precisely what proportion of the families in their counties earn less than they do. We may find that in County A, 20% of the families have lower incomes than the Grahams, whereas in County B, 10% have lower incomes than the Parkers. A statewide program to supplement the income of families in the lowest 15% of the income scale in every county will help the Grahams but not the Parkers—even though both families are in the same financial circumstances. With a little bit of elementary statistical advice from a sociologist, such injustices can be avoided.

Other descriptive statistics enable us to learn even more about a population. They enable us to compute the strength of relationships between two or more variables, or to determine how much impact a number of different factors has upon a variable in which we are interested. They enable us to determine, for example, how strong the relationship is between pollution and life expectancy. Where such relationships are already known for each of several kinds of pollution (say from toxic wastes, motor vehicles, pesticides, and heavy industry), more complex statistics permit us to combine the effects of each kind of pollution and determine their total impact.

Thus we could predict life expectancy in different counties, depending on their level of pollution. The results of these predictions will be clearly understood by everyone when, for example, they see life expectancy is 3 years lower in Lester County than it is in Bowie County and 5 years lower than in Mitchell County. This example shows how we use statistics to summarize complicated experiences with just a few numbers.

Inferential Statistics

Inferential statistics enable us to take descriptive statistics about a group of cases and generalize what we have learned from the group to a much larger group. The group we know about is called the *sample,* and the group we generalize to is called the *population.* The sample cannot tell us exactly what is going on in the population; we get only an approximation, but it saves us the time, money, and hassle of surveying everyone in the population. The following illustration shows how inferential statistics are used.

Suppose a citizens' group has heard about alcohol usage at their local high school. They commission us to find out what proportion of students have a serious alcohol problem. We agree to survey a sample of the student population. I would begin by clarifying what the group means by "serious alcohol problem" and then design a simple questionnaire for each student in the sample to fill out.

I set the sample size before I give out the questionnaire. Larger samples (up to a certain point) give us greater precision and more confidence in our results; but money, personnel, and time constraints generally force us to limit sample sizes. With formulas and tables in a statistics text, I can determine how much precision and certainty we can get for any given sample size. The citizens' group would likely be satisfied with a "ballpark estimate." It would be close enough to determine an appropriate intervention strategy. With a sample of 300, we can be 95% certain that the proportion of the sample with serious alcohol problems I find will be within 6% plus or minus (called a *confidence interval*) of the actual proportion in the student population. Most frequently, we report our results at this 95% *level of significance,* as clients are usually satisfied with 19:1 odds that the information they are receiving is correct.

Suppose I administer the survey and get usable responses from 283 students. Of them, 43% fit our definition of having a serious problem with alcohol. From this result, I infer that we can be 95% certain that somewhere between 37% and 49% of all the students in the school have serious alcohol problems. I report this to the citizens' group.

Inferential statistics have many other uses as well. They enable us to determine whether differences we observe between scores are *statistically significant* — that is, whether or not we are willing to bet they do not occur by chance. Now suppose further that on the basis of my survey results my clients implement an intensive counseling program. To test its effectiveness, 6 months later I take another survey. The proportion in this sample with serious alcohol problems may be 31% or 28% or 37% or whatever. The proportion is lower, and I do a statistical test to see if it is "significantly" lower.

Based on the test, I can report (usually with the same 95% of certainty) whether their program was effective. This is a simple example of a rapidly expanding field, known as *evaluation research,* in which social science practitioners evaluate the effectiveness of policies or programs for agencies, corporations, or other organizations.

Qualitative Analysis*

Unlike quantitative methods, qualitative methods are not highly formalized. Qualitative analysis is used to discover *themes and variations* in social life and to explore how different patterns of social organization emerge from social interaction. Its basic logic involves the identification and comparison of *categories* of social phenomena, whether they be roles, strategies, processes, relationships, or groups.

The typical approach is for the researcher to take extensive notes recording what is noticed in field work, interviews, participant observation, or study of available materials. Then we go over our notes and "code" them for basic categories or processes.

For example, we might scan through a few pages of notes to sensitize ourselves to "what's happening" there, and then go over them, line by line, trying to fit a label or name to "the action." These are often penciled in on the margins of our notes. After doing this, we go back and scan our marginal notations looking to see what crops up again and again, what the patterns and variations seem to be.

Some researchers make a habit of making several copies of their field notes; they take one copy and actually cut it up into pieces that seem to "hang together," physically sort these pieces into piles representing a single pattern or set of categories, then sort these piles into subpiles representing stages of a pattern, categories, or variations of a category. This tactic allows one to continually sort and re-sort material.

The researcher seeks to determine what different kinds of actions or interactions are represented by this material; how they are linked or related; and, when variations or different lines of development are observed, where these split off from one another. It is much like working out a flow chart in computer programming. The result is a *substantive theory* or "model" of what a process or phenomenon is like or how it works in practice. I (Straus) can briefly illustrate this from my own research as a graduate student.

I was unconvinced by the accepted view of cults and other new religious movements as conspiracies on the part of hypocritical "insiders," who nab gullible youths and "brainwash" them into mindless, robotlike

---

*Material in this section concerning qualitative analysis was contributed by the editor, Roger A. Straus.

"true believers." I therefore contacted members of every "trip" I could locate around Davis, California (where I was a student) and conducted intensive, 2-to-3-hour interviews with 17 people, probing for exactly how they got into their "trip" and how they kept themselves in the group. My interviewees ranged from Scientologists to Jesus People.

What I discovered was that a person who was dissatisfied with his or her life or self or relationships might start casting about for a means of change. Gradually, in a process I termed "creative bumbling," the person comes to see himself or herself as a "seeker." Combing through networks of friends, chance acquaintances, and available information about different alternatives, the person comes to settle on a possibility. She or he then proceeds to "check out" the trip, perhaps by hanging around with group members. Eventually, if satisfied with what is observed, the person may then decide to join the group. This is typically done in an experimental, "give it a try and see" fashion— remember the group offers recruits a means of changing one's life that can only be gotten by taking this plunge. Then the person tries to make his or her new self real by deliberately acting the role of a letter-perfect, true-believing "convert," often to the amusement of more established members (Straus 1976).

Although it is a fairly primitive model, which I have since expanded, this was the first study of its kind. Since then, my model of active seekers interacting with group members to convert themselves has become an accepted "paradigm" among researchers into religious conversion. An exercise in pure research, it has nevertheless changed our conceptualization of how cults work—which has definite social and legal implications—and has provided me with many useful concepts and approaches that I later adapted to my clinical work.

Methods of Explanation

The term *cause* means the explanation for that which we seek to explain, which is what we mean by *effect*. We use methods of explanation to relate causes and effects or to describe the nature of qualitative relationships.

Case Studies

We use case studies (including life histories) either to explain things in a qualitative way or to generalize from one, two, or a few cases to a whole population of cases, or both. Sometimes we know our case studies are representative because we are familiar with a lot of cases. At other times we have the opportunity to study only the case or cases at hand, and rely on our sociological intuition to infer that they typify many other cases.

For example, a few hours of unintended field work in one place became the only illustrative case study for someone else working on an entirely different project. I am referring to observations I made on my first day in the Amazonian jungle in Ecuador. I was on my way to a field site to study the effects of white colonization on the lives of the indigenous people. The bus I was on became mired in mud near the headquarters of the crew that was extending the road into the jungle. I watched the road crew extricate the bus, and observed the sociological features of the crew, their headquarters, the people on the bus, and the environment.

After completing my own study, I introduced my report with a few pages about the mired bus, the efforts to free it, and the road. My point was the pervasive effect of the region's continual rain. I noted humans did all the labor, and described how wheelbarrows were trapped in the mud. A colleague who was studying road building in the Andes saw my report. Mine was the most detailed firsthand description he had seen of the difficulties of Amazonian jungle road maintenance. He used my observations as his only case study. His familiarity with the subject enabled him to draw information about the general problems of road maintenance from just the single example. I had fortuitously included enough of the descriptive details he needed to make his generalizations.

Causal Analysis

We use *causal analysis* to find the cause or causes of a particular effect. Social scientists use the term *independent variable,* or X, instead of "cause," and *dependent variable,* or Y, instead of "effect." The simplest type of causal analysis explores the relationship between one X and one Y to see if differences in X can explain differences in Y.

When he commissioned my voting rights survey, my client wanted to know if at-large election systems prevent the election of blacks to public office. The independent variable was election system and the dependent variable was the election of blacks to office.

I divided my independent variable into two categories of election system, "at-large" and "ward," and compared counties in Georgia that had at-large systems (all candidates run against each other throughout the whole county) with those that had ward systems (the county is geographically divided into wards and each ward elects one official). I also divided my dependent variable into two categories. One was for counties that had elected at least one black county commissioner since passage of the Voting Rights Act in 1965, and the other was for counties that had elected none in that same time span.

I had data on both variables from 55 counties with large concentrations of black residents. I found a black commissioner had been elected in only 5% of the counties with at-large systems, compared with 38% of the counties with ward systems. The percentage in counties with ward systems was more than seven times greater, indicating a strong relationship between *X* and *Y*. This was the first step in determining whether the election system, *X,* was part of the explanation for election of black officials, *Y.*

Correlation (our technical term for "statistical relationship") is not enough to establish that *X* helps explain *Y.* We have to find *how X* affects *Y.* I found part of the explanation to lie in white "racial bloc voting" throughout the state, meaning that whites will not vote for *any* black candidate, period. The only chance blacks have to win elections is to run where the overwhelming proportion of voters are black. Even then they might not win, but at least they have a fighting chance.

Only one county in the state has such an overwhelming proportion of blacks — and blacks regularly win elections there. Sections of other counties have high concentrations of blacks who are swamped by whites in at-large elections as a result of racial bloc voting. When, however, the county is divided into wards and some wards coincide with black population concentrations, at least some blacks get elected.

Blacks do not always vote for black candidates, but they are the only group that will vote for blacks. Thus a necessary condition for the election of blacks is the presence of a large majority of blacks in the electorate. The at-large system prevents this, while the ward system facilitates it — and blacks get elected from some wards. This explains why a much greater percentage of counties with ward systems have had a black commissioner than have counties with at-large systems.

One independent variable is rarely the whole explanation of a dependent variable; *multicausal explanations* tend to be the rule in real life. Election systems are but part of the explanation why blacks were not elected in the counties I studied. I looked for other explanatory variables and found additional correlations between lack of black commissioners and low black registration and voter turnout, which in turn correlated with discriminatory registration practices, intimidation at the polls, and reprisals against blacks who run for office, to name a few. Each is part of the multicausal explanation for my dependent variable: the lack of elected black county commissioners.

We usually have *hypotheses,* or knowledgeable guesses, about which independent variable or variables explain our dependent variable. We then gather the information, as I did with my survey, to "test the hypothesis," to see whether our guesses stand up to the empirical evidence. Hypotheses come from familiarity with the particular problem or issue and from general knowledge about causal relationships in social life.

Finding a statistical relationship between *X* and *Y* does not always mean that *X* explains or "causes" *Y.* Sometimes, as in the following example, it is incidental to the real explanation. This is known as a *spurious* relationship. Some people argue that *race* is the independent variable that explains low black registration and voter turnout. They say characteristics of blacks, such as apathy, cause their lower rates. This simply does not hold up under scrutiny.

On the other hand, part of the explanation is the continued resistance by whites to black political participation; as resistance declines, the evidence shows that the relationship between these rates and race also declines. Thus resistance (expressed as discriminatory practices) and not race is a real explanatory variable. Some of the explanation also lies in other sociological variables. Those with lower incomes have lower rates because they are less likely to get time off from work to register and are less likely to have transportation to registration and voting sites. Since blacks, as a group, have lower incomes than whites, it follows that they have lower rates. Thus income is another part of the explanation of lower rates, whereas race is only incidentally related — a spurious relationship — because blacks have lower incomes.

Experimentation

Experimentation is particularly well suited to clinical sociology. Common to all experimentation is trying something and observing what happens. We compare the effects of something we do to what happens when we do not do it, or when we do something else.

We use *controlled experiments* when we want to see if a certain independent variable affects a dependent variable we are interested in. In its simplest form, this is done by comparing the effects of variable X upon an *experimental group* with what happens in a *control group* not exposed to X. The variable X can be something we do or some condition we change.

If we wanted to investigate the effects of counseling on drinking behavior, we might use two groups of people. First, we establish some kind of measure of our dependent variable, "drinking behavior," and test all our subjects to establish their drinking behavior prior to the experiment. Next we divide subjects into two groups, one that is given counseling and one that is not. Then we test all our subjects again and statistically analyze any difference between these measurements for experimental and control groups, looking to see if our X variable has caused a significant effect.

When we design a controlled experiment, we want to keep all other factors and conditions constant so that we can observe the effect of our independent variable and nothing but our independent variable. Otherwise, we lose certainty that counseling is, indeed, what is causing that effect. Ideally, a well-designed experiment "controls" for all possible sources of variation other than the selected independent variable.

One very important source of unwanted variation can be differences in the composition of the experimental and control groups. If all the subjects in our experimental group were teetotalers, and all those in our control group were heavy drinkers, our results would be spurious. Therefore, experimental researchers take care to control for this possibility in much the same way that survey researchers do—by randomly assigning subjects to experimental or control groups.

This kind of rigorously controlled experiment is obviously most feasible in a laboratory setting. It is also far easier to perform when your subjects are not human beings whose behavior will often change for the simple reason that they know they are participating in an experiment. Nevertheless, some sociologists do perform laboratory research on human subjects using full experimental design. In the field, we try to come as close as we can to that ideal, even though we cannot fully control all conditions or randomly assign subjects to experimental and control groups.

My hypothetical citizens' group wanted to see if their program of counseling would reduce alcoholism. They try the program and observe the results; if the results show it works, they make the program permanent. If the program does not work, they can try another.

I would recommend that they try two programs, such as one emphasizing counseling and one emphasizing information about alcohol abuse and its effects; then compare the results. If one is more effective, they should adopt it. If not, we can experiment with different versions of each, combinations of the two, or new approaches, and implement the one that produces the most satisfying results. This would be closer to a fully controlled experiment.

We use *open experiments* when we want to change current conditions but do not yet know what the more desirable alternative is. We try alternatives and study their consequences, hoping each experiment brings us closer to a desirable alternative. Open experimentation is trial and error based on educated guesses.

For example, I do experimentation with music. I started out to extend the definition of musical situations and am now at a point at which I have created a musical form with different sociological characteristics than music in our society. Through experimentation, I have found a way to make aesthetically pleasing music that requires no preparation, finances, instruments, or training. I call it "available resource music" because it is made by whoever is available, wherever they are, with whatever resources are at hand.

I want to increase the kinds of situations in which music can be experienced. This is both a sociological and a musical issue. As a sociologist, I understand music as a phenomenon that exists when culture defines it to exist, and for more than 10 years I have been using my clinical experience in changing definitions of the situation to vary the definition of music.

In my first experiments, I handed out small percussion instruments such as maracas, tom-toms, and finger cymbals in my classes and to groups in my apartment building for collective improvisation. Most tried to play music they associated with the instruments; they imitated familiar styles and resorted to clichés.

Next I experimented with sets of instructions that newly defined the musical situation. Explicit instructions eliminated clichés. The music was more like the available resource music I had hypothesized could be developed, and I concluded that new instructions were one causal variable. Through further experimentation, I learned that more careful explanations of instructions increased participants' commitment, which led to more satisfying music.

In the next step I replaced the instruments with available sound makers, such as hubcaps, wooden bowls and utensils, cooking pans, etc. Our music now had more originality and zest. I then eliminated the sound makers by asking participants to make sounds with whatever they found in the room.

At this point I felt I had succeeded in creating a method that would regularly produce the music I was looking for. I wanted to see how it would work in different environments, such as parking lots and stairwells, and made a record to document the results. Currently I am experimenting with what it takes to get people I do not know well to participate. The open experiment continues. I try something, observe the results, think about them, reach conclusions, and try something else. Each new experiment leads to unanticipated discoveries.

Conclusion

Rather than present a dry explanation of sociological methods as something we do "because we're social scientists," I have tried in this chapter to share with you my excitement in actually doing methodology as a clinical sociologist. By focusing on how I actually use them in real-life cases, I hope I have been able to show you what the major methods are, how they work, what they mean, and how they apply both to doing something about real-world social problems (e.g., racial discrimination) and in facilitating our understanding of everyday life.

Review Questions and Exercises

1. Compare and contrast 6 of the 12 methods discussed in this chapter, explaining when each is most useful or appropriate and giving a real and imaginary example of a "pure" or "clinical" research project using each method.

2. Suppose you applied either to a professional school or for a job and were turned down, despite the fact that you are eminently qualified for the position. How might you go about investigating whether you have been discriminated against because of your personal characteristics (age, sex, race, ethnic background, family or class background, regional background, life style, etc.)?

3. Work with a group of at least four students. Go to the library and obtain a copy of a sociological journal. Select a research paper you find interesting and understandable and analyze the methods employed in it. Write a short description of what the paper was about, what the findings were, and what method(s) it employed. Explain how they relate to the material in this chapter. Each group member should try to find an example of a different application of sociological method and discuss his or her example with the group.

Readings and References

Curry, G. David. *Sunshine Patriots: Punishment and the Vietnam Offender.* South Bend, Ind.: University of Notre Dame Press, 1984.

Fashing, J., and T. Goertzel. "The Myth of the Normal Curve, A Theoretical Critique and Examination of Its Role in Teaching and Research." *Humanity and Society* 5 (March 1981).

Layne, Ben, and Dennis Thompson. "Questionnaire Page Length and Return Rate. *Journal of Social Psychology* 113 (1981): 291-292.

Loewen, James. *Social Science in the Courtroom.* Lexington, Mass.: Lexington Books, 1982.

Mills, C. Wright. "On Intellectual Craftsmanship." In C. W. Mills, *The Sociological Imagination.* New York: Oxford University Pres, 1959.

Paasche, Gottfried. "A Case for Experience and Description in Sociology." *Human Affairs,* Spring 1982.

Sanders, Ed. *Investigative Poetry.* San Francisco: City Lights, 1976.

Sherman, Brian. "Drawing the Lines: A Reapportionment Primer." *Southern Changes* 5 (October/November 1983).

_____. "Done and Left Undone: A Survey of Local Electoral Practices and Politics in Georgia Fifteen Years after the Voting Rights Act." *Civil Rights Research Review* 9 (Fall/Winter 1981).

Starr, Jerold, and Judith Handel. *Humanistic Perspectives on Participant Observation.* Special issue. *Humanity and Society* 3 (November 1979).

Straus, Roger A. "Changing Oneself: Seekers and the Creative Transformation of Personal Experience." In J. Lofland, *Doing Social Life.* New York: Wiley-Interscience, 1976.

Vidich, J., J. Bensman, and M. Stein. *Reflections on Community Studies.* New York: Wiley, 1964.

Chapter **3**   SOCIOLOGY AND YOU:
GOOD LIVING
Harry Cohen

Jack and Jill climbed up the hill. Jack fell; so did Jill. I say they fell in love.
And soon after they fell again — out of love. It is a pain many people share.
  Many of our nation's communities report a 50% divorce rate. Some
areas nearly double that record (Coleman and Edwards 1980:5). And those
who stay married and avoid divorce do not all find the joy they wish with one
another. Painful couple relationships are common among the unmarried too.
These numbers of unhappy couples are not recorded in official statistics. Nor
do we have a full count of breakdowns of good human relationships
elsewhere, such as at work and between groups of people.

Culture and the Pathology of Normalcy

  When we consider the extent of trouble between people, we can say
that poor human relationships seem to be a normal part (and result) of
culture. By "culture" sociologists mean the complex whole of learned ways
of thinking, having, and doing that are common in a society (Bierstedt
1970:123). One part of culture emphasizes that good people get along well
with others. Another part obviously does not teach enough about how to
accomplish this. And some parts of culture may actually lead us away from
our goals of peaceful, harmonious relationships.
  Many sociologists prefer to conduct research on what people do and
have as part of culture and society. Working from a clinical perspective,
however, we consider these data, we learn about culture and what people
normally do, *and then go a step further.* Where elements of culture put people in life conditions in which they suffer pain instead of finding joy, where
elements of culture are discrepant and thus push people here and there,
tearing them apart so they find little joy no matter what they do, the clinical
sociologist looks to change culture and teach people how to relate more
sanely within it — which changes culture.
  When statistics are compiled about human behavior in a society, we
can determine the average, what people normally do. What is perceived as
average looks normal because it is common in the culture. But what is normal (as average) can also be pathological. There is such a thing as the
pathology of normalcy (Fromm 1965).

My mother graduated only from elementary school, but she understood the pathology of normalcy. In my youth I demanded the right to do what all the other children did. I adopted the standards of what other people did as being "right," and I used it as a lever to try to get my mother to let me do what everyone else was doing. Sociologically stated, if it was part of culture I felt the need and the right to conform to it. "Everyone else is doing it. Why can't I?" I would ask. She used to respond, "If everyone else jumps out of windows of tall buildings, do you also have to do this?" She was explaining that what "people do" and what "they say," while average and normal in culture, are not the only standards for choosing personal behavior. She meant that we have the right and obligation to choose our own sane behavior and do not have to follow cultural dictates blindly. We can follow *cultural norms* (i.e., ways of doing things patterned into a culture and its people as standards and expectations for behavior) when they do not harm us, but we do not always have to follow them. We can choose our own behavior.

Is the cultural norm leading people to the sane goals they desire? Are they reaching those goals in unnecessarily painful ways or in relatively joyful and fulfilling ways? What are the personal and social benefits of the goals and the means by which those goals are attempted and attained? What are the costs? Do the costs outweigh the benefits? The clinical sociologist tries to maximize the benefits and decrease the costs of meeting life goals. Costs in life are unavoidable. The clinical sociologist tries to increase the benefits, to shift behavior toward less painful costs, to lessen some costs and to make others more bearable.

It is part of the scientific sociological *subculture* (portion of a total culture) to avoid values as standards of "good" in research. Some sociologists wish to research and report "what is," not "what should be." But values must be considered when clinically *using* sociology. A clinician does not only study behavior, recording what people do and avoiding discussion of what they might do for more healthy living. In order to know what to change *from* and what to change *toward,* the clinical sociologist — and any other person — needs to consider what makes for a good life and what detracts from it. Some standard of "good" has to be considered by the clinical sociologist, or there is no basing point for what to work toward and what to eliminate while helping clients.

A student or anyone else can apply a clinical perspective to his or her life. Do research on your life and where you stand in it now. Is this where you want to be? Should you set different standards of good living and ways to reach those standards? What are the goals of your life — and the goals of life itself? What are the costs and benefits of your behavior? What are the *consequences* (results with costs and benefits) of your behavior for yourself and for other people? What is your culture and subculture? Are the cultural and subcultural standards concerning how to relate to your body and mind, or to men and women, teachers, parents, friends, and employers, or to nature itself leading you (and others) to personal and interpersonal costs of pain rather than benefits of fulfillment? What changes could lead to more joy and fulfillment?

Is it part of your peer subculture to take the easy way through school rather than to read, research, study, learn basic skills, and treat teachers and others with respect even while you disagree with them? The benefit of following peer-group norms of little work might be a degree with "no sweat," but the costs may be educationally empty school years, boredom, a bad conscience, a lack of pride in oneself, few solid accomplishments, and lifelong deficits in skills such as reading, writing, and critical thinking. Researching and analyzing the student subculture may show a pathology of normalcy.

Is this true for your peer group? Do some sociological research. You can do similar research about the costs and benefits of the culture, sub-culture, and behavioral patterns and goals of your family, dating relation-ships, networks of friends, and even of the government. Where group norms set a path toward ignorance and wasted time, the clinically oriented student can set another path toward scholarship and fulfillment. Such students refuse to follow the crowd blindly. They take ownership of, and responsibility for, their lives. When friends, teachers, and parents do not set good *role models,* such students model their own roles or choose other people as models.

The sociologist teaches that culture is learned behavior, including norms that regulate conduct. Patterns of human action are set by culture and then become "fixed" into the *social system* as the way to live, as guides for behavior. They become habits of action and reaction followed without much conscious thought or reflection.

Clinical sociologists teach about the culture and its patterned effects, showing people how to make changes for their greater joy, breaking the pathology of normalcy where it exists. People are helped to think about the costs and benefits of following aspects of their cultures and subcultures, and are then advised to choose which social elements they wish to keep and which they wish to change.

The ability to choose what to follow and what to reject from culture is called *autonomy* (Riesman, Glazer, and Denney 1961). The *conformist* blindly follows the pattern of group culture; the conformist who is happy is satisfied, and if unhappy, does not know why and suffers. The autonomous person takes ownership and responsibility for his or her life and works to make personal and societal changes toward happiness.

It may not be worth the time and effort to conflict with the dominant culture about some things. Consider, for example, the question whether to wear a tie. Here, I personally do what the culture tells me to do — I wear a tie in certain situations — even though I think it is a silly custom. We can avoid wasting our energies fighting over ties, for example in job interviews where not wearing one can lead to immediate rejection. But we can marshal our energies to refuse to cheat our teachers, employers, customers, or ourselves, even though we may see that cheating is becoming the normal expectation in a subculture where "everyone is doing it."

⟶ The Consequences of Behavior ⟵

There are consequences deriving from any behavior. For example, if you cheat, you may suffer guilt and related anxiety for the possible gain of higher grades or more money. If you do not cheat — and possibly earn lower grades or less money — you may feel better about yourself. Socrates made this point centuries ago: "justice" is a matter of balance. The just person benefits by a clear conscience in a healthy mind — which modern research shows is connected to healthy bodily functioning — as well as the support of people who like and trust such a person. The unjust person, however successful at collecting money and power, suffers the costs of an unbalanced mind and the hatred of those (s)he hurts.

From a systems perspective, it is interesting to note that imbalance may be seen as *dis-ease,* a fallen, crooked condition of no balance of parts. Disease as disease is painful; there are costs. Balance leads to an "upright" or "right" or "righteous" life with the benefits of a balanced connection of parts in the whole person and society. That which is whole is not dis-eased or diseased: whole, hale, health, heal are all words with common roots. The costs of injustice are the pains of an unbalanced, dis-eased personal state and social system. The benefits of justice are balanced, healthy people in a well-functioning personal and social whole.

One isolated episode of being unjust may yield costs of dis-ease in emotion, body, and group that come and go rapidly. Many episodes of being unjust build accumulated pressures and may take a greater, long-term toll in poor mental, physical, and social health. A few unjust actions with a lover may lead to a few negative feelings; but whenever such feelings arise, pleasure decreases in the relationship. Unjust actions between people switch their relationship onto a *negative track.*

Take a walk on a beautiful day with a beautiful lover who feels bad about you — because of something mean that you did — and your pleasure flies away with the wind. Accumulated consequences of repeated injustices may destroy the relationship. It becomes unbalanced and dis-eased and breaks, giving the couple a great deal of pain in its fall. A person might think s(he) is "getting away" with injustices but pays in his or her own self and in poor social relationships.

Changing Tracks

A person who does not wish to own up to negative feelings for unjust behavior, or for anything else, commonly tries to pin these feelings on someone else. This is called *projection*. Projections are very destructive. They help groove relationships into negative *tracks*. If I am in your presence, and instead of your saying, "I feel hurt," you project your anger on *me* for talking about something that in reality bothers *you,* blaming me for "making you feel bad," I may get "hooked" into anger. I perceive injustice and tend to feel bad about you. "Your anger makes me angry." Actually, I should say, "I feel hurt when I perceive your anger, and I feel unjustly treated." Otherwise, my response will arouse you to further anger; it will just be another projection. Your statements arouse anger in me. My response inflames your anger. We are on a two-way negative track that affects our social relationship negatively. At some point we may even forget the reason for our mutual anger. The anger gets grooved into our relationship. It becomes part of our daily lives together. We treat one another poorly without even knowing why. This process is very common — in families, among lovers, at work, and between groups of people (e.g., different ethnic groups). Social relationships often become diverted onto negative tracks. The negative tracks "make" everyone angrier — without any resolution of the real problems coming between the people involved.

This example illustrates the kind of analysis that can be made of human social behavior. It is one way in which sociological understandings can be used for clinical work, trying to teach people how they may be tracked into negative relationships, and how the track can be switched toward positive relationships. Rather than projecting your feelings onto others, for better living I suggest that you autonomously change to *"I messages."* For example, say "I feel angry when . . ." instead of "You make me . . . ."

A sociologist studies the relationship between human actions. Every *act* of life is an *act*-ion (action). An action leads to a re-*act*-ion (reaction). A person acts; another person reacts to that act; the original actor reacts to that reaction. This is social life. Actions and reactions stand in relationship to one another. Action causes reaction. Actions and reactions make inter-*act*-ion (interaction). An act of life is played out. You act. I re-*act*. This makes our inter-*act*-ion. I can re-*act* to your act of anger with anger, or I can react with forgiving understanding. We have the power to change social relationships by acting or reacting differently.

The autonomous person takes responsibility for actions, reactions, and interactions, and for their consequences. Study actions and reactions in your relationships at work, when dating, or in the family. If you do not like the consequences — because there are too many costs or too few benefits—change either the action or reaction. We have the power to build positive tracks into our social relationships.

Analyze the act↔re-act = inter-act-ion process in your social life situations. If you look long enough and deeply enough, you will see an intricate web of relationships hanging together. This web consists of tracks of actions and reactions making interactions. Repeated behavior in grooved tracks of actions and reactions makes an organized pattern of social relationships called *social structure*.

Buildings are all structured. But they are structured differently for different functions. The pieces are put into different patterns of *social organization*. In social life, one couple, family, school, or corporation is socially structured in a different fashion from another. They are all organized, but they are structured differently. The relationships follow different tracks of actions↔reactions. Thus the *functions* are different, following differently tracked structures. If the act↔react process is building an unbalanced structure in which the actors (participants) function poorly with too many costs and too few benefits, we can restructure that situation. When we restructure, actions follow other tracks and function differently—one hopes with more benefits and fewer costs.

Study in any group the intricate web of action↔reaction tracks and how they stand in relationship to one another. As you learned in Chapter 1, what you are describing is a *social system*. As the actions↔reactions of people repeat, the tracks are grooved into a structure. If the consequences are not balanced, if there is dis-ease, change the grooved structure to other grooved tracks. The action↔reaction pattern changes. The structure changes. You have restructured the relationship—the relationship of parts in the system.

Jack and Jill may be in a relationship—that is, a tracked structure of actions↔reactions—where Jack commonly says something that "hooks" Jill's self-esteem negatively. That is his "act." She commonly reacts by feeling anger, projecting her anger onto Jack to accuse him of "being stupid," to which Jack reacts, punishing Jill by saying something that "hooks" her self-esteem again. Hurting one another is a grooved track in this act↔react = interaction system.

If Jack and Jill could stop bothering each other—stop the movie of life—to pick out a few frames of action and reaction, studying what leads to what, and the consequences, they could break their negative track, substituting a positive one in its place. The structure would be changed, and the consequences would change. Jack and Jill would no longer blindly run on tracks that give them trouble but would autonomously choose the tracks necessary to build the consequences of love and joy that they wish. Their relationship would be fixed, or more technically said, "restructured."

Jack learns not to say things in a manner that "hooks" Jill's self-esteem. She learns not to provoke him into it. Jill learns not to let her self-esteem get "hooked" or be dependent on what anyone says. They both learn not to project their negative feelings onto one another but to own their feelings. And they learn to switch the track of act↔react to forgiveness instead of "paying back" and "getting even." "Getting even" leads only to escalating pain as each "pays back" the other on a grooved-in negative track of giving and getting trouble. They learn to set tracks of forgiveness and of working out their troubles, not running trouble up and down their interactive tracks. They build their own socially tracked railroad to bring them to the destination of peace, joy, and love. They lay tracks so their relationship does not track trouble and pain. They avoid flipping from the tracks into a breakdown or crackup.

A mechanic studies the structure of an engine and how each part acts on and reacts to other parts. If something is not balanced right and the relationship of parts suffers symptoms reflecting the dis-ease of imbalance, the mechanic clinically restructures the parts for another tracked relationship. He may tighten one part, loosen another, and add lubricant. Architects, medical doctors, chemists, and other specialists employ a similar vision. So do clinical sociologists. This vision can be used with all social relationships.

Everything in a relationship leads to and connects to everything else in it. In our culture we are trained to look for "who is to blame" when things do not work out in our lives. This leads to pathologies. It sets a track of making blame. I suggest you do not look for who is at fault. Instead, for better understanding and for improvement in social relationships of every kind, analyze what action leads to what reaction, determining how the relationship is structured. If the structure of the relationship leads to malfunctions (problems), then change the structure.

Jack and Jill learn to stop blaming each other. They learn that they are part of an act↔react = interaction matrix (social structure) in which each holds responsibility for functions because they are each part of the causes and effects in it. They learn to cut out the blaming track from their interpersonal systemic structure. They substitute in its place a track of studying the issues that come between them. This is one way to place social relationships on a positive track.

The Balancing Act

A young boy ran away from home several times. Yet it seemed as if his parents treated him well at home. It looked as if he was at fault for running away, not appreciating his good family life. Instead of looking for blame, a therapist tried to determine the act↔react process. Since interviews were not successful in eliciting feelings and relational patterns, the therapist decided to use a form of sociodrama (described at length in a later chapter) to show visually how the act↔react structure of the family was perceived by family members. The therapist asked the boy to play a game of "statue" with his parents. She asked him to move his parents around the room and mold their bodies as he wished. They were to remain "statues" just as he left them. Then he was asked to do the same for himself.

The results were striking. The boy positioned the parents on the far side of the room, arm in arm, free arms waving as if saying goodbye. He positioned himself, dejected, standing by the door, ready to leave. In the boy's perception he was not running away from home, but his parents were in an alliance with each other and were pushing him out. He perceived the family structure as mother and father tracked together with him as an outsider being told goodbye. So he followed the track of the outsider and left. And he was caught and blamed for leaving. So he felt more the outsider and left again. The parents were asked to "sculpt" their feelings toward their son. The therapist took this into account, too, in her clinical attempts to restructure the family in order to eliminate the running away.

If the parents are indeed allied with one another to push the son out, the clinician will have to determine by research the reasons why. She will try to align the family structure so that all three family members feel "in." The parents have to be tracked so that they can interact closely and privately with one another and still make room for the son to interact separately with his mother, separately with his father, and with both mother and father together.

It is a balancing act, realigning the act↔react = interaction structure so that husband and wife belong together — are tracked together — at the same time the son has tracks to each separately and together. This family was dis-eased. The parts were not balanced. The symptom of the disease was the running away and the trouble connected with it. This led the family to the therapist, who worked to restructure the family to the point where the parts stand in a balanced relationship in a healthy whole.

The therapist can try to help the boy change his behavior so his parents do not react to his act by keeping him out so much. He can be taught to change his act by saying, "I feel unloved," when he perceives his parents are keeping him out, instead of reacting to their act by running away from home. The therapist will try to change the parents' behavior so the son does not react to *their* act by acting in such a way that they feel the need to react by excluding him. They might be taught how to show love for the son while showing love for each other. If it is determined that they find it hard to love their son, he can be taught that he does not have to react by getting his self-esteem "hooked." That his parents have a problem with love does not mean that there is anything bad about him.

This may sound very complicated, but it proves simple if you trace the act↔react tracks. This is what a clinician does. Once we "map" the tracks in this family structure, we can reroute the family along tracks that reach the goal of a happy wife, husband, and son. We can cut out tracks and add tracks. The relationship of parts in the family system is restructured.

The Definition of the Situation

The sociologist wants to see and unravel the many threads in the web of social interaction. Many of the threads in the social network of a family or any other social relationship come from *perceptions*, as with the runaway son's perception that his parents were pushing him out, while they perceived they were not. At some point in human interactions it no longer matters whether the original perception is true or not because the consequences of the perception take on a reality of their own.

We act and react on the perceptions as well as the actual behavior of others. You may be insulted by my writing, perceiving that I make you angry. I do not wish to insult you or make you angry; I wish to interest you, teach you, help you. But your perception and the consequences of your anger are real. If I am in your presence, you may well show me these consequences. I am insulted and angry in return. Your perceptions — untrue according to what I intended — are real to you, and they have real consequences for me and for you. Sociologists William I. and Dorothy Swaine Thomas wrote a long time ago that if people "define situations as real, they are real in their consequences" (1928:572). This is known as the *Thomas Theorem*.

The Thomas Theorem is very important for the understanding and improvement of human relationships. Sometimes you can change someone's behavior to effect changed consequences, but you can also change perceptions to change consequences. If someone does something, and you feel hurt because you perceive insult, and that person will not change his or her behavior to your liking, you can perceive that someone is bothered by you because of his or her own reasons, which do not have to connect negatively to your feelings of self-esteem. It is their act, not your own. Your changed perceptions will thus change your feelings and actions. Other people tend to react to your changed reactions, and the relationship changes.

Define a situation differently, and the consequences change. If I am yelling, you can perceive that I am a nasty man who is insulting you. The feeling of insult is a real consequence, leading to a whole stream of actions↔reactions = interactions. Change your perception to that I am yelling, not because I am nasty, but because I am in pain, and your feelings can change from insult to compassion for my pain and my foolish way of expressing it. Completely different actions↔reactions = interactions will flow from these changed feelings: perceive insult and we have a negative track in our relationship; perceive my hurt, and we have a positive track — all with the same yelling. Why not autonomously choose definitions that yield consequences of more benefits and fewer costs?

Value Judgments and Self-Fulfilling Prophecies

I suggested the need for considering values and setting standards of "good" living. But I am not suggesting that we make moral judgments about people and their behavior. I have not said that unjust people are "bad" (a moral judgment). I did say that research on the consequences of their behavior leads to the evaluation that there are costs — payments to be made — for being unjust.

Clinical sociologists and all others who wish to better understand, help, and get along with people must not *value-judge* people but must *evaluate* behavior (Hegarty and Goldberg 1980). A value judgment jumps to conclusions based on flimsy evidence, and often comes from limited past experiences, prejudices, and a lack of full awareness. An evaluation is based on research, on seeing many sides of something (seeing the whole), on consideration of the facts. A value judgment often leads to accusations and fault-finding. Evaluation leads to understanding. You value-judge me as nasty because I am yelling; yet an evaluation based on careful research might show that you did not understand what I meant, I did not express myself well, or I am a troubled person because of poor treatment in my life. Value judgments are not scientific and are often unjust; evaluation is scientific and leads to understanding.

I do not value-judge that people with marital problems are bad or failures. I make an evaluation based on research and analysis and find that a marital relationship can fall into an unbalanced, dis-eased state because of certain act↔react = interaction processes, some of which are based on pathological cultural teachings of how to get along with people. Clinicians can intervene to change perceptions and act↔react processes, thus switching the relationship to a healthy, positive track. If the general culture does not provide couples with the skills for balancing their relationships, they can be taught how to do so from another cultural pattern, the subculture of the clinician. The clinician — whether sociologist or medical practitioner — avoids value-judging clients, but evaluates dis-ease with the aim of achieving health.

People often make mistakes. It is common in our culture for people who make mistakes to suffer problems of low self-esteem and a poor self-concept, a feeling that they are total failures. They value-judge themselves instead of evaluating their mistake and using what they learn from it for better living in the future. They compound objective failure on a task such as an exam with a subjective feeling of lack of self-worth. They react to the *act* of failure with the perception—a value judgment—that they *are* failures. This is likely to become a *self-fulfilling prophecy* (Merton 1980). That is, they are likely to act as if they are failures, with the consequence of making that negative self-definition come true. From one failure, some people define their full selves as failures and begin to react to most events as failures. A person refused one date may react by acting like a failure, playing the act of avoiding interaction with the opposite sex. "No one wants me." This is a value judgment; evaluation would show that one person said no to going to a movie one single time. Is this a total failure of self? The consequences of a perception of being a total failure are very real. The person who says, "No one wants me. I am a failure," and who avoids social contact, will be very lonely. The Thomas Theorem is operating here in the form of a self-fulfilling prophecy.

Coping with Failure

I suggest that it is more healthy to separate failure at a task (objective consequence) from personal feelings of being low in self-esteem (subjective consequence). I also suggest that it is more healthy (balanced) to change the cultural judgmental perception of 'failure" as only negative to the evaluative perception that failure holds potential for success. Changing this definition of the situation allows people who fail in something to see failure as positive feedback about errors that, if corrected, can lead to beneficial consequences (Samples 1978).

I failed many times in many tasks and human relationships. But I learned from these mistakes and became a better person and even a scholar of people's troubles from my mistakes. Had I not learned from my mistakes and failures, I could not write this chapter. Much of what you read in my writings comes from scholarly study *and* from my experience of failure. So, were my failures totally negative experiences, or were they successes? A value judgment would say that they were negatives. An evaluation would show that my failures gave me bad times, yes, but also that they taught me a great deal, leading to many successes.

We need to learn how to research "what is happening and why" (evaluation), instead of saying, "You are wrong," or, "You are a failure" (value judgment). Evaluation of marital discord or other conflictual relations shows that social relations became unbalanced. But the participants do not have to pin the label of failure on one another or on themselves. Failures can also be analyzed in terms of costs and benefits. In our culture we emphasize the costs of failures and forget about the benefits. I see this as pathological and unbalanced, giving people a great deal of personal and interpersonal pain and dis-ease. Where the culture pins the label of failure on a person, that person should autonomously unpin the negative label and choose a positive label of an "O.K." person who has made a mistake and who will learn from it.

It is the same with school grades. You may receive an *F,* which is an evaluation of your work on an examination, but you need not feel like an *F,* a failure, which is a value judgment of being dumb or bad. You "have" an *F,* but how can you "be" an *F?* You are a human being with many dimensions who did poorly only at one task. American culture often confuses "having" with "being." As my former student Molly Watkins pointed out to me, if "having" is the mark of "being," why don't we call people "human havings" instead of human beings? There is a difference between "having" and "being."

If I have a good job, good looks, powerful connections, high grades, a beautiful lover, lots of money—all the things defined as desirable by the culture—then I might think that I *am* great. This might be true, or I might *have* all these things and actually *be* in a low condition of dis-ease from unjust actions, low in self-esteem, unable to enjoy what I have. Many people have many things and are still unhappy. These people do not find that "having" equals "being" happy.

Divorced people, poor people, people fired from jobs, students with low grades—all may suffer because of their objective life conditions. I would advise them to evaluate themselves and their conditions toward the goal of changing their positions in life—without accepting the subjective judgmental perception of themselves as *being* failures. They do not have to fall into the cultural pathological trap of value-judging themselves bad, low, unworthy people. Fail an exam, learn from your mistakes—but keep your self-esteem high. You *have* a low grade, but you can still *be* a beautiful, worthwhile, happy person!

Communication Problems

Social structure is made (tracked) by behavior, by perceptions, and by communication too. What we do, perceive, say, and hear are all part of the act↔react = interaction process. Communication problems lead to misperceptions that track trouble into the structure of social relationships. It is necessary to communicate directly and clearly for good social relationships. If Jack says, "You are stupid," when he means, "I feel hurt," Jill will probably react to hearing "stupid" and will not react to Jack's hurt in the manner he needs and wants. She may snap back at him, and if so, he does not get the support and comfort he wants. Jack and Jill build a social structure that leads them off the track of joy and on the track for arguments.

Communication problems are frequent. This is one reason poorly tracked (dis-eased) relationships between people are so common. Instead of Jill saying, "I want to see a movie. Do you?" she says to Jack, "You would like to see a movie, wouldn't you?" Or she says, "It would do you good to see a movie." Jack may react by answering, "Stop telling me what I like and what I should do!" Jill reacts with tears, and says, "You never [by which she means not often enough for her liking] take me anywhere," to which Jack reacts by saying, "That's not true. We had dinner out two weeks ago." He rationally confronts her on the incorrect "never," but misses Jill's real point (unstated) that going out every two weeks is not often enough for her liking and that she is in the mood to see a movie. They have a long argument—when all that is necessary is, "I want to see a movie. How about you?" Jill might even go off her track by saying, "There's a new movie house down the street," to which Jack, not knowing what to make of it, reacts by saying, "How interesting." This frustrates Jill because he is not responding to her desire to see a movie, but to the fact of a new movie house (Satir 1967:15).

In our culture many people talk past one another. They miscommunicate. They do not connect. Do some research by observing and listening carefully in a deep manner. Listen to how people talk on dates. Listen to how people express themselves in their families. Listen to students in hallways, at parties, talking over the dining table. Are all the participants aware of what is really meant? Are they talking *with* one another, or just running on their own private tracks? Do they talk by hinting? Do they take care to say what they mean? Do they hear what the other is trying to say?

A 16-year-old son asks his father at 5:30 P.M. on a Friday, "What are you doing tonight, Dad?" His father replies, "You can have it!" The son answers, "I don't want it now." The father snaps back in anger, "Why did you ask?" The son answers with anger, "What's the use?" (Satir 1972:54).

After researching by entering the mind space of both father and son to evaluate what they mean by what they say, we learn that the son wanted to find out if his father planned to watch him play basketball that night. He did not ask his father directly. He was afraid his father might say no, and he would feel hurt because he feels the no as "Father does not love me," hooking his self-esteem. So the son used a hinting method. The father got the message that the son was hinting, but hinting that he wanted the family car for the night. The son got the message that his father was putting him off. The father felt his son's anger (act) and was angry (react) because he felt his son was ungrateful (value judgment) for being given the use of the car. The father and son became angrier (interaction), both perceiving that the other "didn't care" (a value judgment and a definition of the situation with real consequences).

Such exchanges become grooved into a family subculture that creates a family social structure made up of act↔react = interaction tracks where almost all conversations are based on hints. The family structure is based on tracks that often go "off the track." Being "off the track" creates imbalance, feelings of injustice, and family dis-ease. For interactions with fewer problems, we have to retrack this family to make direct communication.

Think about your own communication and its consequences in the relationships in your own life. What kind of act↔react = interaction tracks are involved? How can you improve the ratio of costs to benefits? How often have you found your relationships going off track because of communication problems? How often have you realized, after an argument or a disagreement, that each person did not really know where the other "was coming from"?

Understanding

In order to understand "where a person is coming from" in words and behavior, it is important to practice the skill of *taking the role of the other* in relation to life conditions such as culture, sex, age, health, and occupation. This can be broadly seen as entering by the powers of mind and imagination — and, where possible, by actual research, experience, and observation — the life position and condition, set of mind, feelings, culture, and subculture of another to see "where he or she stands." In a way, you stand in another person's position so you can perceive how things look and feel in that person's perception.

I am writing this during summer residence on the twenty-eighth floor of a downtown San Francisco skyscraper. My writing table is next to a wall-to-wall picture window overlooking much of the western part of the city. I perceive a very special image of urban life from my twenty-eighth floor perspective. I do not think the ghetto residents a few blocks away and down below have the same perception.

The janitor working in the basement of my summer residence is in the same building structure as I am. He also probably sees another view of urban life. Sociological research would determine what these images are. The janitor and I are both at the same address, but our perspectives are different because of where we are — where we stand — in the structure. People occupy different positions in the social structure, and their perspectives are different because of it. Poor and rich, women and men, bosses and employees, teachers and students, husbands and wives and children all may be in the same structure, but their perspectives are probably different.

To stand with another in his or her life conditions is really to under-stand. "Understand" says to stand under, or to uphold a person's humanity from his or her perspective and position. I am not a janitor, and the janitor is not a sociologist and writer. Neither of us should make inferences (value judgments) about how the other lives, thinks, feels, perceives, without asking about and considering (evaluating by research) the special conditions of the positions of each.

Do you think I am lucky living in a skyscraper structure in San Francisco during the summer? Do you envy my perfect life? If so, you are value judging. Evaluation of my life might show that you would not wish to have it. Sociology has concepts (tools) and perspectives (visions) that can be used to understand different people and to explain people to one another.

We can simply ask questions of one another. But asking questions and getting answers often do not give us all the understanding we wish. For more understanding, we can switch roles to determine how it feels. A husband (or boy friend) can take the role of the wife (or girl friend) and do what she does, and she can take his role. But they will still never fully understand each other for many reasons, including the important condition that she never lived or will live with a penis and he with a vagina—and everything else connected to this prime biological sex difference, including the different ways in which males and females are brought up in our culture. But for more understanding, they can take the role of the other *in imagination* to determine how it feels, even when they cannot arrange a switch in fact. Doing this eliminates many value judgments and leads to deeper understandings, thereby solving problems between people.

Taking the role of the other by imagination for research and understanding is especially important when we cannot switch roles and when we cannot ask people what they feel, need, and perceive. How can we understand what an infant feels? Sometimes a cry gives us information. But this is very little information. The baby cannot answer if we ask for more information. Some adults are also at a loss for words under certain conditions, and we are left with the tool of taking the role of the other in imagination for understanding. We can try to remember how we felt when we were babies, but for the most part our memories fail us. So an active process of imagining how it would feel to be a baby is necessary for understanding.

How does it feel—with an immature brain functioning—to commune with the ceiling, looking up, hour after hour, not being able to turn over? Virginia Satir (1972:216-17) takes the role of a baby and writes a lengthy story. I will abstract only one short part:

> One terrible thing is when someone comes to my crib and suddenly puts his big face over mine. I feel that a giant is going to stamp me out. All my muscles get tight, and I hurt. Whenever I hurt, I cry. . . . People don't always know what I mean.

This process—a deep imagining of how things might be and feel for another person—is what the pioneering sociologist Max Weber meant when using the German word *Verstehen,* which is roughly equivalent to our English phrase "deep understanding." As you learned in Chapter 1, *Verstehen* is a basic method in sociological analysis. It is also one of our most valuable clinical sociological tools.

Conclusion

When Jack and Jill met at the well, little did they understand about culture, subculture, the pathology of normalcy, role models, autonomy, balance and justice, imbalance, injustice and dis-ease, projection, the act↔ react = interaction process, self-esteem, social organization and social structure, the Thomas Theorem, the self-fulfilling prophecy, value judging and evaluating, having and being, the need for direct and clear communication and the problems of vague communication, the need to take the role of the other, *Verstehen* — and more. So they fell because of the crookedness of the act↔react tracks making the structure of their relationship.

They went far off the track and had a breakup because of the breakdown of a good social relationship. They were broken, too, losing the joy and love they wished. The clinical sociologist uses basic sociological tools — only some of which I have had the space to cover for you — to help Jack and Jill and the many unhappy people like them at love, work, community, and elsewhere build more satisfying, stable social structures where the tracks lead to joy and fulfillment, not to breakdown and trouble.

Review Questions and Exercises

1. Use the act↔react = interaction model to show why it is better for good social relationships to say, "I feel angry when . . ." instead of, "You make me angry." What is the technical term for someone putting their feelings onto someone else instead of taking ownership of feelings?
2. Use your imagination. Take the role of the other, and use *Verstehen* analysis to write several pages stating as best you can how it feels to be the opposite sex in any three of the following activities. (The work can be done anonymously.)

    a. Discovering one's own body at puberty

    b. Taking a walk on the street in shorts and a light shirt (blouse) on a hot summer day

    c. At the pool in a bathing suit

    d. Nude, on a nude beach

    e. Asking for a date. Refusing a date

Read responses written by men and women. Are there differences? Are there similarities? Discuss the responses with others. Do you feel the need to change your act with men or women after this exercise?

Readings and References

Bierstedt, Robert. *The Social Order.* 3rd ed. New York: McGraw-Hill, 1970.
Cohen, Harry. *Connections: Understanding Social Relationships.* Ames, Iowa: Iowa State University Press, 1981.

Readings and References

Coleman, Emily, and Betty Edwards. *Brief Encounters.* Garden City, N.Y.: Doubleday/Anchor, 1980.

Fromm, Erich. *The Sane Society.* New York: Fawcett, 1965.

Hegarty, Christopher, with Phillip Goldberg. *How to Manage Your Boss.* New York: Rawson, Wade, 1980.

Merton, Robert K. "The Self-fulfilling Prophecy." In Lewis A. Coser, ed., *The Pleasures of Sociology,* 29.47. New York: Mentor, 1980.

Riesman, David, with Nathan Glazer and Reuel Denney. *The Lonely Crowd.* New Haven, Conn.: Yale University Press, 1961.

Rubin, Lillian Breslow. *Worlds of Pain: Life in the Working-Class Family.* New York: Basic Books, 1976.

Samples, R., quoted in John Glass, "Changing Your Life in Twenty-Five Words or Less." *Dawnpoint—in Transition,* 2 (Winter 1978).

Satir, Virginia. *Conjoint Family Therapy.* Rev. ed. Palo Alto, Calif.: Science and Behavior Books, 1967.

_____. *Peoplemaking.* Palo Alto, Calif.: Science and Behavior Books, 1972.

Socrates, cited in Plato *Republic* I and IV.

Thomas, W. I., and Dorothy Swaine Thomas. *The Child in America: Behavior Problems and Programs.* New York: Knopf, 1928.

4 THE SOCIOLOGY OF
THE INDIVIDUAL
Patricia See and *Roger A. Straus*

From birth, you have become accustomed to seeing yourself at the center of your universe. After all, this only makes sense. Who, then, are you? Who else but you, yourself. Again, this seems obvious to us.

But then you run into problems. How do you explain it? If you are like most people, you will figure it this way: When things don't work out the way you want them to, when things happen to you that you can't seem to do anything about, that's your tough luck. Or maybe somebody else is to blame—but, in any case, it's all your own personal problem.

The bad things that happen to you might not be your fault, but surely you could have done something to avoid them, surely you must have done something to bring them on yourself? Perhaps you deserve it. Maybe it has to do with your inborn nature. . . . Perhaps the source of your problems and difficulties, and your failures and successes as well, in life lies within your own mind. *What's wrong with you?*

We are socially and culturally conditioned to look at ourselves and our problems in this fashion. It is known as *common sense.* Common sense also tells us to look at other people and their problems in the same way.

People are what they are and do what they do because that is the *type* of person they are, isn't that so? If they have troubles, if they cannot cope with the "real world," that is literally their problem, isn't it? If you have what it takes, you will make it; if you don't, you won't; that's that, isn't it?

Think about all the times you have approached your own problems and those of other people in this fashion. Has it ever really helped you *do* anything about them? Perhaps there is something wrong with this whole way of looking at human problems as if life is a game of chance in which we are fated either to be winners or losers.

Sociology offers us an entirely different way of looking at people and their problems. Based on the observation that we each find ourselves alive in a world already inhabited by other people, a sociological perspective starts with the fact that not only do we all begin in an ongoing social world but that the world is already organized before we arrive.

"A separate individual is an abstraction unknown to experience, and likewise is society when regarded as something apart from individuals . . .

61

"society" and "individuals" do not denote separable phenomena, but simply collective and distributive aspects of the same thing (Cooley 1909)." The sociology of the individual goes on to explore the fact that we are *literally* social creatures. Whatever else might be said about "human nature," it is certain that people need other people in order to become fully human, that our species is capable of adapting a bewildering variety of collective strategies for our mutual survival through the device of social organization, and that the life of the individual is intimately connected to the life of society.

Our very sense of who and what we really are, the ways in which we think, even the thoughts we think and the things we feel it is "only natural" for us to do—all these things have their origins and their foundations in social life. We must recognize the extraordinary range of possibilities and potentialities manifested in the nearly infinite human variety—and then we must explain it.

Socialization

The essence of sociology lies in making the connection between the organized patterns of social life and both the varieties of people and the kinds of lives they lead within these patterns. A sociology of human individuals must, therefore, investigate how people and patterns come together in the process known as socialization.

Socialization is a lifelong learning process in which a person conforms herself or himself to the patterns of social life. This involves *internalizing* (i.e., making one's own) the ideas, understandings, beliefs, values, expectations for self, self's behavior, and the behavior of others held by members of one's social group. While there are many specific theories of socialization, all revolve around the principle that we tend to adopt the perspectives of those among whom we make our lives regarding life and how to live it.

Based on observation of his own daughters in the last years of the nineteenth century, the pioneering American sociologist Charles Horton Cooley proposed (1902) that this process might be described as "the looking-glass self." We begin, as infants, by observing the behavior of family members; then we try to imitate them, and they respond with positive or negative feedback. Ultimately, the child constructs a self-image on the bases of imagining how others judge her or him to really be:

A self-idea of this sort seems to have three principal elements: the imagination of our appearance to the other person; the imagination of his judgment of that appearance, and some sort of self-feeling, such as prode or mortification. The comparison with a looking-glass hardly suggests the second element, the imagined judgement, which is quite essential. The thing that moves us to pride or shame is not the mere mechanical reflection of ourselves, but an imputed sentiment, the imagined effect of this reflection upon another's mind . . . (Cooley 1902).

According to Cooley and other theorists, this process continues throughout our lives. Our very sense of who we are, what kind of person we are, what we are like, flows out of the history of our social interactions. We live to a very great extent, it seems, in this imagined reflection of ourselves we see in the eyes (and minds) of others.

Have you ever considered how much of your own sense of self reflects how you imagine others see you, or to what degree you base your own actions on how you think others will respond to them? Think about it. It's a real eye-opener!

To the degree that the larger organization of society is reflected in the patterns of behavior exhibited by individual members of that society, socialization provides the means by which each human being is tied into the whole society. We consider these relationships at further length later in our discussion, but it is important at this point to clarify the fact that there is a direct connection between the structure of any particular society and the character of the people who make their lives within that structure.

The particular society provides a general context for the socialization of its members. It both determines the range of possibilities for individuals and, directly or indirectly, establishes the kinds of problems and circumstances with which they will have to deal. When considering the sociology of the individual, however, the sociologist is most typically concerned with the more immediate relationships framing the social life of concrete human beings.

Our evolving definitions of self are not affected equally by all social interactions. We are most strongly influenced by those others with whom we have the most intense relationships. George Herbert Mead (1934), who elaborated Cooley's basic scheme into the Conduct Paradigm described in Chapter 1 of this volume, described such individuals as *significant others*. These are the people who are most important to us, whose respect, approval, judgment, and opinion we value most highly. Significant others, in other words, are those in whose eyes we are most concerned to see ourselves evaluated positively.

Groups and Social Networks

The group is the level of collective life most strongly affecting individual human beings on a day-in, day-out basis. Sociologists define the *social group* as a human system within which each member stands in a more or less fixed role relationship to the others (Merton 1968). Where else, then, are a person's significant others to be found but in the social groups in which he or she participates? For this reason, sociological understanding of the individual cannot be separated from investigation of the groups to which that person belongs.

Some groups are more influential than others, particularly those characterized by face-to-face interaction between members, prolonged and intimate relationships, and a strong sense of belonging on the part of members. These are known as *primary groups,* in contradiction to the more numerous, more formally organized, and more businesslike *secondary groups* to which a person belongs (Cooley 1909). Your "crowd," fraternity, or sorority are examples of college-age primary groups; the students in your sociology course can be described as a secondary group.

The "most primary" of all primary groups in almost everybody's life is the family in which one grows up. We acquire our basic socialization during a period of life in which we are entirely dependent upon parents and other family members; many or most of the patterns for our later life are laid down during childhood, and (as mental health practitioners find again and again) family members tend to remain our most significant others on a lifelong basis. Cooley went so far as to suggest that the reason people of every time and culture exhibit so many similarities — that is, a common "human nature" — is that we are all initially socialized within a primary group.

Social scientists studying the relationship between personal well-being and primary relationships of all types have recognized the crucial role of *social support,* "a set of exchanges which provide the individual with material and physical assistance, social contact and emotional sharing, as well as the sense that one is the continuing object of concern by others" (Pilisuk and Parks 1981). Social support was a major function of the traditional family. However, in today's world an increasing number of adults find their most intimate personal relationships outside the conventional family structure (Leading Edge Bulletin 1982). We are coming to depend more and more on "intentional extended families" comprised of friends, lovers, coworkers, business associates and other people with whom we spend our leisure time pursuing common interests. These relationships, ranging from informal groupings of friends through "natural helping systems" arising within neighborhoods and communities to formally constituted mutual help groups and community systems, are collectively referred to as *social support networks* (Pilisuk and Parks 1983). Thus, to understand a person, we need to study their social support networks as well.

A final point about groups is that they are not only the immediate context of socialization; we live our lives within the context of social groups. The sociologist, in other words, looks at the individual human actor as, above all else, a *group member.* Group membership structures our internal experience, provides us with a social identity, and provides the situations with respect to which we organize our conduct.

Regardless of how we enter a social group—whether as a baby, slave, employee, stranger, adoptee, visitor, peer, family member by marriage, or boss—we are assigned a particular *status* in the system. That is, we occupy a position in that group's social structure that carries with it a specific amount of prestige and authority. Our statuses can rise or fall, but we invariably have an identifiable place in the "pecking order" of every social group to which we belong.

Each status is associated with a *social role,* that is, with expectations for behavior, rights, and obligations. As suggested at the beginning of this section, "role" is a relational term, meaning that every member of a human system "plays a role" vis-à-vis every other person and the group as a whole. As we proceed through life's transitions, acquiring new roles and statuses, our repertoire of role sets (i.e., possible ways of "being ourselves") normally increases.

Our adeptness at managing these transitions and mastering these new roles depends, in turn, on our development of role-playing skills. Many "personal" as well as "interpersonal" problems may actually be problems in *social skills* and may be resolved by sociological counseling sensitizing the person to the facts of group life and training them in the necessary skills. Chapter 3 discusses this theme at length.

Situational Analysis

When we consider what it means to "be yourself," it is essential to recognize the difference between that which lies at the center of your consciousness, looking out, and your *social self*. Mead (1934) described this as the distinction between the "I," that innermost awareness (whatever its true nature), and the "Me," the person you experience yourself to be in the world of other people.

Functionally, one's "self" emerges in the interplay between the subjective awareness of the human organism and its context, the socially organized human world. Each member of society continuously shares in the creation of both the social order and of a "self" within that world as he or she interacts with others in the business of living. As Mead and Cooley so brilliantly argued, mind, self, and society are different aspects of one and the same stream of meaning-filled human behavior.

Interaction with others or the material environment triggers a process whereby an individual examines and evaluates the situation before she or he responds. According to how the individual interprets the situation to "really be," the person then selects the most appropriate attitudes, emotions, and actions with which to respond to that situation so as to positively influence its outcome. Described by W. I. Thomas (1923) as the *definition of the situation,* this is the side of your self that you experience directly, "from the inside."

The sociologist is careful to point out that the definition of the situation is directly tied to the socially organized world in which the person operates. As we have seen, any social grouping *institutionalizes* (incorporates within its framework) a more or less stable set of roles, rules, relationships and shared understandings which we refer to as its *social structure.* It follows, therefore, that society presents individuals with social situations which have already been at least partially structured, providing a limited number of grooves or tracks for one's own behavior. Sociologists, therefore, stress the degree to which situations are defined and, hence, the person's thoughts and actions are shaped by the groups and institutions constituting their special environment.

As you move through group life, you learn the patterns of your social world and proceed to fit your self into those patterns. It is the way human beings are made, in both senses of the phrase: Not only is the stream of our concrete acts dependent on these mental definitions of the situation, but gradually a whole life policy — our "character" — emerges from our repeated acts of defining the situation. As one of the co-authors of this chapter (Straus 1982) has put it, "You are your act."

Thomas (1923) labeled this ongoing process *situational analysis,* stressing that the person one thus becomes is overwhelmingly conditioned by the kinds of situations, social influences, and other experiences progressively encountered by the individual in the course of social life. "Preliminary to any self-determined act of behavior there is always a stage of examination and deliberation which we may call *the definition of the situation.* And actually not only concrete acts are dependent on the definition of the situation, but gradually a whole life-policy and the personality of the individual himself follow from a series of such definitions. (Thomas 1923)." In order to understand a human being, you must, therefore, discover *(a)* how he or she actually interprets the meaning of different kinds of situations; and *(b)* how he or she has come to analyze situations in that particular way.

Sociologists' descriptions of situational analysis and other social-psychological phenomena often give the impression that a person consciously examines and evaluates each situation prior to acting. This, as each of us knows from experience, is not the case. Rather, the mental definition of the situation and its manifestation in objective conduct are stages in a single, flowing act; once the situation is defined, one need generally only *release* action.

The key concept here is *internalization.* As, perhaps through repetition, one becomes increasingly familiar with a way of thinking, feeling, imagining, or behaving, it becomes part of oneself, literally. It becomes more or less habitual, automatic, "right" and "natural" to us, a taken-for-granted element of our analytical and behavioral repertoire (Parsons and Bales 1955). Through internalization, both material reality and the social order become part of our cognitive map of the world, or, as psychologists might describe it, our mental "set."

One consequence of this fact is that the socialized individual's character reflects in miniature the structure of the social world in which she or he lives. This extends beyond conscious awareness to how we define, sort, and organize information in the process of situational analysis (Bateson 1972), as well as to supplying the rules governing how we release the definition of the situation in even our "spontaneous" actions.

Most of the time we are unaware of most of the elements entering into our situational analysis. Yet, these "unknown" definitions have an inordinate influence upon both our self-definition and our construction of action. Louis Wirth (1951) pointed out that the most important thing we can know about a person is what that person takes for granted, and that the most important facts about a society or social group are those that are seldom debated but generally regarded as settled.

An *internalized role*, for example, is one that the person believes without question others expect him or her to enact, whether or not it actually corresponds either to how the person defines the situation or to the person's own self-concept (Parsons 1951). At the same time, in the process of learning one's own role within any human system, the person internalizes his or her understanding of the other, interrelated roles providing its context.

The child, for example, in order to define the boundaries of self must also internalize the roles of mother, father, brother, sister, grandparent, etc., as presented within that particular family group. These personal and situational contingencies, along with the biological variability of the human organism, account for the almost infinite human variety even within a single society.

One can perhaps best understand these things by making the analogy between a person and a computer. These internalized roles, and other definitions of the situation, are not so much "pure ideas" as socially learned scripts for action. When confronted by a concrete situation, the "processor" sorts through its stored information for patterns matching those presented by the situation. This sorting activity is itself governed by rules at least in part "programmed" into the mind by socialization. The "processor" then constructs a composite map or mental model of the situation out of these stored patterns, assembling, in effect, a behavioral "program." This program is Thomas's "definition of the situation." Sometimes, after conscious reflection and modification, but more often without, the program is then fed into the "effector" circuitry of the human organism—its nervous system—and its instructions are released in the form of socially organized action.

The Cultural Connection

Social scientists generally make a distinction between biology, society, and culture: *Culture is the total nonbiological inheritance of a society (or social group)*. Culture itself is usually differentiated into *material culture* and *symbolic culture*. "Material culture" denotes technology and everything created by technology — buildings, T-shirts, highways, books, television sets, cereal boxes, art objects, cyclotrons, and other artifacts. "Symbolic culture" denotes everything else — languages, myths, beliefs, values, all the rules for communicating, understanding, and behaving underlying a particular form of society.

Although culture is most fully developed as a concept within the discipline of anthropology, it is essential for sociological understanding as well, as you learned in Chapter 3. Sociologists are typically more interested in the cultural variations within a society than anthropologists, who characteristically study the culture of entire societies. Sociologists are also most typically concerned with the rules by which a culture functions to carve out a common reality for participants and coordinate their actions.

We generally differentiate these rule-supplying elements of culture into *norms* and *values* (Parsons 1951). In each case, they may be partially or entirely shared by all members of a society or only by members of specific social worlds within the larger society. *Social worlds* are segments of a larger society, sometimes defined by geography, more often by membership in differentiated ethnic, racial, occupational, or economic groups.

We use the term *norm* to refer to the accepted rules or standards for thinking, feeling, being, and behaving shared by the social group. *Values,* on the other hand, are the group's way of defining what is or is not good, desirable, worthwhile, meaningful, and worth striving or even dying for. Generally, norms are based on the values of a social group. Some norms are more binding on individuals of one status than another, and some are more binding on all group members than others, depending on the shared values of that social world.

The principle that norms and values are not universal but specific to the particular society that upholds them is known as *cultural relativity.* Human groups typically consider their own ways the only right, natural, and proper ways; this belief is termed *ethnocentrism.* As long as we have to deal only with individuals socialized within our own culture or subculture, ethnocentrism presents no problem. The moment we attempt to interpret the behavior of people who follow different cultural standards, however, it becomes a very great problem indeed.

For example, schoolteachers in the United States have (at least until recently) been educated to judge students by the norms of "well behaved" white, middle-class children. They know how to interpret the meaning of departures from these role expectations. But now they are confronted with an influx of Hispanic, oriental, and other children raised by entirely different standards—in which, for example, it is a sign of disrespect to look someone of higher status than yourself directly in the eyes.

Teachers who are unaware of these cultural differences might, for example, interpret the Hispanic child's demeanor as a sign of guilt, inattention, or disrespect, and may respond to the child accordingly. Such a teacher's lack of sociological awareness is liable to create a self-fulfilling prophecy, dooming minority children to academic failure.

Few people spontaneously discover this sociological perspective for themselves and break free of their internalized cultural biases on their own. We are all creatures of our own culture. Each of us is on the inside, looking out—which is one of the best arguments why every student should be introduced to the sociological imagination.

Becoming aware of the cultural connection, in particular, explains many things. Not only is the "cultural approach" one of the foundations of the clinical perspective in sociology, but everyone who works with people needs to be aware of it. Utilizing the cultural approach in the practice of counseling, education, public administration, and the health-care and service professions means that special attention is placed on how the individuals one is dealing with analyze situations given their particular cultural backgrounds, social characteristics, and group affiliations.

Life-Style Variations

A *life style* is precisely that, a style of life. In recent years it has become fashionable to consider life style a matter of personal choice. "Pop" psychologists often tell us that the way to solve our personal problems is simply to change our life style. Granted, many aspects of contemporary American life styles are anything but socially, psychologically, or medically health-promoting, but, as Max Weber long ago pointed out, there is far more to life style than "doing your own thing." To a very large extent, one's way of living is shaped by the role expectations associated with one's status and social world (Weber 1946).

For example, one of the co-authors teaches at a college where the student body is polarized into several different status groups. Those who attend the School of Fine Arts are generally treated by others as outcasts. Called "Arties," they are ritually scorned by other students because they tend to look, talk, and act as if they were "Sixties people," generally keep to themselves, and almost never join fraternities or sororities or engage in communal rituals such as attending football games. On the other hand, the "Arties" consider other students to be overly conventional, unimaginative, closed minded, hung up on "making a buck," and find their life styles either objectionable or boring.

It is not that the "Arties" are, whatever their culture says, significantly more or less free than fraternity brothers and sorority sisters to improvise a life style of their own. Rather, their life style comes with the territory — upon investigation, it becomes clear that art majors participate in a separate social world within the academic community. The structure of their curriculum, their personal preferences, and the inherited culture of the group all work together in this respect. The same is true of the other social worlds on campus; a frat brother majoring in business would not get along with *his* crowd were he to look, live, and act "like an Artie." Nor would he probably want to.

In recent years the term life style has taken on a second connotation as well — it is often used to refer to the kind of sex and family life in which one engages. While there is considerable group variation in tolerance for "alternative life styles" in that sense of the word, this aspect of conduct is generally treated as a concern of the whole society. For quite a few years the pendulum had been swinging in the direction of greater permissiveness with respect to sexual freedom, sexual orientation, and experimentation with various forms of family relationships. This was manifested in an increasing number of unmarried couples living together, the gay rights movement, the emergency of a "singles" life style, and so forth.

More recently, cultural reaction has set in, and so homosexuality, alternative families, and other "life style variations" are again being looked upon as threats to the social order. To the degree that individual variability means that different people have different needs with regard to sexuality and relationships and that they will be most effective in social functioning if those needs are satisfied, the attempt to reimpose restrictive cultural norms on this aspect of social life can only backfire, to the detriment of both individuals and the general society.

Although conformity to a single cultural norm certainly makes life simpler for most people and institutions, forcing people to adopt a rigidly defined way of life down to matters of sexuality and intimate relationships creates far more problems than it attempts to solve. Unrealistic standards only create tension between what people are supposed to do and what they do anyway.

Every social world implicitly or explicitly defines a standard for life style, behavior, and character according to its professed values. Violation of the accepted norms governing "your sort of person" causes both social and personal stress, as discussed by Harry Cohen in Chapter 3.

For one thing, such conduct threatens those who accept the values expressed in ideal norms, whose status and sense of identity are based on those values. They tend to defend their interests with a vengeance, placing the cultural violator in a position of having to conceal his or her true feelings or conduct, sometimes even to live a secret life. Except in a few cosmopolitan areas, this is the common plight of the homosexual; an enormous popular and scientific literature documents the injuries and inequities to both individuals and society caused by this one example of cultural rigidity.

When violations of this sort become so widespread that a significant minority of group members engages in them on a "things as normal" basis, the split between cultural belief and actual practice becomes socially disruptive in the extreme. On the one hand, such a split leaves "slack" within which individuals and groups can maintain unfair advantages or advance their interests through corruption. On the other hand, it leads to a situation where individual lives are ruined, children and youth are socialized to be hypocritical, "accepted" cultural norms can be enforced only through the self-defeating mechanism of force. However you interpret the pharmacological facts of the case, consider how the criminalization of marijuana—in essence, a conflict over cultural norms—has adversely affected our lives in just this fashion.

Social Characteristics

An individual's conduct is a reflection of how she or he, based on cultural learning, analyzes situations. One's acquisition of culture depends in turn on *social location,* that is, on one's place in the overall social structure as it is organized at this particular time in history. As sociological investigation has proved, one's social location also tends to determine the kinds of problems and circumstances one will face in life, determines one's chances for success in attaining culturally defined goals, the sort of work one is likely to do, the kind of treatment one can expect from others, the kind of life one will lead, even the probability of health or ill health, longevity or an early demise (Gerth and Mills 1953).

To speak of "social location" is shorthand for saying that every member of a society can be described in terms of relationship to certain structural factors of that society. Among these "vital features" in our own society, according to clinical sociologists Glassner and Freedman (1977), are the person's socioeconomic status, ethnicity, gender, and age. We consider these briefly here.

Socioeconomic status refers to position in the social stratification system. Taking the form of a hierarchical pecking order, this arrangement locates each person or group in a particular "stratum" or level of material wealth, power, and prestige, with specific rights and duties relative to other strata. Thus, a person's socioeconomic status tends to determine his or her circumstances, relative chances at rising or falling within the overall system, the kind of person one is socialized to become, both the kind of life the person is likely to want for self and the manner of life the person is actually able to lead (Blumberg 1972).

One of the most difficult facts of life for most students to accept is the fact that the game of life is rigged; the stratification system is simply not fair. A tiny fraction of the population at the top monopolizes a radically disproportionate amount of the available wealth, power, and resources of society (U.S. Department of Commerce 1982), while those at the bottom have almost no chance of rising out of poverty. Dominant sociological opinion seems to be that socioeconomic status is the most powerful social characteristic in every way, and that the other vital features only modify its impact on the person.

Ethnicity refers to one's hereditary membership in a distinct group with a historically based subculture of its own and a sense of "ethnic" or "racial" identity. Each such group possesses a unique subculture based on its historical experience, with its own set of values, symbols, and beliefs. Sometimes this is tied up with religion, as in the case of the Jews; rather than, other times with racial identity, as in the case of American blacks. Particularly as some ethnic groups are the targets of discrimination because of their unique subcultures, ethnicity has significant influence on the socialization, self-concept, conduct, health, and mental health of the individual (Farley 1982).

Gender is important because human societies universally organize work and family roles according to cultural rules defining the meaning of sex differences, how men and women are to behave, their relative status, rights and privileges. The family is a basic organizing unit of any society, and its nature, structure, stability, and meaning are all vitally dependent on gender-based socialization. In our society, needless to say, the historical subjugation of women has been particularly significant for both sexes.

Age is a vital feature for several reasons. For one thing, our life within society is structured along a time dimension in that we each progress through a sequence of age-related roles such as child, student, youth, worker, parent, and retired person. Children and old people, for example, are socially defined as noncontributing members of society and are therefore granted limited rights. Second, it is useful to consider those of a single age (technically known as a *cohort*) as a situationally distinct social group, since members were initially socialized under similar historic conditions and then progress through life's passages together. This is extremely important with regard to understanding how they analyze situations.

The Problem of Change

Philosophy and physics alike tell us that the most basic fact of life is the fact of change. Social scientists believe that culture is perhaps the most basic means by which human groups adapt themselves to objective conditions. More than that, it is through that part of culture known as *technology* that humans actively conform both the material and social environments to their own interests, goals, and purposes. As these changes progress, the rest of the culture must follow suit, enabling society to adapt to these new conditions.

Sociocultural change (i.e., change in both social structure and culture) has an enormous impact on the individual, especially when the rate of technological change leads to ever-accelerating changes in material conditions, social arrangements, even the most trivial aspects of day-to-day living. These changes are now flowing up and down the nested levels of human systems in our own society at a phenomenally rapid pace. Contemporary American society is a huge, highly diverse system of systems undergoing change at an unprecedented rate—faster than any known group of its size and complexity.

Sociocultural change implies stress and dislocation at every level of society; these pressures, often resulting in conflict between groups and individuals, eventually lead to the working out of new social arrangements and cultural realities. As these changes permeate the society, roles and statuses change relatively quickly, norms and values more slowly; but every element and every relationship within the system undergoes continual pressure in the direction of change.

Change, however, affects some groups and social classes more immediately or more dramatically than others. Thus the effects of social change on any given individual will depend upon his or her social location (Lee 1951).

Economic shifts in the United States, for example, are having far more adverse effect on workers in the steel, automobile, and other "heavy" industries of the Frostbelt than on the technicians and assembly workers in the "high tech" industries of the Sunbelt. Nevertheless, these accelerating changes in the economic structure are so pervasive that very few groups and individuals have not already been significantly affected. Perhaps only those whose statuses are unaffected by day-to-day economic changes, such as the extremely wealthy, and those whose social worlds are structurally insulated from the general society, such as the Amish, and some Native American and Appalachian communities, have so far avoided the impact of accelerating sociocultural change.

In the main, most individuals are trying to operate successfully in new situations with old, previously internalized cultural realities and social-strategies. In a rapidly changing society such as our own, it is not uncommon for individuals to reach early adulthood socialized to deal with sociocultural conditions that no longer exist. They have worked from earliest childhood to master rules and roles that are no longer appropriate to the society, that may or may not match the contemporary society's emerging expectations for them.

Those expectations and values into which we have been most intensively socialized, such as those relating to family and sex roles, and those roles in which we have been successful, are, sometimes tragically, most resistant to change. They have often become so deeply internalized that we no longer even think about them; they have become part of our selves. They continue to color our evaluations, yet we remain unaware of them even while we unconsciously pull them into our situational analyses. Thus, they continue to influence our thoughts, feelings, and actions even while we seek to change our act.

Sociocultural change directly affects individuals in many ways. First, it radically alters the conditions with which they must deal. Often, this creates situations for which they are entirely unprepared, which require them to suddenly shift roles or the entire direction of their lives. Thus, it continually challenges their cultural conditioning, thrusting them into situations where everything they have learned to take for granted is called into question, where the rules and values they have internalized no longer seem to apply, and where they can no longer interpret the meanings of things and events in any way that makes sense to them.

Consequently, rapid change places them under conditions of social stress, for which they have no coping skills. This adversely affects their physical and mental health, strains or totally disrupts their families and other social relationships.

Very likely, you have seen some or all of these effects in your own family. No doubt, you have experienced firsthand the "generation gap" in which your parents cannot accept or understand your tastes in music and dress, the ways in which you prefer to "party," or your attitudes toward work and sacrifice. These things seem only natural to you, since they are part of the cultural reality of your age cohort; they tend to seem unnatural or downright perverse from the perspective of previous generations.

Every student has also encountered one of the most troublesome consequences of rapid sociocultural change in recent years: the instability of contemporary marriages. In some regions over half the students in any classroom will come from so-called broken homes, while about half of all marriages made today will end in divorce. One of the most basic institutions in American society has changed from something you can pretty much take for granted to something you can no longer rely on.

An increasing number of young people feel afraid to fall in love or commit themselves to another person on a lifelong basis, although that is exactly what we have been culturally conditioned to want for ourselves. Historically, the family based on the ideal of lifelong marriage permanently uniting two sets of relatives, has been our most important provider of an intimate group of people who care about us, on whom we can rely for total acceptance, assistance, support, and approval. What happens now? Will your uncle still help you get that job with his firm after your parents' messy divorce?

It is not that people were any happier when they had to marry and could not get divorced. A bad relationship is good for nobody. While there are troubling social, economic, and psychological consequences for both adults and the children of divorce and remarriage, these are very likely related to a lack of social and cultural arrangements adapted to today's objective conditions (Cherlin 1982).

Many people are therefore improvising their own solutions by involving themselves in "voluntary families" drawn from their close friends (*Leading Edge Bulletin* 1978). Thus, self-created support networks may come to fill at least some of the sociocultural void created by the pervasive changes in family structure in contemporary society. In 1982 California's Mental Health Promotion Unit sponsored the statewide "Friends Can Be Good Medicine" campaign to raise people's consciousness in this regard and motivate them to place time and energy in building and maintaining such relationships on their own. Increasingly, however, Americans are seeking professional help in attempting to deal with the consequences of galloping sociocultural change.

The Sociological Counselor

One of the newer professionals to whom individuals can turn is the clinical sociologist. As a counselor, the sociologist employs social theory (most commonly from the systems or conduct paradigm) and sociological research methods to assess the case, obtain *Verstehen* into the client's situational analysis (as the last chapter described), work up a substantive model of what is going on, and explore possibilities for change in the particular situation.

It is essential to point out that these professionals limit themselves to treating social problems that are manifested at the individual or primary-group level. They proceed on the principle (discussed in Wirth 1931) that the problem of an individual cannot be understood outside its social context and that the conduct of individuals, however it may seem to differ from the conduct of others, is always somehow related to the culture of their social world.

More and more commonly, sociologists and other social science clinicians treat individuals' problems as problems of their entire family or other primary group. Often, they will work with the entire human system rather than just the member with an identified problem. Even when the sociological counselor works with a single individual, the focus of intervention will be upon the organization of relationships surrounding the individual, rather than trying to change only the individual.

In other words, faithful to the roots of modern clinical sociology in the Chicago School, the emphasis is upon patterns of social relations, either directly or indirectly, by redefining personal culture. The sociologist may also serve as part of a multidisciplinary team as well. as an independent provider of counseling services. In this context, in addition to face-to-face intervention, the sociologist's role normally involves consultation with other team members with regard to the sociological aspects of the total case.

Sociological Counseling

We shall briefly consider some interventions that clinical sociologists have designed to help individual clients. First, however, we need a client for whom sociological counseling would be appropriate.

Consider the case of an "underachieving" woman college student troubled by feelings of personal inadequacy. She has always believed that her scholastic problems and low self-esteem reflected some internal, psychological deficit of her own. She has tried and tried again to overcome these things on her own, but she has always failed. What she tells the sociologist in her initial interview is that she is afraid she cannot hack it in college and wants to find out what is wrong with her.

The first task of the sociological counselor is to assess this case in order to work out a program of intervention. Normally, one or more of the initial sessions will be devoted to constructing a sociological life history answering these questions: "What is the story [or script] being acted out here?" and "How does the client *do* his or her problem?" This requires the clinician to piece together a model of the client's social world and personal culture, social location and personal background, and the history of the problem — what it is, how it works, and above all else, how the client defines all these things and what he or she wants to get out of the helping relationship.

The co-authors' assessment strategies give some idea of the range of possibilities. Straus (1982) has normally used a simple interview format involving guided conversation. See (1981), on the other hand, developed a method of self-observation in which the client is asked to keep a journal for several weeks in which he or she records every thing experienced — from details of food intake, sleep, and exercise to dreams, social interactions, and reflections on the day's events. Client and counselor then go over this material, searching out the patterns to be found within it. Very typically, these patterns do not conform to the client's own concep- tions and conscious definitions. Here again, what people *say* they do — even to themselves — and what they *actually do* are often very different realities.

The sociological interview process may be as straightforward as a guided conversation or as elaborate as See's "self-observation" technique described above. This "research" phase of counseling provides necessary data and helps the client see how the sociological imagination could apply to his or her case. Thus it is also the first stage of sociological therapy. In the case of the woman student, two interrelated stories will very likely emerge. The first will connect her feelings of personal inadequacy to the consequences of the social and political arrangements of our male-dominated society and (one would suspect) of growing up in an "old-fashioned" family with a workaholic father and a mother who runs the household with an iron hand and has done everything in her power to train the daughter to be a "proper young lady."

The other part of the story might be that, having been a poor student who barely made it through high school, her mother tried to push her to do well in school. At the same time, the mother probably gave off subtle messages to the effect that, being a girl, the daughter should not threaten boys by conspicuously excelling, most particularly in math. With no guidance from her parents, the girl developed erratic study habits, coming to spend a great deal of her time daydreaming about getting married and having a family. While she maintained above-average grades, her "attitude" became a continual source of conflict during her high school years.

Going away to college to please her parents, she suddenly found herself both free to do as she liked and confronted with peers and faculty who encouraged her to excel, to be assertive, to make a career of her own and not simply find a husband to care for her. Now her study habits have become a problem to her, and she has become aware that she does not have to live with that extreme self-consciousness and low self-esteem she had believed to be "only natural."

The sociological counselor would be concerned to help her sort out and redefine her definitions of the situation regarding herself and her role as a woman.

One method might be *sociodrama* (Glassner and Freedman 1979), in which the client is guided to act out the various roles, relationships, and definitions of the situation involved in her problem. Often other people, such as a specially trained assistant, will be asked to take part. For example, in a method called "the auxiliary ego," the client might be asked to coach an assistant to perform the role of a significant other, such as her mother, or to play her while she plays her mother, her father, a math exam, a boy friend, etc.

Clinical sociologists have employed a variety of intervention strategies depending on their personal training and preferences and the nature of the case. Some of these include hypnosis, videotaping, sociometry (diagraming one's roles and relationships), behavioral and cognitive-behavioral therapy, poetic analysis (Black and Enos 1981) and guided conversation. Sometimes, the clinician will prefer to work with an entire primary group using techniques of family therapy, human systems intervention, or both. Had the student in our hypothetical case, or her parents, sought help while she was still living at home, this would really have been the best way to go about it. Such an approach might take the form of improving communication between group members, clarifying their role expectations for one another, sociodrama, or the introduction of mechanisms by which group members may change behaviors to manage problems within their system. This kind of strategy involves changing the client's primary-group context rather than changing the client's self.

Clinical social scientist may also work at another level, as we have suggested in this chapter. Rather than focus interventions directly on the problems of individuals or families, they may help develop or implement intervention programs creating new social support networks or "geared to make use of the kinship and community network whether in crisis intervention, in the recapturing of latent long-term ties or in developing new relations" (Pilisuk and Parks 1983). For example, the sociologists might recommend that the client join a "self-help" group such as Alcoholics Anonymous or AlAnon (for persons who have intimate relationships with alcoholics), or become involved in the activities of a Women's Center or other community support network.

Whatever strategies and methods the sociological counselor employs, the goal of the intervention process will be to help the client maximize life. The clinical sociologist may suggest adjustments to social context to better facilitate the individual's human needs or teach clients strategies and tactics for dealing more effectively with their social context and life circumstances from a position of increased knowledge. By and large, then, sociological counseling is more like an educational or training endeavor rather than "therapy" in the sense of "fixing what's wrong with the client." It illustrates how concepts, perspectives, and methods concerning the sociology of the individual can be effectively used help people do something about social problems as they are manifested in their own lives. It is the practical form of the sociology of the individual.

Review Questions and Exercises

1. Write a short description of how, if you were "just being yourself," you imagine the following people would see you:
   a. Your parents
   b. Your closest friends
   c. Your instructor
   d. Other students who have never met you

Complete this exercise by writing a paragraph or two comparing and contrasting these different images of yourself and considering how each imagined judgment would affect your self-image and your actual behavior.

2. C. Wright Mills (1959) described the "sociological imagination" as the ability to see the connection between society—social structure, social location, culture, and history—and the individual's personal troubles, problems, and circumstances. Select one or more "vital feature" that has

been highly influential in shaping your self-concept, and explain the relationship between your self and society in terms of the sociological imagination.

3. This is a group exercise. Select one student to be the one who is having difficulty coping with school. That student can decide what her or his specific (imaginary) problem is. Now the other group members each choose a role from the following: father, mother, college professor, counselor or adviser, girl friend/boy friend, close friends of the student, others students she or he does not know well. Now conduct a brief sociodrama in which the student tries to get help with her or his troubles from these other people. After doing this (for a period of time to be set by the class instructor), group members should discuss the following:

    a. What occurred?

    b. What patterns emerged?

    c. How did each member of the group feel?

Then each student should write up a short discussion of what family, social support networks, and other groups mean to her or him.

Readings and References

Bateson, Gregory, *Steps Toward an Ecology of Mind.* New York: Ballantine Books, 1972.

Black, Clifford and Enos, Richard. "Using Phenomenology in Clinical Social Work: A Poetic Pilgrimage." *Clinical Social Work Journal* Vol. 9, no. 1 (Spring 1981), pp. 34–43).

Blumburg, Paul. *The Impact of Social Class.* New York: Crowell, 1972.

Cherlin, Andrew. "Remarriage as an Incomplete Institution." In A. S. Skolnick and J. H. Skolnick, eds., *Family in Transition,* 4th ed. Boston: Little, Brown, 1982.

Cooley, Charles Horton. *Human Nature and the Social Order.* New York: Scribners, 1902.

_____. *Social Organization.* New York: Scribners, 1909.

Farley, John E. *Majority-Minority Relations.* Englewood Cliffs, N. J.: Prentice-Hall, 1982.

Gerth, Hans, and C. Wright Mills. *Character and Social Structure.* New York: Harcourt, Brace & World, 1953.

Glassner, Barry, and Jonathan Freedman. *Clinical Sociology.* New York: Longman, 1979.

Leading Edge Bulletin 3, no. 2 (1982). "Peer Network Beginning to Supplant Families."

Lee, Alfred McClung, ed. *Principles of Sociology.* New York: Barnes and Noble, 1951.

_____. *Multivalent Man.* New York: Braziller, 1970.

Mead, George Herbert. *Mind, Self, and Society.* Edited by Charles Morris. Chicago: University of Chicago Press, 1934.

Mental Health Promotion Unit. *Friends Can Be Good Medicine,* Workbook and Training/Resource Manual. Sacramento, Calif.: California Department of Mental Health, 1981.

Merton, Robert. *Social Theory and Social Structure.* Expanded ed. New York: Free Press, 1968.

Mills, C. Wright. *The Sociological Imagination.* New York: Oxford University Press, 1959.

Parsons, Talcott. *The Social System.* New York: Free Press, 1951.

_____. and R. F. Bales. *Family, Socialization, and Interaction.* Glencoe, Ill: Free Press, 1955.

Pilisuk, M., and Parks, S. H. Chapter 6: Social support and family stress, pp. 137–156 in McCubbin, H. I., Sussman, M. B. and J. M. Patterson, eds., *Social Stress and the Family.* New York: Haworth Press, 1983.

_____. The place of network analysis in the study of supportive social associations. *Basic and Applied Social Psychology,* 2(2), 1981: 121–132.

See, Patricia W. "Self-observation and the Change Process." Paper presented at the California Council on Family Relations Annual Meetings, Santa Barbara, Calif., September 22, 1981.

Straus, Roger A. *Strategic Self-Hypnosis.* Englewood Cliffs, N. J.: Prentice-Hall, 1982.

_____. "Clinical Sociology on the One-to-One Level: A Social-Behavioral Approach to Counseling." *Clinical Sociology Review* 1 (1982): 59–74.

Thomas, William Isaac. *The Unadjusted Girl.* Boston: Little, Brown, 1923.

U.S. Department of Commerce. Bureau of the Census. *Statistical Abstract of the United States. 1982–83.* Washington D.C., 1982.

Weber, Max. *From Max Weber.* Edited by H. Gerth and C. W. Mills. New York: Oxford University Press, 1946.

Wirth, Louis. "Preface" to Karl Mannheim, *Ideology and Utopia: An Introduction to the Sociology of Knowledge.* New York: Harcourt, Brace, 1951.

_____. "Clinical Sociology." *American Journal of Sociology* 37 (1931): 49–66.

Zurcher, Louis A., Jr. *The Mutuable Self: A Self-Concept for Social Change.* Beverly Hills, Calif.: Sage, 1977.

Chapter **5** UNDERSTANDING
ORGANIZATIONS AND
THE WORKPLACE
John F. Glass

Have you ever felt grateful that, unlike many of your high school classmates, you have not been forced to jump directly into full-time work? How do you feel about what lies ahead for you, when you have completed your education and must, finally, enter that phase of life? Harsh as it may be to contemplate, the fact remains that there will come a time when you lose your protected status as student, leave school, and enter the world of work.

It isn't easy out there — why else do you think others often envy your life as a student? Most of your adult life will be spent earning a living, struggling to make ends meet, trying to better yourself in the world of work. Sociologists consider that work is the proving ground against which we define ourselves, our identity, and our value as adults.

From the beginning, therefore, the sociological discipline has been deeply concerned with the social organization of work as a key issue in understanding society and social life. Karl Marx, for example, felt that the way in which work is organized is the single most important sociological fact about any society. Perhaps Emile Durkheim's most influential contribution centers on his analysis of the ever-increasing *division of labor* (i.e., of job specialization). Max Weber's monumental synthesis of interpretive sociology was entitled *Economy and Society* (1968a, b).

The sociological imagination teaches us that human action and experience can be understood only in its structural context. Consequently, contemporary sociologists have been especially interested in the social arrangement of the workplace. Since, for most of us, our work life takes place in offices, factories, agencies, hospitals, schools, businesses of various kinds, the sociologist is most interested in this kind of "formal organization" and seeks to understand its functioning — how people make their lives and careers within the organization, and the ways in which it can be changed to become both more humane and more effective.

Formal organizations ("organizations" for short) are complex human systems deliberately established to fulfill a defined purpose (Caplow 1983). Pioneered by Max Weber, the sociological study of organizations investigates how they are structured, how people behave in them, how they are led and managed, how they relate to their social and material environments, and what makes some organizations more successful than others.

81

Formal Organizations

Today's sociologists generally analyze organizations from the perspective of systems theory. Human systems of this scale are often described simply as social systems; that is, organizations are viewed as social systems consisting of a number of individuals organized into a network of work groups and other lesser systems. Like any other system, organizations can either be considered as a whole or analyzed in terms of their component parts and relationships. They may be viewed in terms of either *process* or *structure*.

Historically, social systems have been most commonly analyzed in functional terms. Derived from the analogy between human systems and biological organisms, this approach conceptualizes organizations as sets of interdependent parts in a state of equilibrium maintained by the operation of specialized subsystems, each dedicated to fulfilling one or more needs of the whole. More recently, insights from general systems theory have shifted emphasis to a more dynamic view of the organization as *a chain of activities in continuous transaction with its environment* (Buckley 1967; Capelle 1979).

Looking at a factory as a process of transforming raw material into a finished product is an example of the general systems approach. Activities are analyzed in terms of *input* of information, material, and personnel; *processing* of these inputs; and then *output* of products, services, or information. Every such system also incorporates *feedback* mechanisms through which the organization detects and adjusts to changes in both its environment and its internal states. Systems concepts are discussed at greater length in Chapter 1 of this book.

Systems-as-process and systems-as-social-structures are two sides of the same coin. The *social structure* is the framework of the organization; to analyze its structure is similar to analyzing the anatomy of a living organism. In both cases, structure provides forms and patterns for coordinating and conducting the activities (or "functions") of the system.

Perhaps the most basic way of understanding social structure is to consider its internal division of labor — how the tasks of the organization are distributed among its component individuals and groups of individuals. "Roles" and "positions" are the building blocks of organizational structure in this sense.

Role refers, in this context, to a set of expectations for behavior defining how a person within the organization is to function. Roles are always considered in terms of how they relate to others' roles around them: boss/worker, parent/child, and teacher/student are common examples of such role relationships. In organizational analysis, emphasis is placed on role relationships more than on the content of the roles themselves; for example, on the subordinate/manager relationship where one person is held accountable for the performance of another in a work setting (Jaques 1976).

A *position,* on the other hand, is a social location within an organization whose task or function is determined by that organization's nature or goals. "Waitress," "chief surgeon," and "senator" are examples of positions. The position of waitress in a restaurant, for example, carries with it a set of behavioral norms or rules for performing the role, such as those concerning taking orders, filling orders, serving customers, or preparing certain food items. All these *norms* (expectations for behavior), taken together, define the *role* of waitress, the set of expectations for behavior associated with that position.

Positions and roles are not the same; a position is defined in terms of role relationships and is filled by a person hired or assigned to perform a specific role within the organization. A position can exist without the performance of its associated role, as when a position is vacant.

Every position in a social structure carries with it a *status*, that is, a unique place in the organization's *hierarchy*, or pecking order. Status is usually thought of in terms of the authority it carries. *Authority* refers to *the right to make decisions or demands, exert influence, give directions, or apply sanctions.* "Higher" positions generally have formal authority over lower positions, as in a "chain of command." Sergeants are allowed to give orders to privates; the role and status of sergeant carries with it this authority. Whether or not the sergeant's orders are actually followed, however, depends both on the subordinate's acceptance of that authority and the sergeant's power to influence his behavior.

Power can be defined as *the ability to act and to influence either the behavior of others or the outcome of events.* Although power and authority often go together, they are not the same. Power is an attribute of an individual or a group of individuals, not something inherent in a position. Authority is always vested in positions rather than individuals. For example, the person occupying the position of "supervisor" has the right to assign work, give orders, and hire or fire workers. The individual has this authority solely by virtue of filling that position; because the person is their supervisor, workers will normally accept this as a legitimate exercise of authority.

In practice, however, one might have authority and no power, or vice versa. A policeman, for example, who is disarmed by a robber has the authority to arrest the criminal but may not in that situation have the power to exercise this authority; while the armed robber has power to influence others but no authority to do so. In everyday life people generally follow rules, orders, instructions because they voluntarily agree to accept the authority of those in positions to give such directions.

Organizational Structure

An organization, then, can be looked upon as a hierarchical network of positions each carrying specific role expectations and a formally or informally defined level of status. The number of positions and hierarchical levels is closely associated with organizational scale. That is, in small businesses and similar organizations, a few people take on many roles; sales, service, and bookkeeping may all be done by a single individual. Status hierarchies tend to be minimal in such cases, compared to the large organization in which there is a great division of labor. The automobile assembly plant is a prime example of this, where each worker does just one or two tasks, and several echelons of supervisory and management personnel are required to coordinate all these people in accomplishing the organization's task.

The structure of an organization has significant consequences for its functioning at all levels. Since the organization is a social system, the relationships between positions are of utmost importance. Organizations have problems when roles are not clear, when their structure is not compatible with their task, or when individuals are not clear about who is accountable or responsible for what.

Common sense might tell you that structure is structure; to analyze organizational structure, all one would have to do is to consult an organization chart, the charter or legal code formally establishing that organization, its bylaws, or other documentary evidence. This is what Elliott Jaques (1976), a leading British clinical sociologist, terms the organization's *manifest social structure.*

Jaques has found, however, that in organizations, as elsewhere in social life, things are not necessarily what they seem. It is essential, he has shown, to consider three other aspects of organizational structure. The first is the *assumed social structure,* how the participants in the organization see its role structure, what they believe or assume to be the current situation. Second, he stresses, the sociologist must also analyze the *extant social structure.* This refers to how things actually function, which can be determined only by systematic research. This generally leads to a description of the organization that is very different from its manifest or assumed structure. Finally, from the perspective of a sociological clinician, Jaques differentiates the *requisite social structure* of an organization. This is a conceptualization of the organization as it would need to be in order to maximize its effectiveness in realizing its objectives.

Some Consequences of Organizational Structure

A classic example of sociological practice from the work of William Foote Whyte can illustrate many of the concepts we have been discussing.

Demonstrating how the structure of social relationships decisively influences behavior within organizations, it also shows how sociological investigation can lead to useful change (Whyte 1948; Porter, 1962).

In the years after World War II, Whyte was retained by a restaurant chain to help them with pressing problems of inefficiency, low morale, and high employee turnover. Waitresses were breaking down in tears; cooks were walking off the job; and managers, needless to say, were upset. After applying his expertise in field research methods (described in Chapter 3) to investigating the situation, Whyte determined that the root of the problem lay in the high levels of stress during busy periods, which affected the relationships between waitresses and customers, waitresses and cooks, waitresses and managers, managers and cooks.

Upon examining the extant social structure and observing interactions between these roles, Whyte found that the situation violated nearly all aspects of requisite structure. The setup was simply inappropriate. The cooks, who were males, earned more money than the waitresses, who were females. They also had higher status—in the manifest structure, that is.

In actuality, Whyte observed the waitresses giving orders to the cooks. This violates the rule that persons of higher status give orders to those of lower status, not vice versa. Moreover (remember, this was some 40 years ago), women were giving orders to men.

Whyte suggested an elegant, and amazingly simple, solution: the *spindle*, that round metal band with clips on it to hold written "orders" now found in almost all restaurants. This innovation allowed the waitress to place a customer's order before the cook without having to give the order verbally.

The effect of this suggestion was to change the social system of the restaurant. The spindle served as a memory device for the cook, who no longer had to remember all the orders. This made his work easier, especially during rush hours. The spindle was also a buffer; several waitresses could put up their orders simultaneously without having to fight for the cook's attention. By restructuring the relationship between cooks and waitresses, this device led both to feel differently, behave differently, and experience their work roles with less stress and internal conflict.

It also had the practical effect of enabling the cook to get to each order at his own work rate. The spindle held orders in the sequence received, while allowing the cook to look them all over by merely turning the spindle. This made it possible to coordinate the preparation of all the orders, reducing errors.

What Whyte did was to look at the restaurant as a social system rather than look only at the positions and processes making up the system. A systems approach, then, investigates the dynamic configuration of the whole organization; how roles interact, how work flows, how information flows. Systems-level solutions are sought for systems-level problems.

The spindle restructured the *relationship between positions* in the restaurant chain. By facilitating a change in the pattern of interaction between people in the social system, Whyte thus solved a problem that had exhibited itself through individual behavior in forms that were good for neither the organization nor the individual.

Common sense might have suggested a psychological explanation and solution for the problem, but it actually lay in the way the work was organized, how positions were filled, cultural biases concerning gender, and how roles interacted. In short, it was a sociological problem.

> The structure of relationships between roles has a decisive effect
> upon . . . the people who occupy them, and upon the quality of
> their social interactions. Change the nature of this structure of
> social relationships and you change behavior and the quality of
> social life. The same people act and go about life differently . . .
> In short, social institutions produce powerful effects on human
> behavior and relationships: they are never neutral or innocent
> (Jaques 1976:14).

Bureaucracy as a Kind of Organization

Sociologists have investigated many kinds of organizations, large and small, formal and informal, voluntary and coercive, to name just a few. In our society today, the workplace is predominantly some form of "bureaucratic organization."

First studied by Weber, this kind of organization is designed to accomplish large-scale administrative tasks by systematically coordinating the work of many individuals in a rational manner. By "rational," sociologists mean both cost effective and scientific. This contrasts with the old-fashioned "Mom and Pop" operation where business was conducted on the basis of personal relationships, common sense, and the owner's "feel."

Bureaucracy is identified with such features as impersonal management by formal rules, a hierarchy of specialized positions organized in terms of status and function, the principle that the position is separate from the person appointed to fill that job description, and so forth. This form of organization may not be appropriate for neighborhood enterprises such as the "Mom and Pop" store or in professional and educational situations where efficient administration and production is less important than quality of relationships or where roles cannot be performed within a hierarchical structure.

In most other cases — the majority of contemporary work situations, in fact — bureaucractic organization promotes efficient operation, eliminates favoritism, and provides career opportunities based on expertise and specialized knowledge. It has become popular to associate bureaucracy with "red tape," inertia, and inefficiency, but these very real problems are related to the imposition of this form on situations where it is simply inappropriate, or to inappropriate organization of the bureaucracy itself.

Not only is bureaucracy here to stay but it represents the most efficient way of structuring large organizations ever developed. Therefore, when we consider how sociologists can apply their knowledge, perspectives, and methods to working with organizations, we are generally speaking about working with bureaucracies (Blau and Meyer 1971).

We may find ourselves frustrated by corporate or governmental bureaucracies as they exist at present, but there is simply no better way. Jaques, whose work represents perhaps our greatest advance in understanding this form of organization since Weber, argues that bureaucracies can be made both more humane and more effective through, among other things, restructuring roles and authority patterns.

Working with Organizations

Since economic production and government administration are the life's blood of modern societies, there has been a long tradition of organizational-scale interventions. The dominant approach in industry was, until recently, the *scientific management school*. This approach is exemplified by the work of F. W. Taylor around the turn of the century. The prototypical "efficiency expert," he sought to improve factory performance by "rationalizing" work—that is, by breaking down jobs to their smallest elements so as to make tasks as quick and efficient as possible. These tasks were then quantified, generally in terms of output rates, and the worker was offered a bonus for "increased productivity." The goal of the efficiency expert was to get workers to do exactly as management wanted them to do. The method was based on stopwatches and individual psychology, not systems theory. "Scientific management" was interested in one thing and one thing only: how much one worker could do, day in and day out, if he or she were shown the most efficient way of doing the job.

Increasingly, however, emphasis has been placed on management rather than efficiency of production. Here, a rudimentary systems approach has been employed that is, in many ways, compatible with the structural-functionalist model. Consultants employing this perspective concentrate on the organization's needs, goals, structure, and functioning. The assumption is that the healthy state of a social system is one of equilibrium and that this harmonious condition will naturally follow if only people are adequately socialized to accept the values of the organization. The organizational structure, they believe, should therefore be determined by the functional needs of the system.

This "structure-systems" approach for understanding and changing organizations is typically management oriented. After all, the consultant is hired by management to help them with problems in employee relations, productivity, profitability, and so forth. The expectation is that employees will "be reasonable," as defined by the organization or the policies under which it operates—meaning, of course, "by management." The legitimacy of managerial authority and the necessity of "rule from above" are simply taken for granted.

Policies based on these presumptions, however, can evoke strong feelings of anger and frustration when those within or served by the organization feel that their needs or their situation are not being considered. Such individuals create problems for the organization that often cannot be resolved through the approaches we have discussed so far.

It should be noted here that sociologists who work with organizations tend to share a common set of values that emphasize the individual's well being within the organization. Often denoted by the term *organizational democracy,* this set of values views worker and management alike as "citizens" of the organization. It defines the purpose of intervention as facilitating such things as self-regulation, participation in decision making, innovation, trust, openness, and collaboration. These stand in contrast to the conventional values of regulation from above, "top down" authority (following orders), reliance on standardized procedures, mistrust, secrecy, and "minding one's own business."

Indeed, sociologists (and others as well) have been vitally interested in organizations from the viewpoint of the individual. Goffman's classic study portrays the mental hospital as an institution in which patients learn to "make out" and in a myriad of ways to evade the formal rules and controls and protect their behavior which often is at odds with the goals of the organization (Goffman, 1961). Studs Terkel's (1975) best seller, *Working,* tells the stories of workers in a variety of occupations through their individual feeelings and experience with regard to their jobs and the organizations they work in. A more recent study of how men and women differ in their experiences, work, and careers in large corporations is reported by Rosabeth Moss Kanter in *Men and Women of the Corporation* (1977).

Interaction in the Workplace

In 1978 a book by a then unknown sociologist, Robert Schrank, created a sensation by suggesting that, for many workers, what makes work pleasant is the chance to socialize with other workers, to *schmooze.* What Schrank has to say runs directly counter to the conventional wisdom regarding how to manage the industrial concern to maximize productivity and, hence, profitability. At the same time, it illustrates precisely our point that the workplace can, indeed, be made both more humane and more effective.

Schrank's credentials are not those of an "armchair expert." Instead, he put in some 25 years as a blue-collar worker, union organizer, and bureaucrat before he entered college and earned his Ph.D. in sociology.

Schrank questions much of the conventional wisdom about worker satisfaction and life in the factory. High absenteeism, he argues, does not necessarily mean dissatisfied workers but may reflect the fact that workers can afford to take a day off to go fishing. As a manager, Schrank himself closed shop and "took inventory" the day hunting season opened.

Getting workers to work for you rather than against you can be accomplished through such simple tactics as keeping toilets clean, having pleasant dining areas, and improving the social atmosphere of the workplace. While Schrank is pessimistic about management's ability to make repetitive work interesting and enriching, he suggests that giving workers a chance to *schmooze* will at least make the day less dull for them. He suggests that the workplace can easily be rearranged to facilitate this:

> If you have a crew or workers assembling parts at desks and they keep turning around craning their necks to talk to the people behind them, turn the desks around so they face each other. . . . Turn your machines around so people can talk to each other like normal human beings (quoted in *Successful Business, 1979:41).*

Redefining the situation, even in this simple, physical sense, initiates a redefinition of behavioral roles within that environment. How? The work environment had previously been structured to block interaction between workers, quite effectively defining their roles (as opposed to those of office staff) as not involving socialization on the job. Schrank merely removes this element of the situation, effectively unblocking the flow of interaction between workers.

Allowing even the production-line workers to engage in social interaction "like normal human beings," Schrank feels, will have a meaningful impact on morale and, hence, productivity throughout the system. What is perhaps most startling about these ideas is that they are indeed radical! Yet, you can notice that when people are given a chance to socialize while they work, they will do so and report that it makes their jobs tolerable to do so. This same principle is illustrated by the use of CB radios by long-haul truckers; it breaks up the monotony, keeps them awake, and provides a sense of community to those in a particularly solitary occupational role.

The Human Relations Approach

Schrank's perspective is an example of the *human relations approach* in business and industry. He believes, for example, that work teams that have some autonomy over how and when they will do the work are more satisfied and more productive. He believes, moreover, that managers should talk to their employees and find out what they think. In many cases, employees can be left to organize work themselves. People will work harder and be more satisfied in a workplace where people are friendly; where there is warmth, a supportive atmosphere, and a good reward and feedback system that considers the needs of the people who constitute the organization.

Schrank is especially critical of the attempt to "be scientific" by simply quantifying everything; this is precisely what Taylor tried to do. Rather than study as organization from the management's perspective, through questionnaires or other so-called empirical methods, Schrank prefers to take a worker to a local bar and, over a couple of beers, ask him to talk about his job. In this way, he attempts to gain *Verstehen* into how the system is or is not working from the perspective of those who are doing the actual work.

This has led Schrank to propose some unusual innovations. He suggests, for example, putting telephones in factories so that blue-collar workers have the same opportunity to call or be contacted during the workday as white-collar workers have. Most production workers, one must realize, operate in an almost military atmosphere in which they are permitted only one or two breaks a day, by the clock, and in which their activity often is entirely controlled by the flow of the assembly line. When a Canadian company added telephones on a production line, it found that the average worker made or received only two or three calls a week, and that this did not interfere with production at all. In fact, assembly-line workers covered for their buddies who were on the phone, and an informal norm developed that it was unfair to inconvenience others by spending too much time on the phone.

The human relations approach remains perhaps the best-known application of sociology to organizations and the workplace. Its roots lie in pioneering studies by industrial sociologists during the 1930s at Western Electric's Hawthorne telephone equipment plant outside Chicago. There, Elton Mayo, Fritz Roethlisberger, and others found that workers set informal norms about production, trade-off jobs, and establish their own work rules, generally unknown to management and often contrary to official company policy (see Landsberger 1958).

The human relations school stresses the importance of working with these informal patterns and networks; this is in direct opposition to the older way of thinking, where only the manifest structure of the organization is considered, and then only from management's point of view. Recently, this approach has been extended to consideration of *organizational culture* (Deal and Kennedy, 1982). Theorists and practitioners investigate the norms and values shared and passed on by those who work in the organization on the principle that both problems and successes can be better grasped if one has *Verstehen* into the way in which members of the system understand the social world of their organization.

Recent books by Peters and Waterman (1982) and Kanter (1983) investigate extremely successful corporations to see what they have in common and what distinguishes them from less successful ones. "Excellent" organizations exhibited a conspicuous and coherent culture maintained through stories, slogans, myths, and legends. Like the anthropologist who seeks to understand societies through their cultures, the clinical sociologist can glean invaluable information about an organization by studying its corporate culture.

What are the shared values? Are they innovation, product quality, and service? Does the organization treat employees well? What is the climate of the organization—open, closed, authoritarian, democratic, repressive, or growth oriented? What myths have sustained the organization over the years? The Bell Telephone Company, for example, deliberately maintained the image of itself as a service company rather than a telephone company; in both its advertising to the public and its internal communication, "Ma Bell" instilled in its employees and the public the belief that it was a public service rather than a manufacturer and distributor of telephone equipment.

Most innovative companies believe that their individual employees, from top to bottom, are the best source of new ideas and energy. Highly innovative organizations reward people for being collaborative. They view the task of management as one of creating climates and environments hospitable to people's natural inventiveness. Harrison (1983) believes that balance and harmony are keys to organizational vitality. The support of individuals by one another and by the larger whole comes through a sense of mutual responsibility and caring in such organizations.

"The Quality of Work Life" Approach

Another contemporary sociological approach to both studying and working with organizations focuses upon the *quality of work life* with special emphasis on the interaction of human systems and technology. The relationship between workers and technical systems is viewed as a system-of-systems, or a *sociotechnical system.*

The concept of sociotechnical systems implies that we must look at both people and technology in understanding and changing organizations. Hospitals using state-of-the-art equipment, offices using electronic computers, and factories of almost every kind are all workplaces where humans interact with machines. The engineer automatically assumes that these operations involve technological systems; the sociologist has only recently added the idea that the people who work with those systems are themselves organized into human systems.

Organizational sociologists who employ this perspective focus specifically on the *work group* as the human systems level that directly interacts with technology. This contrasts dramatically with Taylor and the "scientific management" school's concentration on the individual job holder. Moreover, at the sociotechnical systems level, the focus is on work systems as sets of interrelated activities, rather than on single jobs.

An example of how the sociotechnical systems concept works can be seen in an intervention related by Trist (1981). For many years, the Norwegian shipping industry has been concerned with problems stemming from the traditional segregation of personnel into officers, petty officers, and crew (including deck personnel and engine-room personnel). Guided by sociotechnical systems thinking, they have experimented with new ways of designing ships that would facilitate the establishment of a single shipboard community among people who must live together under isolated conditions, 24 hours a day. Some of these design features include common recreation and dining halls where all ranks and ratings can socialize, as opposed to separate facilities for each group, and the deliberate reduction of status differentials between officers and crew.

"Quality of worklife" (QWL) is a term coined in the early 1970s and describes a way of thinking about people, organizations, and work based on the sociotechnical systems approach. QWL can be broken down into (*a*) a concern with the impact of work on people as well as organizational effectiveness; (*b*) the idea of participation in organizational problem solving and decision making at various organizational levels. Much of the interest in QWL stems from the concern of American management to compete more effectively with Japanese firms that have already put into practice many of the principles developed by sociologists of the human relations school.

One of the best-known QWL-related innovations is *quality circles,* small groups of workers and managers from the same work area that meet voluntarily on a regular basis to analyze and solve problems in that area. These might be problems in production, in flow of work, in work roles, or in worker–management relations; problem solving might be directed at increasing productivity, improving quality, meeting production schedules, improving the work environment, making jobs more creative, giving workers a stake in enhancing profitability, etc. Ultimately, any concerns that the work group has and that are amenable to discussion and can be solved are potential subjects for quality circles.

QWL, then, is the use of a systems model to examine social and technical factors in relation to each other. The isolation, fatigue, and stress that can be experienced by word processor operators is a present-day example of a new problem for QWL efforts.

The restaurant-spindle intervention described earlier was a very simple but clear example of a technological innovation that had an effect on the social structure of the workplace. Modern QWL thinking stresses how the development of worker potential and the creation of satisfying working environments are no less important than technological and economic factors when considering organizational structure and work design.

Organizational Development

The approaches we have been describing, although based on and employing sociological insights, have generally been conducted by consultants with business backgrounds or by management itself. In contrast, *Organizational Development* (OD) is a relatively new field primarily originating from the work of applied social and behavioral scientists.

The term OD is really an umbrella covering a variety of intervention activities and techniques. One of its roots was industrial "human relations" research and practice based on small groups, such as T-groups and leadership training, which became popular in business and industry in the 1950s and 1960s. Another was the social psychologist Kurt Lewin's development of *action research*, an approach based on the idea that people participating in research on their own behavior are more likely to act on the results.

As the OD field has grown it has become more self-consciously sociological in orientation; its focus has progressed from small-group dynamics to changing whole social systems. In their introduction to the field, French and Bell (1977) state that it deals with the possibility that people within organizations can collaboratively manage the culture of the organization in such a way that the goals and purposes of the organization are achieved along with furthering human values of the individuals within it. The organizational development specialist, then, is a change agent, an action researcher who studies an organization, gathers data, and helps the organization use this information to create desirable changes.

The Sociologist as Change Agent

As you can see from our preceding discussion, the trend has been toward an ever more clearly sociological form of organizational intervention. Whereas in the past, sociologists have been more interested in studying organizations and organizational changes than facilitating them, today's clinical sociologists are increasingly becoming organizational change agents. Taking the role of consultant rather than applied researcher, evaluator, manager, technical or task specialist, the sociologist acts as a *sociotherapist* whose client is a social system rather than an individual, and who therefore directs intervention at roles, relationships, organizational structure, analysis and functioning of the ongoing system.

One of the earliest models of sociological practice at this level, *social analysis,* was developed by Elliott Jaques while associated with the Tavistock Institute of Human Relations in Britain during the 1940s. We have already discussed some of his concepts. Although he is also a trained psychoanalyst, Jaques's approach is distinctly sociological, focusing on social structure as opposed to personality factors or group process. The social analyst looks at role relationships and how they are perceived in order to learn about the organization. Jaques has found that specifying and clarifying accountability and authority in manager–subordinate role relationships is essential to organizational success and individual well-being. Specifying roles is therefore an important sociological task in organization design, analysis, and change.

Social analysis is based on the fact that things do not always work the way they are supposed to work and that the way they are supposed to work is always subject to redefinition, anyhow. The method, as it has been developed over the past 40 years, is quite elegant (Jaques 1982).

The social analyst is invited into some unit of an organization experiencing problems. The analyst then discusses the situation with those involved, both as a group and individually, working up a summary of their views, which is then presented to the group as a whole. The analyst's role is to help members clarify their views, teasing out the important ideas and supplying concepts when necessary, and then to help the group systematically conceptualize their situation and possible resolutions. Often, this will be worked up into a report, which is then presented to the next higher unit of organization and the process repeated at that level of the system.

Jaques worked with a single company, Glacier Metal Works, for over 30 years. During this period – probably the longest-term study of a single organization yet conducted – he did social analysis with the company's Work Council on a wide range of projects. These included methods of payment, managerial organization, trade union representation, industrial relations, promotion procedures, and employee participation. As a result of this work, Jaques's expertise has been called upon time and again when large organizations are considering structural changes. His group has done social analysis, for example, with the Church of England, the British National Health Service, and the U.S. Army.

Another approach, developed by Ronald Capelle, who is a marriage and family therapist as well as an organizational consultant, combines the social systems perspective with behavioral tactics of intervention and analysis. Called *human systems consultation,* this involves programmatic strategies of analyzing the organization as a behavioral system and working out and implementing a plan for change. In this approach, Capelle stresses the systemic relationships between seven levels of human systems: intrapersonal, interpersonal group, intergroup, organizational, interorganizational, and community-scale systems.

Capelle's concern with systems of systems is the focus of several specifically sociological approaches to organizational change. It is, in fact, the root of a model for intervention unique to the work of clinical sociologists and termed *integrated levels of focus* by another sociological practitioner, Jonathan Freedman (Straus 1983/84). In this approach, the sociologist deals with the system or subsystem with the identified problem in terms of its systemic relationships to other social systems levels from that of individuals and their groups, to subcultures, communities, and entire societies.

Intervention by those subscribing to this model will generally attack the problem systematically, through some combination of strategies working at several of these levels. In Capelle's practice, the "dimensions" of objectives, structures, roles, communication, reward system, power, and time and space at each level are taken into account. Thus, when the client is a family or work group, for example, intervention will be directed at both the levels of the individual and at interpersonal relationships with respect to all eight of these dimensions.

The concept of integrated levels of focus has also been employed in developing *indirect* forms of sociological intervention, where changes targeted at one systems level are used to create changes at another level when a direct approach is inappropriate or not feasible. For example, Freedman (described in Straus 1983/84) was involved in a project to reorganize a statewide mental hospital system so as to shift an increasing proportion of clients to community and outpatient facilities. The approach selected including redesigning a record keeping system by introducing a new form. The form itself was instrumental in redefining roles and the organizational culture in such a way as to promote both the kind of treatment and the view of the patient which would facilitate transfer of patients from overloaded mental hospitals back into community settings.

The Sociology of Organizations

The sociology of organizations as an academic subject and a field of practice is based on the fundamental principle that human behavior is influenced by the social contexts in which it occurs. This concept is the beginning of understanding and creating change. If our behavior is shaped by social structure, culture, and environment, then it can be changed by changing any or all of these three.

Whether or not he or she is a clinical sociologist, the change agent needs an accurate understanding of an organization's structure and process in order to pinpoint problems and facilitate appropriate interventions. As one is dealing with a complex, goal-directed social system, a *sociological* approach is the most likely to yield the information needed to guide such change.

If you were a sociological change agent, the sort of approach you might take in *diagnosing an organization's work structure* would very likely involve applying *field work* and *participant observation* tactics such as these:

1. *Talking* to people in the organization
2. *Watching* what they do and how they do it
3. *Reading* reports, bulletin boards, policy statements, organization charts, etc.

You would be looking to answer such questions as these:

1. What is the formal and informal structure of the organization?
2. What symbols, rituals, and other evidences of the organization's culture can you discover?
3. What do people like most and least about their jobs?
4. How are work tasks organized?
5. Are decisions made at the level where the most adequate information is available?
6. What is the climate and level of trust in the organization?
7. How are differences and disagreements handled?
8. When changes are made, are the people affected by the changes asked for their ideas?
9. Do people desire to contribute their talents and abilities to their work as fully as they can?

This kind of information would allow you to understand and assess the organizational system and design the most appropriate intervention to help the organization function more effectively—both to achieve its goals and to maximize its potential as a workplace for human beings.

The sociological challenge is to discover which social arrangements contribute to human growth, health, and well-being. Problems may have psychological, technical, economic, or political dimensions, to be sure—but we must not forget the more subtle influence of social context. Human systems are interrelated; problems in one system or aspect of a system affect all others.

Unclear organizational objectives can contribute to poor work-team performance. Work problems can affect family life, and family problems can affect work life; both are affected by the nested social systems forming their sociocultural context. A clinical perspective on the sociology of organizations, therefore, means more than using sociology for creating change; it means studying how organizations affect our lives and using that knowledge to improve the quality of our lives and those of our fellow human beings.

Review Questions and Exercises

1. What are the differences between a social systems approach and an individual psychology approach to improving organizational productivity?
2. What is the role of the bureaucratic form of organization in contemporary American life? Consider both the positive and the negative aspects of governmental and private-sector bureaucracies. How could the negative features be eliminated or reduced and the positive features enhanced?
3. Take the role of a sociological change agent. Either act out in a group or write how you would go about diagnosing the work structure of an organization of your choice, what you might find, and the sorts of changes you might recommend to improve both the human qualities and the overall effectiveness of this system. (If possible, gather data on an actual organization for this exercise.)

Readings and References

Benne, Kenneth D., et at., eds. *The Laboratory Method of Changing and Learning.* Palo Alto, Calif.: Science and Behavior Books, 1975.

Bennis, Warren G., et. al, eds. *The Planning of Change.* 3d ed. New York: Holt, Rinehart, and Winston, 1976.

Blau, Peter, and Marshal W. Meyer. *Bureaucracy in Modern Society.* New York: Random House, 1971.

Capelle, Ronald G. *Changing Human Systems.* Toronto: International Human Systems Institute, 1979.

Caplow, Theodore. *Managing an Organization.* New York: Holt, Rinehart, and Winston, 1983.

Dalton, Melville. *Men Who Manage.* New York: Wiley, 1959.

Deal, Terrence E., and Allan A. Kennedy. *Corporate Cultures: The Rites and Rituals of Corporate Life.* Reading, Mass.: Addison-Wesley, 1982.

Durkheim, Emile. *The Division of Labor in Society.* New York: Free Press, 1964.

Fordyce, Jack K., and Raymond Weil. *Managing with People: A Manager's Handbook of Organization Development Methods.* 2d ed. Reading, Mass.: Addison-Wesley, 1982.

French, Wendell L., and Cecil H. Bell, Jr. *Organization Development.* Englewood Cliffs, N.J.: Prentice-Hall, 1973.

Glass, John. "Renewing an Old Profession: Clinical Sociology." *American Behavioral Scientist* 23 (March/April 1979): 515–530.

Goffman, Erving. *Asylums.* New York: Anchor Books, 1961.

Gouldner, Alvin. *Patterns of Industrial Bureaucracy.* New York: Free Press, 1954.

98   USING SOCIOLOGY

Harrison, Roger. "Strategies for a New Age." *Human Resource Management* 22 (Fall 1983): 209–235.
Jaques, Elliott. "The Method of Social Analysis in Social Change and Social Research." *Clinical Sociology Review* 1 (1982): 50–58.
———. *A General Theory of Bureaucracy.* New York: Halstead Press, 976.
Kanter, Rosabeth M. *The Change Masters.* New York: Simon and Schuster, 1983.
———. *Men and Women of the Corporation.* New York: Basic Books, 1977.
Landsberger, Henry A. *Hawthorne Revisited: Management and the Worker.* Ithaca, N.Y.: Cornell University Press, 1958.
Levinson, Harry. *Organizational Diagnosis.* Cambridge, Mass.: Harvard University Press, 1972.
Lindenfeld, Frank, and Joyce Rothschild-Whitt, eds. *Workplace Democracy and Social Change.* Boston: Porter Sargent, 1983.
Perrow, Charles, *Complex Organizations: A Critical Essay.* 2d ed. Glenview, Ill.: Scott Foresman, 1979.
———. *Organizational Analysis: A Sociological View.* Belmont, Calif.: Wadsworth, 1970.
Peters, Thomas J., and Robert H. Waterman, Jr. *In Search of Excellence.* New York: Harper & Row, 1982.
Porter, Elias H. "The Parable of the Spindle." *Harvard Business Review* 40 (May/June 1962): 58–66.
Ritti, R. Richard, and G. Ray Funkhauser. *The Ropes to Skip and the Ropes to Know.* 2d ed. Columbus, Ohio: Grid, 1982.
Schein, Edgar. *Process Consultation: Its Role in Organization Development.* Reading, Mass.: Addison-Wesley, 1969.
Schindler-Rainman, Eva, and Ronald Lippitt. *The Volunteer Community.* 2d ed. La Jolla, Calif.: University Associates, 1977.
Schrank, Robert. *Ten Thousand Working Days.* Boston: MIT Press, 1978.
Steel, Fritz. *Consulting for Organizational Change.* Amherst: University of Massachussetts Press, 1975.
———, and Stephen Jenks. *The Feel of the Workplace: Understanding and Improving Organizational Climate.* Reading, Mass.: Addison-Wesley, 1977.
Stein, Barry A., and Rosabeth M. Kanter, eds. *Life in Organizations.* New York: Basic Books, 1979.
Straus, Roger. "Changing the Definition of the Situation: Toward a Theory of Sociological Interventions," *Clinical Sociology Review* 2 (1983/84).
Successful Business, Spring, 1979. "Schmoozing with Robert Schrank: An Interview with a Common-sense Sociologist."
Terkel, Studs. *Working.* New York: Avon Books, 1975.
Trist, Eric. *The Evolution of Socio-Technical Systems.* Occasional Paper No. 2, Ontario Quality of Working Life Center. Toronto: Ministry of Labor, June 1981.
Weber, Max. *Economy and Society: An Outline of Interpretive Sociology,* vol. 1. Translated and edited by G. Roth and C. Wittich. New York: Bedminster Press, 1968. (Originally published 1925.)

_____. *Economy and Society: An Outline of Interpretive Sociology,* vol. 2. Translated and edited by H. Gerth and C. W. Mills. New York: Bedminster Press, 1968 (Originally published 1922.)
Whyte, William Foote. *Human Relations in the Restaurant Industry.* New York: McGraw-Hill, 1948.

Chapter **6**   MEDICAL SOCIOLOGY: THE
CLINICAL PERSPECTIVE
David J. Kallen and *Christopher A. Pack*

The medical sociologist practicing sociology in medicine translates the discoveries of sociology into activities that positively affect the quality of health care provided to patients. These activities may range from working with doctors and patients to improve the quality of their interaction to helping to shape national health-care policy. There is a long tradition in sociology of research on the delivery of medical care, on the ways in which the structure of the health-care setting affects the delivery of care, and on the training of health-care professionals. At the same time, however, medical sociology has been more concerned with the production of knowledge and understanding than with its uses. The application of this body of knowledge is the special concern of the clinical sociologist working in health-care settings.

This chapter touches on seven basic themes in medical sociology:

1. Concepts of disease and illness
2. Medicine as a profession
3. The clinic as an organization
4. Doctor–patient interaction
5. Identity loss and the hospital as an institution
6. The sick role
7. Health-care policy

The patient's experiences in seeking and receiving health care illustrate all these themes, as well as showing how a clinical sociologist may have an impact on the practice of medicine for the benefit of all involved. Therefore, this chapter leads you through a series of typical experiences as you seek and receive health care. A description of the experience is given and then analyzed in terms of what is known sociologically about similar situations and in terms of interventions by clinical sociologists. All the interventions described are the work of sociologists at present employed in medical settings. Since this approach to sociology is new, a number of applications have yet to be developed. This chapter reviews what is known sociologically about selected aspects of health care and discusses the clinical sociologists' solutions to today's problems. It can only suggest possible contributions that future sociologists may make to improving medical care.

Concepts of Disease and Illness

You wake up one morning not feeling well. You are feverish,
feel like vomiting, and have a pain in your abdomen. You go
back to bed for a while, but by noon, when you don't feel
any better, you decide that maybe you ought to see a doctor.
You call the clinic and are given an appointment for three
o'clock that afternoon.

The decision to seek medical help indicates that you think you are *ill*.
Sociologically, there is a difference between *illness* and *disease*. *Disease*
refers to a physical or psychological condition. It is a recognition that the
body or the mind (or a combination of body and mind) is not working pro-
perly. *Illness*, or *sickness*, refers to the individual and social recognition
that the condition is a problem.

The difference between disease and illness (sickness) is cultural and
social. Not all diseases are illnesses, nor are all illnesses disease. For example,
in Western culture, people who startle easily are not considered to be ill.
Yet, in Malaya such individuals are thought to have a mental illness called
latta. Similarly, in our own culture, conditions such as alcoholism, mental
illness, and obesity are not considered true diseases, although each may be
considered a sickness.

The difference between illness and disease is important because it has
an influence on behavior. For example, a busy executive may come to work
with a high fever, stopped-up nose, muscle aches, and other evidence of the
flu. He may have a self-perception of being diseased ("Keep away, I have
the flu") but not sick enough to stay home from work. His colleagues may
define "the flu" as an illness and suggest to the executive that he go home so
that co-workers will not be exposed to the disease.

In medicine, normalcy is absolute; in social life, what is normal is
relative to the society. Normal body temperature is 98.6 degrees Farenheit,
and a body temperature of 101 degrees is *always* abnormal. A blood
pressure of 180/100 is hypertension anywhere in the world. There are no
cultural relativities to these physiological measures.

In social life, however, what is normal is a function of the society in
which the person is living. While one society may demand that women be
virgins at marriage and severely censor a woman who does not remain
virginal, another may require that the bride demonstrate her fecundity by
being pregnant prior to marriage. As Emile Durkheim (1938) pointed out,
what is normal in a society is what most people do, or regard as normal, in
that society. Social normality is thus relative and flexible, not absolute and
unvarying.

It is often difficult for professionals who depend on the absolute difference between normality and abnormality to understand the relative

nature of social norms (Kallen 1984). *Social norms refer to perceived and shared expectations about how people in given roles and statuses will act* (Newcomb, Turner and Converse 1965). Yet, an understanding of this difference is important if physicians and other health-care workers are to respond adequately to the social and psychological, as well as the biophysicial, presentations of patients. Sociologists working in health-care programs are frequently called on to remind medically trained colleagues of the changing and relative nature of social norms and the differing ideas about what is normal held by people from different segments of the society.

The task of introducing behavioral sciences into the postgraduate training of physicians (i.e., residency training) has fostered a number of innovative approaches. In one program, a behavioral scientist (e.g. a clinical sociologist, clinical psychologist, or medical anthropologist) is assigned as a consultant to a pediatric clinic. The behavioral scientist is available to talk with the clinic's residents (i.e., young physicians who are undergoing special training in pediatrics) about problems they have with patients. One case in which a behavioral scientist was involved concerned a young daughter of a large Mexican American family. The family became upset when the young woman was asked to go into an examining room with a young male resident. The behavioral scientist pointed out to the resident physician that the reluctance of the young woman to go with the nurse was related to the unwillingness of many traditional Chicano families to permit a young woman to be examined by a male doctor without a female member of the family being present. By acknowledging the family's concern and permitting an adult female of the family to accompany the patient, the resident solved the problem.

The behavioral scientist in this role also helps to point out the interplay between social, environmental, and psychological factors in illness and disease. The clinical sociologist may concentrate primarily on the social or environmental stresses in the life of the patient, including social disconnectedness, pressures from peer groups to violate the individual's standards or norms, family problems, or trends in the larger society that are causing social dislocation for the patient. These trends may include unemployment, natural disasters, or other events that disrupt the fabric of social life. Psychologists and social workers are apt to look more at individualized experiences and help the patient work through the psychological stresses that may influence health. All three professions will examine and help alleviate the consequences of the illness itself. These consequences may include *stigmatization* due to disfigurement or socially unacceptable disease (Goffman 1961; Cahnman 1968; Richardson 1971), the creation of stress within the family system because of the illness of a family member, and social and psychological stresses stemming from the cost of hospitalization. Thus, in addition to working as a consultant within a practice, the clinical sociologist may also provide care in the form of individual or group therapy or counseling.

Medicine as a Profession

Like the recognition of disease, the decision to seek out a physician as an expert in illness is also the result of culture and is an illustration of the way sociological factors can affect the practice of medicine. In the scenario described when we differentiated between disease and illness, despite your fever, pain, and vomiting, you may have returned to bed relieved that you had nothing worse than the flu. Yet, although "flu" is an illness that usually does not require a visit to the doctor, 60 years ago influenza was considered much like the plague. Similarly, in 1920, it is unlikely that you would have visited a doctor for the illness. Instead, you would probably have been treated by your mother, your grandmother, or a neighbor known to have a "special gift" for caring for the sick. Only in the past 50 years have physicians increasingly been identified as experts in illness. This expertise goes beyond the physician's knowledge of medicine and defines the doctor as a *professional* in the field (Friedson 1970; Starr 1982). A *profession* has control over its own behavior, has internalized standards of social control, and is generally not accountable to outsiders for its behavior.

The process of professionalization, which has long been of interest to sociologists, takes place in medical school and in the residency training program following graduation. Medical school students are isolated from their peers and are provided with a new identity: "medical student." Over the four years of medical school, they increasingly adopt the attitudes and world views of the faculty under whom they study and work (Becker, Geer, Hughes, and Straus 1961; Merton, Reader, and Kendall 1957). At the same time, much of the original idealism that brought them to medical school is replaced by more pragmatic values about making it through to graduation.

After completing medical school, most doctors continue on to specialty residencies that involve an additional three or more years of training. By this time, former medical students have restricted much of their social interactions to others in the health professions, partly because of the perception that only those experiencing the same stresses can understand what they are going through, and partly because the work schedule of a resident does not permit much free time. Thus their opportunity to meet and interact with individuals who are not in the health-care field is very limited. Most friends are maintained within the same level of training, and many marry fellow physicians or other health-care professionals.

During the course of residency training, residents work under the supervision of more experienced physicians to learn the clinical — as opposed to the academic — aspects of patient care. Throughout this period, resident physicians continue to develop values, attitudes, and appearances associated with "doctor." It is during this period, as well, that the resident is expected to internalize the norms of the profession fully, particularly a dedication to the idea that the welfare of the patient comes above all else in the life of the physician (Bosk 1979). The resident is not likely to be forgiven moral errors — that is, actions that do not put the best interest of patients first. A resident with mediocre technical skills who does not make moral errors is more likely to be retained in the program than is a resident with excellent technical skills who puts other interests (particularly personal concerns) ahead of the well-being of patients.

This concern with the internalization of moral norms during residency is necessary because of the social-control system of medicine. Most of what a physician does is hidden from view. It is done in the privacy of an office, and few if any physicians have detailed knowledge of what a given doctor does to heal a patient. Because medicine is self-directed and self-regulating, it depends on voluntary compliance with its standards of behavior toward patients to ensure good patient care. These standards must be internalized during residency because the residency training is probably the last time that the physician's behavior is routinely scrutinized by others.

Throughout the residency program, the physician develops new skills through assuming greater and greater levels of responsibility. But the education encompasses all aspects of the resident's professional life, including the manner in which the young doctor introduces himself or herself to patients and the doctor's appearance, dress, and approach and attitudes toward patients. The term of residency often includes the passage of informal lessons of practical value as well: how to set up a practice, billing procedures, etc. These lessons will be of use to the doctor after completion of the residency.

Sociology has influenced the professional socialization of physicians in two ways. First, it has described in detail the process of transformation between medical school and residency; it has generalized this process and therefore demystified it. Second, the recognition that training to become a physician is much like other forms of professional socialization (e.g. law school or business school) is valuable in helping young physicians cope with the inevitable stresses involved.

Understanding these phenomena presents the clinical sociologist with an opportunity to have an impact on problems early in their development. As a result, some aspects of medical school have been reorganized to address these issues. For example, programs are being developed to enable the early recognition of "impaired" physicians. Clinical sociologists are working in medical schools and residency training programs to establish peer support groups and provide career counseling to assist in the transformation from student to physician.

The Clinic as an Organization

When you arrive at the clinic for your appointment, you find the waiting room crowded. Despite the fact that you had arrived on time for your appointment, you must wait for some time before anyone calls your name. Finally the nurse leads you to an examination room. Your blood pressure, pulse, height, and weight are taken, and the nurse asks you why you came to see the doctor. You explain to her how you feel, and she makes some notes on the chart. She takes your temperature and pulse, then says, "Doctor will be right in," and leaves you alone in the room.

Like the recognition of illness, the decision to seek help, and the professionalization of help givers, the system that provides health care is an institution shaped by sociological variables. The doctor's office, the objects in the office (down to the cotton balls and tongue depressors on the stand next to the sink), the time allotted for each visit, the progression of clinic personnel through the examination room and their actions and questions – all are routinized to the point of ritual. The behavior of each member of the clinic is organized by this structure. For example, nurse's aides are often assigned the task of showing you to the exam room and recording your blood pressure and weight. The doctor enters the room after these tasks are completed. A nurse may be assigned more specialized duties, such as drawing blood or giving shots.

This division of labor makes sense when the efficiency of patient flow is viewed from the perspective of the physician, who places a high value on his or her time. It makes less sense from the perspective of the patient, who may also place a high value on his or her time. Part of the division of labor is rational, with the less-skilled tasks reserved to less-skilled personnel (aides and nurses, say, as compared to the physician), while others reflect the need of the medical profession to maintain dominance (there are a number of tasks that a nurse or even an aide could do that are reserved for the physician).

In studying patient flow, sociologists often attempt to create a more functional organization. This is done through examining each role in the organization, making it visible, and helping individuals working in the clinic to create a structure that is organized to maximize the effectiveness of the process for the patient and the staff.

Concern with patient flow is important because it affects other aspects of patient behavior. A number of studies have shown that waiting time is negatively related to the willingness of patients to follow doctors' orders. A sociologist concerned with the uses of sociological knowledge may study the flow of patients through the clinic and recommend changes that may reduce waiting time and improve the flow of patients through the system. Are more examination rooms needed? What would be the impact of hiring more nurses? Can patient scheduling be improved? These are questions that the clinical sociologist can answer. Once the movement of patients through the office is studied and understood, the sociologist can construct models of the practice and may intervene to improve the efficiency of the clinic and thus improve the experience of the patient.

Doctor-Patient Interaction

After some time, the doctor enters the room and introduces himself as Dr. Cromwell. He is wearing a long white coat that has several pens stuck in the breast pocket. His stethoscope is hanging out of one coat pocket, and the other is stuffed with papers. He is carrying a manila folder, which he appears to read from as he introduces himself. The doctor begins by asking why you've come to visit him in the office. This is the third time you've been asked this question, but finally you feel that you are telling your explanation to the correct person. The physician seems a bit harried, and you feel that he is rushing you through the interview. He cuts short your answers to his questions, regardless of their length, and your answers are reduced to one or two short scribbles in the medical record. You feel that the doctor is not really listening and won't let you finish your description of your illness.

In recent years, sociologists have been working with physicians to improve the quality of doctor–patient interaction. Clinical sociologists trained in interactional analysis work with doctors in medical school and during residency training to improve the physicians' interviewing skills. *Interactional analysis* refers to the study of the nature of verbal and nonverbal interactions, with an emphasis on the reciprocity of meaning, of physical gesture, and of symbolic gestures. Patient interviews are videotaped and reviewed. Physicians are taught how to ask open-ended questions, listen for pertinent information, and direct the flow of conversation in a natural and conversational manner. Techniques are also demonstrated for focusing the interview without routinizing it. Under the guidance of a clinical sociologist, by observing themselves on videotape doctors are able to see how body postures and orientation, as well as the use of material objects such as the medical record, can influence doctor–patient rapport and improve the quality of information the doctor receives from the patient.

There are several other important aspects of interaction. One is for the physician to listen to and acknowledge the concerns expressed by the patient, and to respond to them even if the physician is concerned with a different set of symptoms. Korsch, Gozzi, and Francis (1968) found that when young mothers brought a sick child to a pediatric clinic, it was important that the physician respond to the *manifest* reason for the visit even when the medical diagnosis involved a different problem. For example, a mother might bring her child to a clinic because she was concerned about his coughing. The physician might decide that the problem that really required treatment was an ear infection. Yet, the mother was more likely to do what the doctor indicated was necessary to treat the ear infection when the physician also acknowledged the problem created by the cough and discussed it with the mother than when he ignored it and dealt only with the ear infection.

Another important determinant of compliance with physicians' orders is how humanely the patient feels treated by the health-care system (Kallen and Stephenson 1981). Young women who felt that their physicians did not treat them humanely were less likely to be satisfied with the pill or to use it as a contraceptive than those who felt they were treated as persons by their physician.

Treatment style is only partly the result of a physician's personality. It is largely a product of the social organization of the health-care setting. For example, the ability to see the same physician on successive visits has a positive impact on patient compliance. Personal relationships with the health-care giver and the ability to get to know the physician are important parts of medical care. Similarly, the extent to which the physician is familiar with the patient helps in the diagnostic process of separating stress from physiology and illness from disease. Finally, a sense of trust that is helpful in the healing relationship and that adds to the sense that the physician is concerned about the patient is established through interactions occurring over a period of time.

Prepaid group programs often have difficulty in providing the physician with sufficient time to behave in humane ways. Since the physician has little control over the scheduling of patients, and receives no rewards from working excessive hours, there is no benefit to the physician from staying over the allotted time and patients are apt to be put on an assembly line. In fee-for-service practices the physician is more able to control the amount of time to be spent with each patient and to charge accordingly (Mechanic 1975).

The group or clinic program may assign a different physician on each visit, or may assign the same practitioner whenever practicable. Prepaid practices are more likely to have less time available for the patient per visit. On the other hand, the quality of care may be better in multispecialty group practices because members of the group have a greater knowledge of what each physician in the group is doing than is true of solo-practice physicians (Ross and Duff 1978).

Patients, of course, vary in the kind of health care they prefer, and some might prefer a more impersonal level of care. While it might be assumed that patients in prepaid practices, which are more bureaucratic and less personal, would be less satisfied than patients who receive care in other settings, this is not necessarily true. One study found that patient satisfaction was, in part, a result of the number of years they had been in the care setting, and that patients who had been in prepaid practices more than three years were as satisfied with the care they were receiving as were patients in other settings. Moreover, the rapid development of walk-in emergency centers in shopping centers and other easily accessible locations suggests that, at least for some problems, a large number of patients prefer quick service from any physician over service that requires a longer wait from a physician they know.

Clearly, the preceding sections suggest a number of ways in which the sociologist can help in the organization of health-care practice to ensure that the patient follows the physician's orders. One of the most important techniques is constantly to remind the physician that patients act in ways that make sense to them, and it is important to the patient that the provider understand how behavior that appears to be careless or irrational makes sense to the patient. (One reason this is often difficult for the physician is the difference in the definition of normality discussed earlier.) For example, a pediatric resident was complaining that a young mother obviously did not care about the health of her child because she did not bring the child back to check on the progress of an ear infection. When the mother visited the clinic two or three weeks later, she was asked why she had missed the previous visit. She replied, "Why, my husband needed the car that day to go to work, and I am not near a bus line. I would have had to walk a long way with my baby. The baby was feeling better, and it was raining very hard that day. I couldn't see any sense in taking a well baby out in the rain to see a doctor."

Other techniques to improve compliance include making sure that the patient understands what she or he is supposed to do; both the language used and the sequence of instructions should be clear. Little techniques, such as providing the patient with a written sheet on which instructions are clearly given, and making sure that medicines are fully labeled, help a lot. The sociologist can point out to the health-care provider that people have different life styles; simply telling a patient to take medicine with meals may mean that the patient takes the medicine only twice a day, rather than the three times a day the physician expects.

Many of these techniques seem to be simply common sense. Some of them are. Nevertheless, the relevance of various interventions to improve patient satisfaction and patient compliance did not become apparent until sociologists and others began to analyze how health systems functioned and how and why patients behave the way they do.

Identity Loss and the Hospital as an Institution

The doctor completes his examination and tells you that he wants you to go to the hospital immediately because he is concerned that you may have appendicitis. You arrive at the hospital and are processed by the admitting desk. At the desk you are given a plastic bracelet with your name, the date of your birth, and a series of numbers on it. After some time, you arrive at your room and are told to take your clothes off. You are given a hospital gown—a loosely shaped piece of cloth that ties in the back and doesn't quite reach to your knees. Although there is a person in the other bed in your room, introductions are not made. During your first hour in your hospital room a number of people come into your room—someone who draws blood, some nurses, and a doctor who repeats everything (including a painful examination of your stomach and a rectal exam) that your clinic doctor did that morning.

The hospital is a total *institution* in which the inmates (patients) are treated as objects to be processed rather than individuals expected to respond to and follow directions. Staff and inmates (patients) are separated, and each functionary in the institution has authority over the inmate. *Institutionalization* involves a process through which the individual loses identity as a person and becomes one of a class of objects. The total institution and the processes of institutionalization and *depersonalization* have best been described by Goffman (1961). Some of the features of this phenomenon, translated into the hospital situation, include:

1. The person is assigned an arbitrary identity. In the hospital, this is the wrist tag with the name and number of the patient. This lets the person know that he or she is unimportant as an individual; without the arbitrary identification, no one would know who the person is, and with it, anyone can see how the institution classifies him or her. (Certainly in the hospital the absolute identification of patients is vital to their well-being; some checks of identity are to ensure that patients get the correct medicine or that the wrong person does not undergo surgery. But the consequences of the need for certainty include depersonalization as well as protection.)

2. The patient is given a uniform. The clothes that people wear are an important part of their identity, a way of proclaiming, "This is me!" The removal of personal clothing and the provision of a uniform strips individuals of this important part of their *self*. (The *self* is the person as he or

she is known to himself or herself; the self is formed in social interaction as a result of the information others give the person about who he or she is and what he or she is able to do (Mead 1934). Again, it does not matter that the motives for this stripping are of the highest — sanitation, the protection of clothes from soiling or contamination — the effect on identity is the same as in less benign environments. The hospital gown serves to make the social identity of *patient* immediately apparent to everyone who comes in contact with the patient.)

3. Objects are not given the same courtesies as persons. The lack of privacy given the patient, as evidenced by the ubiquitous failure to knock on a patient's door before entering the room, is another aspect of deperson-alization. Only social persons require acknowledgment when entering their presence. (Keep in mind that, in some ways, not knocking on the door and waiting for a reply before entering is functional. If the patient is sleeping, for example, walking in without knocking is a way of ensuring that needed rest will not be interrupted; if the person is too ill or too weak to respond, it ensures that care will be provided anyway.) The lack of privacy may be reflected as well in the denial of modesty — bodily functions are monitored, body cavities invaded, and so on. Again, while this is usually functional to the treatment of the patient, it is not necessarily functional for the self.

4. Loss of identity is also shown by the habit of referring to patients by disease and location rather than by name. Thus you might become "the appendix in Room 307" rather than J. Student, the patient with appendicitis in Room 307. The disease becomes a *label,* the essential characteristic of the patient to which others respond; other individual and personal characteristics are regarded as unimportant.

Patients may be labeled in other, less favorable ways, such as the "crank" who is constantly demanding more care than is reasonable, or the "crock" who is not "really" sick but has endless complaints. Labeling of patients as mentally ill or suffering from psychosomatic diseases is particularly damaging, since all future symptoms are apt to be responded to as if they were signs of mental illness, even when they are clearly based in physical problems.

Clinical sociologists working within medicine can prevent this loss of patient identity. First, hospital personnel can be made aware of the effects that total institutions have on patients, and of ways in which those effects can be countered. Ward staff can be taught new behaviors, such as knocking when entering patients' rooms and being sure to move on down the hall rather than stand around the bed or in the doorway when talking about the patient. One physician always referred to the patient by formal title — Mr. or Ms. or Dr. — when examining parts of the body not usually scrutinized by others, even when he was on a first-name basis with the patient in other situations. These may seem like simple tasks, but assisting people in changing institutionally supported habit patterns is never easy. Not understanding the reasons for the change or the bad effect of the old pattern on the patient may leave the staff supporting the "more efficient" behaviors they are used to. When the clinical sociologist is able to be with ward staff over a continuous period of time, the mere presence of the sociologist serves as a reminder and reinforcer to the staff of needed and appropriate changes in behavior.

Patients also need to be taught how to protect their own identities. This is a difficult task because the patient who is seen as too demanding will be negatively stereotyped and receive fewer services than the patient who is seen as cooperative. But patients can be encouraged to personalize their surroundings through wearing their own clothes and bringing in other items that identify them as specific persons. (Of course, this may be more important during long stays than during brief hospitalizations.) Patients can also be encouraged to ask questions and to insist on choices, including refusing procedures if they are not adequately explained. Patients may also ask staff to call them by their names (and to insist on equality of address) and to display other aspects of their identities.

To bring this increased personalization about, the clinical sociologist needs to work with both patients and staff. If may be necessary to have staff members role-play being patients for a period of time, since many health-care givers have not had the experience of being patients. It may also be necessary to keep reminding staff why the changes in behavior are beneficial to the treatment process. At the same time, patients may be reluctant to behave in nontraditional ways without considerable support and encouragement from the sociologist. A very effective way to bring about change is to show both staff and patients that these new behaviors make everyone's life easier and reduce the time needed for the patient's recovery.

The Sick Role

You have surgery and your appendix is removed. Twenty-four hours after your surgery, you are told by the nurse that it is time for you to get up and walk around. You protest because you are still really tired and you hurt a lot, but the nurse insists, saying, "After all, don't you want to help yourself get well?"

In urging patients to do what is good for them in order to get better, the nurse is requiring patients to conform to the requirements of the *sick role*. The sick role, as described by Parsons (1972), has a number of important aspects. Understanding the sick role is important to the clinical sociologist so that she or he can understand how and why the patient deviates from the sick role in ways that are harmful to recovery. There are several aspects to the sick role:

1. The person is not responsible for his or her condition. However, people who harm themselves are not to be granted this exemption from normal responsibilities.

2. The person is exempted from normal role responsibilities while sick. This protects the person, who then may spend the required energy getting well, and protects the social group from contamination by the sick person.

3. The sick person has a claim on others for assistance and care, and has an obligation to seek assistance from those who are most qualified to provide it. That is, the person has to do the best he or she can to get expert help in getting better.

4. The person has an obligation to cooperate with the expert in order to get well as quickly as possible. As noted earlier, in our culture this expert is usually a physician. The sick person is expected to do what the physician suggests, and secondary gains from being ill are not permissible.

These requirements of the sick role are appropriate for persons with short-term, acute illnesses, particularly when the role behaviors involved are clear. They are less appropriate for people with chronic disease or long-term illnesses, where the required role behaviors are less clear. It is necessary to understand both the nature of the sick role and the ways in which it may be altered to fit different circumstances. For example, while exemption from usual role requirements is appropriate for someone hospitalized with an acute illness, a man who is hospitalized with a leg in traction can do a great many things for himself. Many of these things are done by the caretakers in the hospital because of the exemption of the sick from normal role requirements. Nevertheless, having patients do as much as is reasonably possible for themselves becomes one way of maintaining individual identity and rejecting the social identity of "sick person." It may require a good deal of work with the nursing staff, for example, before they are willing to give up an important aspect of their own role identity — providing nurturing care for the sick person — to aid the patient in the maintainence of a nonsick identity.

A second modification of the sick role is the provision for as much continuity with the pre-sick role as possible, with exemptions granted only for those specific role behaviors that illness makes impossible. For example, a number of hospitals have created special units for the care of physically sick and injured adolescents. In these units adolescents are expected to continue with their school work to the extent that their physical condition permits. Simply being in the hospital does not free the adolescent from keeping up with school assignments. Clinical sociologists assigned to the hospital may help the health-care staff design specific activities for a given patient by taking into consideration the cultural background of the patient, the nature of the disease, the life setting of the patient, and the structure of the hospital.

Another way in which the sick role is often misapplied is in labeling persons with certain physical limitations as handicapped. In these instances the labels identify the person as unable to fulfull any of the role obligations of normal individuals. This labeling process may lead to *self-fulfilling prophecies* (Merton 1957). For example, it may be assumed that a person with a given physical impairment cannot function in a given job, and thus people with the limitation will not be offered that kind of job. Then the paucity of persons with that limitation in such jobs will be taken as an indication that they cannot perform the job. By understanding the nature of the sick role and the nature of labeling, the clinical sociologist can develop programs that restore the majority of normal role obligations to individuals who have specific limitations on their physical abilities.

Health-Care Policy

After a few more days, you are recovered and ready to be discharged from the hospital. You pack up the few things you brought to the hospital and prepare to leave. A volunteer brings a wheelchair to your room and insists that you are not permitted to walk to the lobby, despite the fact that you have been walking the halls for days. On your way out, the volunteer wheels you to the cashier's office, where you are given your bill. You experience a brief sense of panic. The bill is several pages long, with each page filled with charges. The clerk recognizes your expression and assures you that your insurance company will pay most of the bill.

Decisions, both formal and informal, concerning how much of its resources society should allocate to health care and what the organization of the health-care system should be are referred to as *health-care policy*. It is the product of a combination of ideas about the demand for certain services, the amount of resources people are willing to spend on those services, ideas about distributive justice, and political considerations. Different political groups have different ideas about the extent to which ensuring access to health care is a governmental responsibility.

Health-care policy is changing constantly. Until the mid-1950s health care was primarily a personal responsibility. While some companies provided health insurance for their employees, many people had to pay for their health care themselves; doctors and hospitals took care of the poor for nothing (often in exchange for being able to use them as teaching subjects). The expansion of private health insurance, and the development of Medicare for the aged and Medicaid for the poor, led to most of the population's having major portions of their hospital and other health-care bills paid for by a "third party" payer.

The development of third-party payment on a national basis has had a number of consequences for the health-care system. First, it has resulted in a general increase in access to quality health care for people who previously could not afford it. Second, it has been a major factor in the spiraling increases in health-care costs. Third, it has created a new, more demanding patient. Before the wide availability of third-party payments for health care, poor persons were often expected to be grateful for the health care they did receive, and were reluctant to be too demanding of health-care personnel. Now, poor patients regard health care as a right, rather than a privilege, and they expect the same courtesy and care that more affluent patients always received.

In the mid-1980s cost containment has become a major emphasis in health-care policy. The cost of health care is approaching 10% of all goods and services in the United States, and health-care costs are rising at a rate much higher than the inflation rate. Hence there is a renewed emphasis on keeping health-care costs reasonable. A variety of efforts are being made.

New organizational forms are being created, including the *Health Maintenance Organizations (HMOs), Preferred Providers Organizations (PPOs),* and other forms of group practice. In an HMO patients receive all their care from a single organization that hires the physicians, nurses, etc. Patients pay a set fee each year, and this fee covers the complete costs of health care. Patients must receive all their care from the HMO. Costs are spread over a large number of subscribers, some of whom, of course, will not use all the services to which they are entitled. Physicians are salaried, thus helping to keep costs down. The PPOs are a slightly different form of insurance, in which the subscriber must use a physician on a panel approved by the organization; the physician charges members of the PPO less than other patients, in exchange for being guaranteed a certain number of patients by the organization. Other forms of prepaid health care are being developed in efforts to keep costs down.

Third-party payers are limiting what they will pay for. For example, one company will pay the full cost of surgery if the patient gets a second opinion prior to the operation, but only 80% if a second opinion is not obtained. Most insurance carriers will cover the cost of a semiprivate room in the hospital, but not of a private room. Routine tests are no longer permitted; instead, the physician must order (and, if necessary, be able to justify the reason for) each test.

Each of these new organizations and new rules is designed to control the cost of one aspect of the health-care system. Some of them may alter the system in unexpected ways, however. For example, many insurance companies reimburse patients for visits to a hospital emergency room but not for visits to a doctor's office. As a result, emergency rooms are filled with cases that might be better cared for by a family physician, or could be cared for at less cost in a walk-in "ready-clinic." The quality of emergency-room care for routine problems is limited because the ER is structured to render acute care for life-threatening conditions. Emergency rooms offer no follow-up care and are almost twice as expensive as a visit to the doctor's office.

The most recent innovation is for the government to pay a fixed amount per diagnosis (prospective payment) rather than pay the cost of providing care (cost-based reimbursement). It is expected that this system will reduce excessive costs and provide an incentive for greater efficiency in the hospital. When the patient stays in the hospital longer than is provided by the diagnosis (DRG), the hospital must absorb the extra cost; but when the patient is discharged earlier than the average patient with the same condition, the hospital still receives the full payment.

Prospective payment first went into effect in October 1982; thus the effects of changing the reimbursement patterns on health care are unknown. Sociologists, because of their commitment to understanding events as part of an integrated social system, are involved in studying the effects of health-care costs and reimbursement. Much of the basic work in medical sociology is relevant to health policy and to an understanding of the changes that health care is undergoing as a result of shifts in public policy.

Of particular concern are shifts in the locus of control in health care. Starr (1982) demonstrated how the professionalization of medicine and the cultural authority given to the physician have given the medical profession great control over health care. More recently, a consumers' movement has arisen among the public, and those who use health care have gained power in determining the nature of the health-care system. Now, a new source of control seems to be arising: the purchaser of health care. Those who pay the bill, rather than those who provide the care or receive the care, are assuming ever-greater control over the health-care system. State and federal governments, large-scale industrial bureaucracies, and unions are the primary sources of payment for health care today. They are concerned with controlling health-care costs, and perhaps with limiting the cultural authority of the medical profession at the same time. Thus, over time, control of the healing process seems to be going away from the physician who provides it and toward the consumer who uses it and the bureaucracy that pays for it.

How these changes will be brought about are not clear. Nor is the form that the health-care system will take in the future necessarily apparent today. Sociologists will be involved in this process as they study the nature of the health-care system, as they act as social critics to point out the unanticipated consequences of planned changes, and as they work to use sociological knowledge and understandings to create a system that ensures quality health care to all. Thus, medical sociology, as a research and policy science and as clinical practice, can have a major impact on the health-care system of the future.

Review Questions and Exercises

1. Write a convincing argument detailing why sociologists should be hired by medical schools as clinical teaching faculty; and why student physicians, nurses, and other health practitioners should be required to take considerable training in sociology.
2. Describe your most significant experience with the health-care system in terms of some or all of the concepts discussed in this chapter.
3. Visit a local clinic and ask if you can observe what happens when patients are treated (this is often possible in clinics that care for children). If this is not feasible, observe the public areas of a local hospital, student or other clinic, etc. Keep a record of how the providers act toward the patients and how the patients act in turn. If possible, interview one or more patients to find out how they reacted to the visit, and how clearly the instructions given by the provider are remembered.

Readings and References

Bosk, Charles. *Forgive and Remember*. Chicago: University of Chicago Press, 1979.
Becker, Howard, Blanche Geer, Everett C. Hughes, and Anselm L. Straus. *The Boys in White: Student Culture in Medical School*. Chicago: University of Chicago Press, 1957.
Cahnman, Werner. "The Stigma of Obesity." *Sociological Quarterly*, Summer 1968, 283–299.
Conrad, Peter, and Rochelle Kern, eds. *The Sociology of Health and Illness: Critical Perspectives*. New York: St. Martins Press, 1981.
di Matteo, Robin, and D. Dante di Nicola. *Achieving Patient Compliance*. New York: Pergamon Press, 1982.
Durkheim, Emile. *The Rules of Sociological Method*. Glencoe, Ill.: Free Press, 1938.
Ehrenreich, John, ed. *The Cultural Crisis of Modern Medicine*. New York and London: Monthly Review Press, 1978.
Freeman, Howard E., Sol Levine, and Leo G. Reeder, eds. *Handbook of Medical Sociology*. Englewood Cliffs, N.J.: Prentice-Hall, 1972.

Fox, Renee C., and Judith P. Swazey. *The Courage to Fail.* 2d. rev. Chicago: University of Chicago Press, 1978.

Friedson, Eliot. *The Profession of Medicine: A Study in the Sociology of Applied Knowledge.* New York: Dodd, Mead, 1970.

Goffman, Erving. *Asylums: Essays on the Social Situation of Mental Patients and Other Inmates.* Garden City, N.Y.: Doubleday/Anchor, 1961.

_____. *Stigma.* Englewood Cliffs, N.J.: Prentice-Hall, 1963.

Kallen, David J. "Clinical Sociology and Adolescent Medicine." *Clinical Sociology Review* 2 (1984).

_____, and Judith J. Stephenson. "Perceived Physician Humaneness, Patient Attitude, and Satisfaction with the Pill as a Contraceptive." *Journal of Health and Social Behavior* 22 (1981): 256–267.

Korsch, Barbara, E. F. Gozzi, and V. Francis. "Gaps in Doctor–Patient Communication: Doctor–Patient Interaction and Patient Satisfaction." *Pediatrics* 42, no. 15 (1968): 855–871.

Mead, George Herbert. *Mind, Self, and Society.* Chicago: University of Chicago Press, 1934.

Mechanic, David. "The Organization of Medical Practice and Practice Orientations among Patients in Prepaid and Non-prepaid Primary Care Settings." *Medical Care,* 13, no. 3 (1976): 189–204.

_____. *Medical Sociology.* 2d ed. New York: Free Press, 1978.

Merton, Robert K. "Self-Fulfilling Prophecies." In *Social Theory and Social Structure.* Rev. ed. New York: Free Press, 1957.

_____, George Reader, and Patricia L. Kendall, eds. *The Student Physician: Introductory Studies in the Sociology of Medical Education.* Cambridge, Mass.: Harvard University Press, 1957.

Newcomb, Theodore, R. H. Turner, and P. E. Converse. *Social Psychology, the Study of Human Interaction.* New York: Holt, Rinehart, and Winston, 1965.

Parsons, Talcott. "Definitions of Health and Illness in the Light of American Values and Social Structure." In E. Gartley Jaco, ed., *Patients, Physicians and Illness.* 2d ed. New York: Free Press, 1972.

Richardson, Stephen A. "Children's Values and Friendship: A Study of Physical Disability." *Journal of Health and Social Behavior* 12, no. 3 (1971): 253–258.

Ross, C., and R. Duff. "Quality of Outpatient Care: The Influence of Physician Background, Socialization, and Work/Information Environment on Performance." *Journal of Health and Social Behavior* 19, no. 4 (1978): 348–360.

Schwartz, Howard D., and Cary S. Kart, eds. *Dominant Issues in Medical Sociology.* Menlo Park: Addison-Wesley, 1978.

Shapiro, Eileen C., and Leah M. Lowenstein, eds. *Becoming a Physician: Development of Values and Attitudes in Medicine.* Cambridge, Mass.: Ballinger, 1979.

Starr, Paul. *The Social Transformation of American Medicine.* New York: Basic Books, 1982.

Chapter 7   CRIME, DEVIANCE, AND THE
SOCIOLOGICAL IMAGINATION
William M. Hall

The prevalence of crime is one of the most important issues in America to-day. This is evidenced by the amount of coverage accorded the topic on the front page of newspapers and on television. Newspapers have described the gory facts in criminal cases and have cited the concerns of politicians and national experts for decades. But crime persists.

C. Wright Mills once stated, "It is one thing to talk about general problems on a national level, and quite another to tell an individual what to do. Most 'experts' dodge that question. I don't want to" (Horowitz 1963). This chapter discusses what sociologists have to say regarding doing something about the problem of crime in American society. The intervention strategies we discuss are selected because they demonstrate how sociologists think. They illustrate the contribution a clinical perspective can make when we attempt to decrease crime and deal with criminals.

What Do We Mean by Crime?

The study of crime is the study of a special kind of *deviance*. When sociologists speak of deviance, they are referring to a social fact and not a behavior. In other words, sociologists want to be precise and analytic. They realize that behaviors mean different things in different situations.

For example, I had a student who dressed in a wet suit and walked down the main business district of Syracuse, New York. A second student took pictures of her journey. The pictures showed reactions that included business people gawking and a police officer ending the experiment by telling her to change her clothes. It is obvious from this example that wearing a wet suit is not deviant in itself, but where you wear it determines its deviancy. Sociologists therefore use a process-oriented definition, such as: "Deviance is behavior, ideas, or attributes of an individual(s) which some, though not necessarily all, people in society find wrong, bad, crazy, disgusting, strange, or immoral—in other words, offensive" (Higgins and Butler 1982).

The standards used to define offensive behavior, ideas, or attributes of individuals referred to as "crime" are written and codified in the form of *laws*. They are also enforced by government agencies. This does not mean that crime is easier to detect. Although the law stipulates the circumstances

118

under which a behavior becomes a crime, these circumstances must be interpreted in court of law by a judge and often, a jury. Our Constitution guarantees that we have rights that are to be respected; if they are not, we cannot be convicted of a crime. This is made evident when a suspect's right to a speedy trial is violated and a judge dismisses the case because the state has failed to prosecute within a reasonable time.

The trial is a tribunal that allows the behavior of an individual to be defined as criminal. In many instances it is not the behavior that is at issue. For example, if I can demonstrate that a woman was protecting herself, then there is no justification in calling her behavior "criminal."

In a recent case in Allegany County, New York, a woman was on trial for homicide. There was no doubt that she had killed her husband by shooting him while he slept. What was at issue was whether she had believed that this action was the only device she had to escape being killed by her husband. Her defense was that she had been beaten and sexually abused by her husband over a period of time. The result of this experience was the development of a *battered spouse syndrome* that led her to believe her husband's threat that he would kill her and their children.

The jury had to consider a number of issues in this case. One issue was whether the woman was lying about the brutality she experienced. If she was telling the truth, the question remained, "Is there in reality such a phenomenon as 'battered spouse syndrome'?" The woman was convicted. The prosecuting attorney stated after the trial that a tragedy had occurred and that she did not experience any elation at having won the case.

The point that is common to both examples given above is that the behavior was not at issue. Rather, the moral meaning of the behavior was the issue. Both women were defined by an audience as being deviant. This makes the study of deviance very problematic. I think it makes the study of crime interesting and challenging. We cannot go out and discover crime, we must go out and discover how behavior becomes criminal. An area in sociology today that has become popular is the study of jury decision making and what factors influence the outcome of a trial (Hunt 1982).

Many readers of this book may now be sayng to themselves, "Oh, yes, that is interesting — but so what?" I agree. We need to demonstrate how this understanding of the nature of deviance and the social processes that explain its occurrence can be used. The sociologist often uses his or her perspective to show how popular images and explanations are incorrect. The reason that crime occurs has also been addressed by sociologists. Sociologists work with the police, courts, and penal institutions as well. We now discuss how sociologists accomplish these tasks and the intervention strategies that have resulted.

Sociology as an Art in Debunking

An important clinical contribution of sociology is its ability to remedy problems induced by well-meaning people who explain deviance in such a way that they cause harm to be done. When a medical expert induces illness rather than cure , we are often angry, even if the induced illness is the result of a mistake. This is illustrated by the outrage that resulted when people were made aware of the high rates of drug addiction among people being treated for depression. Sociologists have made it a goal to demonstrate the unintentional harm caused by incorrect diagnoses of deviance and deviants.

One way we accomplish this is by *debunking* false beliefs and assumptions. A common-sense belief in American society is that a criminal is someone who is different from the rest of us and is responsible by virtue of his or her criminal *pathology*. This individual is defined as being morally inferior, flawed — and by virtue of this flaw, a threat to the stability of society. The image that portrays the criminal as a pathological being is convenient. It makes the world seem orderly because good is easily defined and bad is easily defined, and so they are clearly distinguishable. This image also provides citizens like ourselves with protection from the possibility that we are like the perpetrator of a crime, a person who could harm others. It is an easy step from saying that criminal behavior is the result of a different kind of person to saying that people who are different or perceived as being different are criminal.

One of the earliest theories of crime in the United States focused on a family that was said to be criminal because of the illegitimacy of a male in the family. We must keep in mind that to be illegitimate in the 1800s was to be morally flawed. Dugdale, the theorist who popularized this notion, stated, "One who is called in these pages Ada Juke, but who is better known to the public as Margaret, the mother of criminals, had one bastard son, who is the progenitor of the destructively criminal line" (Dugdale 1877). I doubt if you would agree with this theory. In fact, you probably wonder how people could think that way. The fact that a child's parents are not legally married is not an indictment of a person.

Think, however, of the image we have of criminals. When you think of the student who donned the wet suit and strolled down the streets of Syracuse, do you have the same image as when you think of the woman who shot her husband? What are the differences?

Physique is often used to portray a criminal. For example, in films the disabled are often portrayed as criminals. John Townsend (1979) found that 25% of television shows that have characters defined as mentally ill depict them as physically violent. When a disability is evident, newspapers often use it in their headlines. For example, *Police Arrest Amputee in Slaying of Doctor* (Bogdan *et al.* 1984).

Sociologists are not arguing that the police, the courts, and the public accuse people of being criminals by virtue of their disability. We are saying that, once accused, the ability to demonsrate that the behavior was not criminal may be dependent, not on legal criteria, but on a person's image. Dion (1972) found that the interpretation of a child's conduct as inappropriate was dependent on the attractiveness of the child.

So what? Yes, it is unfortunate that we associate certain stereotypes with criminal behavior. We should not do this. But what real difference does it make to our safety? After all, don't we want to change the threat that crime poses? Let's find out what pathologies are causing crime and eradicate them.

If you are thinking this, great. I understand your frustration. But there are two problems we experience when we try to eradicate crime by using this logic. First, what if we find a pathology that is related to crime? Does everyone with this condition engage in crime? Do we have a right to intervene before a person commits a crime? Mednick (1980) believes that some people are physically prone to engage in criminal behavior. If he is correct, should we take all children with this condition and perform lobotomies, put them in institutions, place them on probation? Our society believes that a person cannot be punished until he or she has been convicted of a crime. We have no right to limit the freedom of a person unless we believe him or her to be a threat. How many people who will never commit a crime can we incarcerate to ensure that the ones who will engage in crime are stopped?

The second problem we must confront, given our strategy of eradicating from society the pathology responsible for crime, is that crime may result from many facts not dealt with by our intervention. Let me illustrate this point. There was a belief in American society that feeblemindedness was related to crime. A solution to this problem was the sterilization of women defined as feebleminded. In fact, 31 states have had sterilization laws (Kittrie 1971:313). Not only did these laws and the involuntary sterilizations that occurred as a result of them not stop crime from occurring, but they gave people a false sense of security. That is, people believed that this action made them safer.

Today there is a concern for women, as the specter of rape appears regularly in the media. As a result of the belief that psychopaths were responsible for this phenomenon, sexual-psycopath laws were passed in the early 1960s. The result was the incarceration of a few rapists for long periods of time. But these laws did not stop rape or cause it to dcline. In fact, they took our attention away from the factors that are responsible for most rapes. These laws not only reflect our common-sense notions of crime but reinforce the notion that pathology explains crime.

If we step back and review the studies of rape, we may change our image — and more important, the intervention strategies we design to curb this crime. Our first impresion is that the rapist is a stranger with an uncontrollable sex drive. Yet we find that 36% of all reported rapes are committed by acquaintances, and 44% of all women 12 to 19 years of age who were reportedly raped were raped by acquaintances (Bureau of Justice Statistics 1982:45–46). On the other end of the spectrum, sociologists have identified a form of rape known as "date rape," which is often not reported but is nevertheless real. In this variant, the woman wants to stop but the male continues to pursue sexual activity. Studies have found that rapists, in general, are victims of childhood sexual abuse, insecure, and unhappy (Groth and Birnbaum 1979).

This is not the image we have of a rapist, and this new image suggests alternative interventions. There is a need to clarify the rights women have, particularly when they are dating. Second, women should be conscious that rapes occur in places other than dark alleys. Another tactic is the recognition by the police and the courts that the act of rape necessitates a formal routine handling, rather than the assignment of rape cases to a low priority.

As I have been showing you, one important contribution sociologists make to intervention strategies used to combat crime is to debunk commonsense notions of crime. Sociologists also debunk policies that have been implemented by experts. Debunking social policy recommended by experts necessitates more than demonstrating how their assumptions are incorrect. It necessitates the demonstration of how the policies are not accomplishing their goals or are working against the goals of the agencies involved in the intervention. Before discussing how sociology debunks such policies and programs, let us discuss how social interventions are assessed.

The Measurement of Crime

The analysis of interventions designed to curb the incidence of crime seems obvious. I measure the amount of crime that occurs before intervention and that which occurs after. I then determine if an impact occurred by comparing the crime rates. Your reading of the methods chapter in this volume will have familiarized you with some of the problems that must be considered when such an experiment is constructed. Our discussion focuses on the measurement problem itself. Namely, how do we know how much crime exists?

Three kinds of measurements have been relied on to develop a measure of criminal behavior: official rates, victimization surveys, and self-reports. *Official rates* are the number of crimes reported to the police in a particular geographic area. These reports reflect the willingness or unwillingness of people to report a crime. They are also a reflection of a police officer's interpretation of the event, wuch as whether or not the officer defines the event as a possible crime. For example, rape rates are known to be biased because many women are unwilling to undergo the degradation of being interviewed by the police and questioned during a trial. Therefore, an increase in rape after a police rape-crisis unit is set up may reflect an actual increase or may reflect the increased willingness of women to report a rape.

Sociologists often use official statistics on crime to evaluate the working of a police department. Richard McCleary (1982) studied the impact of an increase in the use of detectives to follow up on crimes reported to the police. The department believed this would increase the rate of official crime because more reports could be worked on. The actual consequence was a decrease in the official crime rate. One reason for this was that detectives used a more rigorous definition of crime than did uniformed police officers, and found that many behaviors previously coded as criminal were technically mere "violations" and not "crimes."

A second kind of crime counting, *victimization surveys*, uses survey techniques. Samples of the population that are representative of different groups are asked questions by professional survey researchers. The questions asked include whether the person was a crime victim; the person's vital features, such as age and income; and the residence of the person, whether urban or rural. There are many other questions that include the crime situation and the characteristics of a perpetrator in a crime. These studies find the official statistics underreport crime. For example, only about 50% of all rapes and 55% of all robberies are reported to the police (Bureau of Justice Statistics 1982). Data from this kind of study are also biased, however (Levine 1976). Many people misinterpret situations, and other respondents give answers that they think the researchers want to hear.

A third way crime is detected, by *self-reports*, involves asking people if they have committed crimes and how often. This is done by surveys. Unlike the victimization studies, which are funded and directed by administrative agencies such as the Department of Justice and Law Enforcement Assistance Administration, and official crime rates kept by the police, self-report surveys are done by independent researchers. Practical considerations limit these surveys to well-defined populations and easily accessible populations, such as juveniles still in school. Self-reports are also susceptible to such flaws as respondents' lying about their criminal acts or forgetting what acts they have committed.

We can use the data from these studies to evaluate criminal activity among different populations (self-report), how control organizations are operating (official statistics), and the characteristics of victims (victimization surveys). None of these methods, however, gives us a true picture of crime. No one will ever know what the actual figure for crime is. Therefore, if we wish to determine how effective a solution to crime is, we must use all available data and evaluate our conclusions with the data's limitations in mind.

Doing Something About Crime

I believe that the most important role sociology can play in the field of crime is to demonstrate that a particular intervention is working against some social value. We need to use methods in a creative manner to do this. To demonstrate that society needs to be wary of easy solutions and surefire answers contributes to a healthier system. This does not make sociologists popular among agency personnel required to *do something* about crime. It has led to the development of some productive intervention strategies. In the following section, I discuss how sociologists have shown interventions in juvenile crime to be problematic. I then discuss how a sociological theory has resulted in some productive programs that deal with crime.

The debunking function of sociology has generated policy changes that have radically altered how we respond to crime. During the middle of the nineteenth century, communities in the United States began responding to misconduct by children. Their response was to build structures that housed juveniles in a setting separate from their families and their neighborhoods. The justification for this response was that the disorganized neighborhoods in which the juveniles lived produced their inappropriate behavior, as well as needy, dependent children. We can see in this rhetoric that social reformers of the time were committed to the belief that "evil produces evil."

The consequence was the building of large institutional networks. The purpose of these institutions was to train and care for juveniles. Some of the juveniles had engaged in petty theft; others had a history of serious, repetitive criminal behavior. Juveniles who were abused or had no one to care for them were placed in the same institutions. The reason that these different kinds of juveniles were placed together was a pervasive belief that the unsupervised juvenile would eventually become a deliquent and that to care for him or her before the onset of deliquency was a form of humanitarianism (Platt 1969; Rothman 1980; Picket 1969; Fox 1974).

The system grew until by the late 1960s a network of private and public institutions existed in every state. These institutions exhibited various forms of control and continued to house juveniles who were *status offenders* (i.e., who did not comply with nonlegal rules, such as by engaging in "promiscuous sex" or not going to school), as well as actual *delinquents*, who would have been convicted of crimes if they had been over an arbitrarily selected age (some states use age 21 as the age at which a juvenile becomes an adult, and other states use age 16).

During the 1950s, a sociologist, Erving Goffman (1961), found that *total institutions* were characterized by unintended consequences including the isolation and brutal care of institutionalized populations, or "inmates."

Also, evidence was found that people lose their identity in the institutions, so that when they emerged, they had more problems than when they went into the institution. Polsky began an analysis of juvenile institutions. He, too, found that there were unintended consequences in the institutionalization response: Relationships within the institution were predicated on the ability of some youth to exploit others, and brutality was pervasive (Polsky 1967).

Other researchers found that juveniles were not referred to the institutions because of the acts they had committed. Instead juveniles were referred in some cities because of their racial and class characteristics (Thornberry 1973). Studies continued to be done throughout the 1970s, and the conclusions were similar to those done earlier. For example, a study done on one of the newest, architecturally modern institutions in Ohio found that, despite its sophisticated treatment programs, the same pathological subcultures existed in the institution that had existed in Polsky's earlier analysis (Bartallas, Miller, and Dinitz 1976).

The results of these studies, and many others, forced policy makers to reevaluate the reliance society had placed on total institutions when dealing with juvenile problems. A crisis was precipitated because people were unsure how to deal with juveniles traditionally placed in such institutions. California instituted a plan designed to place juveniles in the community, but under strict supervision. The purpose was to provide care to juveniles within their community. This response demonstrated one of the crucial problems found in any program designed to replace an accepted program. Lerman (1975) found that juveniles placed in the community spent more time in institutions after the community treatment program started than before. How could this happen? Lerman (1975:203) found evidence that probation officers placed the juveniles from a community program in detention, which was an institutional setting, as a form of treatment when the juveniles were not complying with regulations. Blomberg (1980) found that when community programs were started, the system brought more juveniles into the system, rather than redirect juveniles who had been traditionally placed in institutions.

Programs continue to be developed that are advertised as easy solutions to the complex problem of juvenile misconduct. For example, in 1979, Rahway Prison in New Jersey started a program called Scared Straight that was predicated on the belief that by demonstrating the horrid character of correctional institutions, inmates could scare juveniles into "going straight"—that is, not engaging in criminal behavior. The program was praised by people who heard of it, and a television documentary was made that was highly acclaimed and was shown across the country. Many people began arguing that a quick, easy, and cheap answer to juvenile crime had been found. During hearings conducted by Congress, however, experts testified that there was no evidence that this program was effective.

We can conclude from this brief discussion of the institutional response to youth crime that the debunking function of sociology can be very beneficial as a clinical strategy. Alfred McClung Lee has pointed this out time and again (e.g., Lee 1978). Sociologists have demonstrated that a quick and easy solution may not be an effective solution. Sociologists have also demonstrated how some unanticipated consequences, such as the exploitation that occurred in total institutions, may be more harmful than warranted by the desired consequences, such as the reduction of youth crime. New ways of dealing with problems found in social interventions have been suggested by sociologists. Laws have been passed, for example, that prohibit the placement of status offenders in total institutions with juveniles who have been convicted of serious crimes.

Sociological Theory and Social Policy

Although you may be thinking that sociologists are excellent critics, you may also be wondering how they can use their understanding of society to develop strategies to change crime patterns. Sociologists do develop theories designed to modify criminal behavior. Unfortunately, it is not an easy task to demonstrate how a theory designed to explain crime has been incorporated in social policy. This is, in part, because social policy can be implemented only within the moral boundaries of society. A social theory may, for example, suggest that people who cannot both love and discipline children should not have babies. This would be impossible to implement, given our values regarding the freedom to marry and start a family. As you will learn in Chapter 9, on public policy, many other political considerations are involved in policy formation. The development of programs is also contingent on money — if funds are low, this may hurt a program. Finally, the ability to attract quality personnel is essential, and new programs rarely have sufficient funds to hire enough quality people.

The purpose of this chapter is to show how sociologists contribute to crime policies and programs. It is not designed to articulate the various sociological theories relating to deviance and crime. Although I feel uncomfortable discussing only one theory, because various theories provide us with different kinds of insights into the crime problem, we do not have space to cover them all. Therefore, the discussion must focus on how sociologists have demonstrated that *normal social conditions are responsible for crime.* It also illustrates intervention strategies that have been suggested based on this particular theory.

In 1938 Robert K. Merton suggested that crime could be explained as resulting from the structure of American society. He offered a theory that demonstrated how the normal processes in society produce crime. To do this, he built upon theoretical contributions by the pioneering sociologist

Emile Durkheim. Durkheim believed that crime was normal; that is, without crime, society could not exist. For example, without crime, people would be unable to know how to behave. Without crime, there would be no social change (Merton 1938).

Merton focused on the normal conditions of capitalism. He pointed out that in American society we stress the importance of being successful, and we use a person's wealth to assess his or her worth. We also believe that anyone who wants to can get ahead in our society. The strategies we use to get ahead can either take advantage of accepted avenues of success or can involve the creation of different (not accepted) behaviors. Merton believed that people adapt differently to the material goals of society and the standard way of achieving these goals. People who accept the goals and means are called "conformists"; those who reject the material goals are called "ritualists," because they just go through the actions. Some people reject both goals and means; they become "retreatists" or rebels who try to start their own society. Finally, some people's adaptation is to reject the legitimate means to success and try to become wealthy by using illegitimate means. These people are termed "innovators."

Deviants can be found in each adaptation. A woman who took emergency calls and dispatched help recently refused to send aid to a house because the caller was loud and swearing. A conformist, she was so concerned with phone etiquette that she neglected the purpose of her job. The person needing help died, and the dispatcher was fired from her job.

We are primarily concerned with the innovator, for crime is a kind of innovation used to get material wealth. Merton hypothesized that as people experience less opportunity, they will be more inclined to engage in innovation to get ahead. As we go down the class structure—as people get poorer—their chances of getting ahead are more limited. Children whose families are not well-to-do have few symbols they can use to demonstrate their worth. One way a juvenile can become successful in this sense is to excel in sports, but few have the physical qualities required. Others may have special abilities in math or language, but again, they are few in number. A child who has few material rewards and is not successful in school may adapt criminal strategies to get the wealth that is such an important symbol of worth in our culture.

Although we think of school as a fine institution that provides a legitimate avenue to success, the experience of failure in school may result in juveniles seeking other avenues to achieve success. Elliot (1974) found that juveniles having high rates of contact with the police were likely to drop out of school. He also found that delinquency *decreased* after the juveniles dropped out. The implication is that school may contribute to youth crime. Other research has found that the age of *compulsory school attendance* is related to crime in secondary schools. When we compare school districts with compulsory school attendance to age 18 with school districts requiring school only to age 14, those with the higher age requirement experience higher school crime (HEW 1978: Toby 1983). A policy recommendation that follows this evidence would be the elimination of compulsory education legislation, allowing juveniles who do not wish to be in school to drop out and seek more fulfilling (legitimate) channels of goal attainment.

Another policy that has been proposed is the development of programs targeted at juveniles who have special problems and want to drop out of school. One such suggestion would set up alternative academic environments for juveniles who have not succeeded in school and have engaged in patterns of juvenile delinquency. Denver's Project New Pride is one example. The project allows juveniles to work extensively with counselors, who stay in close contact with the juveniles' teachers and social workers. The project strives to establish a positive self-concept among its clients, and to help remedy academic and learning disabilities (McCarthy and McCarthy 1984). In 1980, $9 million were used to fund projects like Project New Pride in other cities.

We can see that criminal behavior is not simply a consequence of poverty, despite the belief that poverty forces people into crime. Nor is it a consequence of inadequate socialization that produces a pathological personality. Rather, crime may be a reflection of relationships that exist between normal social institutions.

Schools, for example, do not produce high crime rates. Nevertheless, in our society the social rewards of schooling are not equally allocated. Some youths are not required to do well in school because they have affluence by virtue of their parents' income. Others cannot rely on middle-class identities, yet they also do not have the required attitudes or skills to succeed in school. Compulsory school attendance laws force these juveniles to experience humiliation, failure, and the anger associated with these experiences. To solve their problem, communities must make a concerted effort in terms of time and money to develop supportive networks for juveniles that provide alternative and legitimate avenues to success. This was done in Denver when Project New Pride was started.

Clinical Sociologists in Clinics and Prisons

Another way in which sociology contributes to efforts to deal with crime can be seen in the work of practitioners who engage in direct interventions rather than research or policy development. It is tempting to describe this as a "new" role, but the fact is that clinical sociologists have been involved in this field since the early years of the present century.

We have been discussing juveniles, and so it is interesting to note that the earliest clinical sociologists were primarily associated with the "child guidance clinics" of the 1920s. According to Wirth (1931), the primary contribution of the sociologist was the "cultural approach to behavior problems" in which "the behavior of the child is seen as a constellation of a number of roles, each oriented with reference to a social group in which he has a place. . . ." Emphasis was placed on the fact that the juvenile was a member of many intersecting and conflicting groups and that behavior identified as a problem from the perspective of the family or the community at large might actually represent conformity to the norms of other groups, such as his gang.

The focus of the sociologist's contribution was not merely obtaining diagnostic insight into the juvenile's motives, attitudes, situational analysis, group and cultural participation but also in controlling and reconstructing the juvenile's behavior (Wirth 1931). Furthermore, the original statement of the Thomas Theorem (described in previous chapters) was made in the context of a volume by clinicians William I. and Dorothy Swaine Thomas (1928), *The Child in America: Behavior Problems and Programs,* which presented one of the earliest statements of a sociological approach to juvenile delinquency.

More recently, the focus of clinical sociological intervention in criminal justice seems to have shifted to work with prisons and inmates. Bruce Berg (in press), for example, helped establish the Youth Advocacy Program (YAP) at New York State's Auburn Prison as an alternative to Scared Straight, in which inmates, themselves trained in principles of clinical sociology, deliver sociodramas for delinquents to try to keep them "straight." A unique feature of this program is that it is run by the prisoners themselves, who circumvent the problems of frequent transfers to other institutions and the possibility that authorities will confiscate written materials by working entirely within an oral tradition passed on from one inmate group to another.

Another example of clinical sociology in prisons was the group training program developed by the late Frances Cheek of the New Jersey Neuropsychiatric Institute. In this program prison inmates were trained in relaxation, self-image enhancement, assertiveness, and social skills. The objective of the program—similar to others Cheek developed for correctional officers and their families as well as New Jersey State Policy Officers—was to enhance self-control and stress management skills. Previous programs developed by nonsociologists had attempted to "condition" inmates into going straight. Not only was this ethically and legally questionable, it was just plain ineffective. Cheek's strategy was to offer inmates a way to get what they wanted out of life while bringing about the unlearning of antisocial and inadequate attitudes and social behaviors that had led to incarceration and that were only reinforced in prison, and "the subsequent learning of a new set of behaviors and attitudes of a more socially acceptable and constructive nature" (Cheek and Baker 1977).

Sociological Intervention and Social Control

The sociologist as critic, as policy adviser, and as clinician are important roles; there is yet a fourth role that sociologists play. This is the adviser role for organizations involved in the control of crime. Sociologists have a history of taking on advisory tasks. In fact, there has been an Office of Socioloist-Actuary since 1933 in the Illinois penitentiary known as Statesville.

The role sociologists play as advisers depends on the position they have in the organization and the personal values of the sociologist. Some sociologists become employees of the justice system and work as police officers, judicial administrators, or institutional staff. Other sociologists are employed to evaluate programs; still others are employed on a full-time basis to use their perspective to help accomplish a particular goal, such as increasing efficiency. Our discussion now turns to how sociologists have contributed to the operations of one organization responsible for the control of crime, the police.

Let's take a look at how the sociological imagination can provide us with a better understanding of how the police function. "Function" has two implications. First, we want to know what the police actually do, and second, we want to know what the consequences of their actions are. Once we know this we need to recommend changes and determine the impact of those changes.

Before I continue, you should know something about why I am interested in police behavior. Although I am a full-time faculty member at Alfred University, I also work part-time as a police officer. I do this not because I need the money, but because I want to develop an understanding of the police from an insider's perspective. This does not mean that, as a participant observer, I am more knowledgeable about the police than researchers who are not policemen, but I have a unique perspective. Two issues I have become concerned with in my endeavors to understand the police are the usefulness of patrol and the efficient allocation of police officers as a resource in the community.

The police have traditionally been viewed as control personnel. Their existence paralleled the declined in reliance on severe punishments, such as drawing and quartering or cutting off a thief's hands as a means of deterring crime. It has been a belief that the presence of police on the street maintains social stability. When I walk down a street, everyone knows who I am by virtue of my uniform, and most people realize that to commit a crime one must look out for the police.

Sociologists have begun studying the impact that police presence has on crime. The methods are weak because, as noted earlier, it is hard to detect the "dark figure of crime." Areas of a city can be defined that are similar in composition and data can be collected using similar indicators for each. Researchers in Kansas City compared 15 patrol areas after three kinds of patrol were initiated. In one kind of patrol, called "reactive," the officers patrolling their beats (areas) responded only to calls for service. In five "central" beats, preventive patrol was maintained at its usual level. In five "proactive" beats, preventive patrol was increased from two to three times its normal level. The researchers concluded: "Given the large amount of data collected and the extremely diverse sources used, the overwhelming evidence is that decreasing or increasing routine preventive patrol within the range tested had no effect on crime, citizen fear of crime, community attitudes toward the police, on the delivery of police service, police response time, or traffic accidents" (Kelling *et al.* 1974). In other words, if the police patrol less and merely react to problems, they will be as effective as if they were patrolling to make an area secure.

This finding does not mean we should not have the police patrolling streets. It does suggest that, when on duty, police officers would serve the public better if they performed specialized services. For example, special units could be set up for monitoring areas that show very high rates of crime. Special units could consist of officers trained in "sting" operations. Other units could be trained to educate the public in how to make an area secure, such as developing a "neighborhood watch" program. Still other units could specialize in domestic disputes.

Programs like these have been explored in some large metropolitan departments. For example, New York City experimented with a Family Crisis Intervention Unit (FCIU) developed by Morton Bard (1970). The officers were trained in skills associated with crisis intervention and conflict resolution. Results of the experiment demonstrated that more families sought help in the district patrolled by the FCIU, there were fewer assaults on family members, and there were no assaults on officers.

Many police departments do not have the money to evaluate job performance and do not have the manpower to train special units. I am working with one small department to develop programs and policies that will increase the department's ability to meet its goals more efficiently. My ability to use the computer and evaluate the consequences of a change in the departmental policies has resulted in their compliance with my suggestions. I am interested in using these data to test hypotheses I have about the consequences of various management changes. The result is that we work together; the department receives feedback on its policies and I develop a better understanding of how rural police departments operate.

An example of how this relationship works was provided by the present chief's desire to enforce a policy mandating giving a traffic ticket when an infraction occurs during an accident. In the past, officers often ignored any violations and concentrated on the task of making sure traffic continued to move around the accident and that an adequate report was written. Shortly after the present chief took office, a memo was issued stating that all traffic infractions were to be ticketed, including all traffic accidents. This meant that the officers had an added obligation, namely, to write up traffic infractions if they occurred during an accident.

The chief requested that I analyze the department's records to determine the impact of the memo. I studied all the accidents to determine the number of tickets given each month over a 2-year period before the memo and a 6-month period after. The results indicated that after the memo, the number of tickets given in accidents increased. The increase was not dramatic, but it convinced the chief that his policy had the intended impact. My goal is to determine if the policy had other impacts, such as a reduction in traffic accidents or a change in community perception of the police (Hall and Margeson 1984).

A second project we are working on is to determine the need for police service outside the traditional police jurisdiction. The local department is responsible only for a geographically defined political unit and is supported by tax revenues from that locality. The State Police service the surrounding community. The village police department wishes to determine if a need exists to change its legal responsibility from the village to the larger town of which the village is a part. Recent months have demonstrated that more calls are being received by the village because the outside region is too vast for the State Police to cover. The political problem is that the town government will be expected to help defray the cost of police services if they are officially extended beyond the village boundaries. I am now working with the police department to determine if a need can be shown to exist. We are using a survey to determine the perception of need on the part of citizens in the town. If the survey indicates that citizens in the town that surrounds the village feel they need more services, the police department will seek funds to increase its force and patrol a larger area.

This description of my involvement with the police is limited and does not address many issues. I have, however, shown how sociologists use their skills to analyze, intervene, and evaluate police behavior. The books written by sociologists explaining how people engaged in criminal enterprises work and think also influence the police. Finally, sociologists may work as police officers.

Concluding Remarks

Sociologists are often characterized as theorists who sit back and observe the world going by. I resent that image, as the historical tradition in sociology has been that of an active discipline. People may or may not be in a position to notice that the police are responding to calls for assistance faster, but they are doing so because of interventions developed by sociologists.

I have tried to demonstrate the important role sociologists have played in debunking myths about deviance and crime. I hope the next time you see a person who has a disability, the moral stigma often attached to a disabled person will not be a factor in your interaction with him or her. And when crime statistics are used to support a social policy, do not accept them at face value but ask how the crime rate was determined. Most important, when you hear someone suggest a quick and easy solution to crime, think of the complexities involved in understanding crime and some of the problems that are the consequence of quick-and-easy solutions.

Review Questions and Exercises

1. What distinguishes crime from deviance? What distinguishes deviance from "normal behavior?"
2. What are the implications of Merton's theory for sociological interventions in crime? How, in the light of the discussion of this approach, would you justify the phrase "crime is normal?"
3. Review 10 classic horror stories and list the traits of the villain. How many villains are "normal" physically? psychologically? What are their social characteristics? Write a short essay or engage in a group discussion on the topic of how these images of criminals have affected our understandings of, and policies related to, crime.

Readings and References

Bard, Morton. *Training Police as Specialists in Family Crises Intervention.* Washington, D.C.: U.S. Government Printing Office, 1970.

Bartollas, F., S. J. Miller, and S. Dinitz. *Juvenile Victimization: The Institutional Paradox.* New York: Wiley, 1976.

Berg, Bruce. "Inmates as Clinical Sociologists: The use of sociodrama in a non-traditional delinquency deterrent program." *International Journal of Offender Treatment and Comparative Criminology.* In press.

Blomberg, Thomas G. "Widening the Net: An Anomaly in the Evaluation of Diversion Programs." In M. Klein and K. H. Teilmann, eds., *Handbook of Criminal Justice Evaluation.* Beverly Hills, Calif.: Sage, 1980.

Bogdan, Robert, D. Biklen, A. Shapiro, and D. Spelkomon. "The Disabled: Media's Monster." *Institutions: Investigative Newsletter on Institutions/Alternatives* 6, 8 (1983).

Bureau of Justice Statistics. *Criminal Victimization in the United States, 1980.* Washington, D.C.: U.S. Department of Justice, 1982.

Cheek, Frances E., and James C. Baker. "Self-control Training for Inmates." *Psychological Reports* 41 (1977).

Dion, Karen. "Physical Attractiveness and Evaluation of Children's Transgressions." *Journal of Personality and Social Psychology* 24 (1972).

Dugdale, Richard. *The Jukes: A Study of Crime, Pauperism, and Heredity.* New York: Putnam, 1877.

Elliot, Delbert, and H. L. Voss. *Delinquency and Dropout.* Lexington, Mass.: Lexington Books, 1974.

Finkenauer, James. *Scared Straight and the Panacea Phenomenon.* Englewood Cliffs, N.J.: Prentice-Hall, 1984.

Fox, Sanford. "Juvenile Justice Reform: A Historical Perspective." *Stanford Law Review* 22 (1970).

Goffman, Erving. *Asylums: Essays on the Social Situation of Mental Patients and Other Inmates.* Garden City, N.Y.: Doubleday/Anchor, 1968.

Groth, N., and H. J. Birnbaum. *Men Who Rape: The Psychology of the Offender.* New York: Plenum Press, 1979.

Hall, W. M., and S. Margeson. "Police Administration Mandates and Policy Analysis." Paper presented at the meetings of the Criminal Justice Educators of New York State, 1984.

Higgins, Paul C., and Richard R. Butler. *Understanding Deviance.* New York: McGraw-Hill, 1982.

Horowitz, Irving L. "Introduction" to C. Wright Mills, *Power, Politics and People,* edited by I. L. Horowitz. New York: Oxford University Press, 1963.

Hunt, Morton. "Putting Juries on Trial." *New York Times Magazine,* August 8, 1982.

Kelling, George, et al. *The Kansas City Preventive Patrol Experiment: Final Report.* New York: Police Foundation, 1974.

Kittrie, Nicholas. *The Right to Be Different.* Baltimore: Johns Hopkins University Press, 1971.

Lee, Alfred McClung. *Sociology for Whom?* New York: Oxford University Press, 1978.

Lerman, Paul. *Community Treatment and Social Control.* Chicago: University of Chicago Press, 1975.

Levine, James. "The Potential for Crime Overreporting in Criminal Victimization Surveys." *Criminology* 14 (1976).

McCarthy, Belinda, and Bernard McCarthy. *Community Based Corrections.* Monterey, Calif.: Brooks/Cole, 1984.

Mednick, Sarnoff. "A Biosocial Theory of the Learning of Law-abiding Behavior." In E. Bittner and S. Messinger, eds., *Criminology Review Yearbook.* Beverly Hills, Calif.: Sage, 1980.

Merton, Robert K. "Social Structure and Anomie." *American Journal of Sociology* 44, no. 3 (1938).

Pickett, Robert S. *House of Refuge: Origins of Juvenile Reform in New York State, 1815–1857.* Syracuse: Syracuse University Press, 1969.

Platt, Anthony. *The Child Savers.* Chicago: University of Chicago Press, 1969.

Polsky, H. W. *Cottage Six: The Social System of Delinquent Boys in Residential Treatment.* New York: Krieger, 1962.

Rothman, David. *Conscience and Convenience.* Boston: Little, Brown, 1980.

Thomas, W. I., and D. S. Thomas. *The Child in America.* New York: Knopf, 1928.

Thornberry, T. P. "Race, Socioeconomic Status and Sentencing in the Juvenile Justice System." *Journal of Criminal Law and Criminology* 12 (1975).

Townsend, John. "Stereotypes of Mental Illness: A Comparison with Ethnic Stereotypes." *Culture, Medicine and Psychiatry, 1979.*

Toby, Jackson. "Crime in the Schools." In J. A. Wilson, ed., *Crime and Public Policy.* New Brunswick, N.J.: Transaction, 1983.

U.S. Department of Health, Education, and Welfare. *Violent Schools—Safe Schools: The Safe School Study Report to Congress.* Washington D.C.: U.S. Government Printing Office, 1978.

Wirth, Louis. "Clinical Sociology." *American Journal of Sociology* 44 (1931).

Chapter **8**   COMMUNITIES: MAKING
THEM WORK
Jan Fritz

An article in *Community Jobs* (1983), the national newspaper for those interested in community change, profiled three people who work for social justice. One of them, an environmental writer for a Kentucky newspaper, advised college students to put more energy into finding jobs that are consistent with their values. In other words, he said, find organizations that are out to solve the world's problems.

Many sociologists face the same dilemma; they want to use their skills to work for social justice. Those who are teachers make sure that the content of some or all of their courses touches upon or focuses on social justice issues. Others contribute by conducting research that will help change initiatives succeed; still others work within or outside academic institutions to make those changes happen. In some cases the sociologist explores all these avenues of social change. This chapter gives you some background on current interests in the area of community and introduces you to some of the clinical sociologists who work on behalf of the community.

Establishing a Definition of Community

Many of the founders of scientific sociology—including Auguste Comte, Ferdinand Tönnies, Emile Durkheim, and Karl Marx—were fascinated by the idea of community. Those who wrote at the time of the Industrial Revolution were concerned about the different kind of community that was developing around them, and some went on to talk about its alienating effects.

Tönnies described this as a change from *Gemeinschaft* ("community" in German) to *Gesellschaft* ("society"). The first refers to a form of social relations in which the individual is embedded in a matrix of tightly knit primary groups, such as family, church, and kinship networks. Characteristic of preindustrial societies, it can still be found in some rural areas of industrial societies. The second refers to a more businesslike form of social relations—often associated in art, literature, and political rhetoric with urban life—in which primary bonds have been all but replaced by impersonal, contractual secondary relationships.

By and large, small-town life in the United States is treated with nostalgia; big-city life is associated with all the evils of the modern age. In sociology, Tönnies established the idea that this shift meant a crucial "loss of community" with negative consequences for individuals and society in general.

The question whether we have lost "community" is still not settled. According to Barry Wellman (1979), there are three main points of view on this subject. The "community-lost view" holds that tightly knit primary groups have been replaced by impersonal, contractual secondary relationships. The "community-saved view" contradicts the first by pointing out the survival of primary-group relationships, particularly among poor people and minorities, in even the largest cities. The "community-liberated view" finds that primary-group relationships still exist and are highly valued but that they are now based on work and friendship rather than geography. The feeling of belonging now comes from social networks people have formed by choice rather than from neighborhoods. By "community liberated," then, Wellman emphasizes how a person chooses his or her own community.

Just as scholars hold divergent opinions about whether we are suffering from a loss of community, they also may define the concept in differing ways. It might be helpful, in establishing a definition for use here, to look at the four kinds of communities identified by Calvin Redekop (1975):

1. The *geographic community* refers to an aggregate of people situated in a rather definite ecological area. In this view of community, there is a strong tie between the social system that develops and the territorial unit.
2. In the *spiritual community* people are not bound together geographically but by a solidarity that comes through friendship, religious belief, tradition, and/or language. Examples of this kind of community include the Jewish, intellectual, and religious communities.
3. The *purposive community* refers to those who live, work, or meet together because of common objectives or purposes. Members of a corporation, a mental hosptial, or a college are referred to as communities in this sense. A purposive community has a geographical base, but this factor is not the basic characteristic of this kind of community.
4. The *intentional community* is quite different from the other three. In this case, the collective is formed for its own sake—to become a community. This is the aim of most contemporary communal movements, as well as classical Christian communes such as the Shakers.

When sociologists give a general definition of community, they usually refer to and build upon what Redekop has defined as the geographical community. We follow this approach by defining a community as *a collection of people within a geographic area among whom there is some degree of mutual identification, interdependence, loyalty, and common social organization of activities.* The clearest examples of communities in this sense of the term are villages, neighborhoods, and small towns.

The Nature of Contemporary Communities

As sociologists from Comte's time till our own have observed, industrialization drastically changed living patterns, first in Europe and then in the United States. According to the U.S. Bureau of the Census (1981), the percentage of our population living in *urban areas* of at least 2500 inhabitants grew from 6% in 1800 to 51% in 1920. Concerned about this change from a predominantly rural and small-town population to an urban society, many Americans came to villify the city as the cause of ever-growing social problems.

University of Chicago sociologists developed a novel *sociological* approach to the study of urban life, as mentioned in Chapter 1. They discovered that "the city" was really a conglomeration of *natural areas,* each with its own community, problems, and life styles. These include wealthy areas, ghettos, ethnic neighborhoods, slums, and commercial areas. They investigated the processes by which natural areas form — the *segregation* of distinctive groups into separate areas; *invasion* of new groups into existing areas; and *succession,* the process by which natural areas change character as they are invaded by different groups (Park, Burgess, and McKenzie 1925).

They investigated land-use patterns and their ecological relationship to natural areas, developing a highly influential theory of city growth. Louis Wirth (1938), a pioneering clinical sociologist, also explored *urbanism* as a distinctive way of life characterized by sophistication, individual freedom, change orientation, and diversity at the cost of the sort of *Gemeinschaft* relationships characteristic of rural life styles.

Since World War II, the structure of American communities has undergone a further shift from centralized, densely populated cities to *metropolitan areas,* which are defined by the Census Bureau as counties or groups of counties with one or more central cities of at least 50,000 population, a density of at least 1000 people per square mile, and outlying areas whose social and economic life are linked to that of the urban centers. By this definition there are some 318 "standard metropolitan statistical areas" in the United States today. Nearly 69 million Americans live in the 20 largest such areas, according to the 1980 Census.

The rapid growth of metropolitan areas was made possible by the mass production of automobiles and the government-sponsored creation of modern highway networks enabling "commuters" to live anywhere within 50–100 miles away from the urban workplace. While this allowed the middle class to achieve the "American dream" of owning their own home and land, it increasingly concentrated the poor in the rundown inner cities and enabled business and industry to sprawl beyond the old commercial centers.

This pattern is known as the *megalopolis,* an area of urban and suburban development often covering hundreds of miles, such as "Bos-wash," stretching between Boston and Washington, D.C., on the East Coast, or the urbanized belt from just north of Los Angeles to the Mexican border on the West Coast. Five-sixths of the U.S. population may live in such areas by the end of the century.

In the past few years as well, growth has shifted both from the old industrial centers of the Northeast and Midwest to the Sunbelt of the Southwest and West Coast, and from densely populated urban communities to more "suburban" communities spreading throughout what were previously rural areas outside the metropolis. This trend affects mainly the more affluent sectors of the population — those who can afford the increasingly high prices of suburban homes and are able to commute to work — or those who can find jobs in offices, retail, or service businesses no longer tied to centralized industry and commerce.

Each of these trends in the American community has contributed to the conditions sociologists since Tönnies have described as "loss of community." That is, we find an increasingly mobile population living outside traditional — rural and small-town — patterns of primary relationship. More and more people either choose to be, or find themselves to be, anonymous both where they reside and where they work.

At least, that is how it *seems* on the face of it. As mentioned, however, sociologists continue to find older forms of primary-group belonging alive and well in both city and suburb. In addition, they have observed the emergence of alternative "network" structures in which people create their own community relationships in conformity with the demands of present-day life styles. Let us turn, then, to a consideration of what this term "community" means outside the small town, on which our ideas are so strongly modeled.

The Mobilization of the Community

City dwellers often participate in many levels of social organization — the block, the neighborhood, the section, as well as the city as a whole — each of which may fit our definition of a community. Each unit is a "collective representation" that exists in the minds of the inhabitants rather than as a geographic region. A physical barrier such as a bridge, a road, or a railroad track may be used to define the edge of a community, but the boundary may also be the north side of a particular street, if that is how people view it. It is the *labeling of the area as a community* that has real consequences.

We stereotype sectors of a large community (such as a major city) because this helps us understand the complex whole. In so doing, we cannot possibly be completely accurate; yet we may grow up believing in the truth of our stereotypes. For instance, we see one section as rich, another as integrated, and a third as only for poor people. These stereotypes may be so strong that, while we are proud to tell what city we are from, we may be less willing, or even embarrassed, to name our neighborhood because of what it "means" to be from there (Milgram 1972).

Each of us identifies more strongly at any particular time with one or another level of community organization. For some, the whole town is important; for others, it is the specific block or neighborhood. External realities, like a crime wave or a natural disaster, are among the factors that help increase identification with a community.

As this identification grows, so may a strong desire to control the forces that shape the lives of the inhabitants of the community. Under what circumstances and in which communities does this *mobilization,* or desire for control over one's own community, develop? Let us now examine the conditions under which mobilization of a community takes place, and investigate the relationship between these conditions and what is referred to as "community development."

Many kinds of projects fall under the label community development (Christenson and Robinson, 1980:3). A state government official might think of flood disaster relief or new roads. A local public official might talk of industrial development or revitalization of an area in the central part of the city. A community activist might think about making jobs, training opportunities, and housing available to the poor, or organizing against construction of a nuclear power plant. Environmentalists might talk of slowing commercial development and preserving natural areas, while an agent from the Cooperative Extension Service might discuss educational programs or organization of groups to study community needs. All these activities have been categorized as community development.

According to the United Nations (1963:4), *community development* is

the process by which the efforts of the people themselves are united with those of governmental authorities to improve the economic, social, and cultural conditions of communities, to integrate these communities into the life of the nation, and to enable them to contribute fully to national progress. This complex of processes is, therefore, made up of two essential elements: the participation by the people themselves in efforts to improve their level of living, with as much reliance as possible on their own initiative; and the provision of technical and other services in ways which encourage initiative, self-help, and mutual help and make these more effective. It is expressed in programmes designed to achieve a wide variety of improvements.

The problem with this UN definition is that it stresses the nation-state as the context of development and suggests that what is deemed desirable by governmental authorities corresponds to the needs, interests, and values of all groups of people in the society. This definition also excludes any consideration of conflict or dissension. A more sociological approach would simply define community development in terms of *action on the part of some group to change programmatically economic, cultural, social, or environmental conditions of that community.*

In recent years, in developed and developing countries, there has been growing interest in community development. But as Roberts (1979:xiii) has noted, the aim has not always been to encourage the involvement of citizens: "In many cases, such as the American Model Cities programs, these workers were employed to serve the interests of the employing agencies rather than to facilitate real participation by the people."

In writing about the new directions in community development, urban affairs expert Hans Spiegel (1980:230) has discussed the current trend toward more decentralization and neighborhood-oriented programs. He says that this trend "represents a golden opportunity for community development." As this golden opportunity develops, however, it will be important to emphasize continually the basic commitment to facilitating citizen participation. This becomes particularly important in troubled economic times as practitioners who work, for instance, for such organizations as public utilities and those who are community activists may find it difficult to remain within the same organizations and continue talking together.

The sociological approach to community development sees it as a process beginning when community groups or members recognize that there is some kind of tension but does not have a real grasp of the problem. The next step is to learn about the problem and then formulate a set of goals or objectives. This might be done with the help of a clinical sociologist or other practitioner, who will facilitate thorough empirical investigation of problems and assessment of community resources, pinpoint weaknesses or skills (such as organization, communication, problem solving, and recordkeeping) that need to be learned, and then help community members formulate specific goals or objectives. Only after these steps have been taken should the community act and evaluate the extent to which goals have actually been met — and the degree to which action has reduced or not reduced tensions.

If a community moves too quickly from the initial phase of "tension" to action without systematically going through the intermediary stages, there may be unsatisfactory results. This frequently has been the case. When clinical sociologists or social scientists with similar training are involved, the chances increase for successful problem solving by the community.

Collective Action

Another element the sociologist contributes to the community development process is the concept of the *social movement* as a mobilizing force in community change. Most community development experts exclude from consideration those social movements that go through a process that leads to violent confrontation. But other forms of collective behavior—such as demonstrations, celebrations, boycotts, presenting demands, and symbolic acts—can give voice to tensions and concerns among community groups whose needs and interests are not effectively represented or considered in the formal community development process.

According to Neil Smelser (1962), six conditions usually exist before there is an episode of collective behavior. The first of these six factors is *structural conduciveness.* The organization of the community—for instance, a good communication network and an open administration—sets the stage for certain forms of collective activity.

When the structure of a society is conducive to collective behavior, *social strain* becomes a precipitating factor. Strain may develop from a sudden disruption to the existing order (a tornado), from persistent and increasing value conflicts (as between economic classes or religious groups), or when some event takes place and the culture offers no guidelines for responding (seepage from a nuclear facility).

Before a collective action takes place, a *generalized belief* usually develops to explain the social strain and anticipate consequences. In the case of radioactive seepage, for instance, there may arise a belief that the facility was improperly designed and that the radioactivity will cause cancer and birth defects. Then something may happen—a *precipitating event*— that confirms the generalized belief. Now *mobilization of the participants* may take place, and that activity may or may not be under the influence of a leader.

The last factor that Smelser discusses is *social control.* Control often is used to stop or redirect a collective action or eliminate its causes. It may also backfire, however, provoking a situation, as sometimes happened when the police attempted to halt civil rights or peace marchers in the 1960s. The form of control very much influences the direction, timing, and outcome of collective activity.

Even when a number of these conditions are met, a community may not take collective action. This does not necessarily mean that a group does not have a desire for change. Rather, the reason may lie in the relative prosperity of the community. In general, more prosperous communities often start with a higher feeling of confidence in their own power to influence change.

In the next two sections of this chapter we explore ways in which clinical sociologists encourage community action through research and consultation.

Community Research

Sociologists are scientists trained in qualitative and quantitative research methods. For example, you will find sociologists conducting in-depth interviews with community organizers about the strategies they use, videotaping meetings to study effective negotiating strategies, working as participant observers in rural communities about to become boom towns, or using sophisticated computer techniques to analyze data that have been collected about demographic trends.

Often, those who describe themselves as "applied sociologists" limit their activity to such research. Academically oriented community researchers may study interaction patterns, institutions, norms, and roles for no other reason than to learn about them or test theoretical hypotheses. Clinical sociologists go beyond this, concerning themselves also with application. They study an area because an individual, organization, or community can benefit from an analysis of the situation, and because the research will help further the planning process or help decide a course of action.

When the intent is to have an impact on the planning process, it is generally felt that it will take more than one study to have that effect. As Lindblom and Cohen (1979:5–6) have noted:

> It may be that the principal impact of policy-oriented studies, say, on inflation, race, conflict, deviance or foreign policy — including those specifically designed to advise a specific policy maker at a particular time — is through their contribution to a cumulating set of incentives (many studies with like results) for a general reconsideration by policy makers of their decision-making framework, their operating political or social philosophy, or their ideology.

Douglas Biklen (1983), author of *Community Organizing,* says that "when researchers amass enough evidence, in study after study, they can topple a whole way of thinking, but it is a slow process."

To enable you to examine this process, we review here two research projects: a case study of the social impact of a flood, and a study of black participation in Georgia local electoral politics.

The Buffalo Creek Flood

The devastating Buffalo Creek, West Virginia flood occurred on February 26, 1972. A huge dam owned by the local coal company (an absentee landlord) collapsed. Water traveling in waves 20 and 30 feet high swallowed Buffalo Creek's 16 small towns, leaving more than 125 people dead and over 4000 homeless.

Sociologist Kai Erikson (1976:193-94) was called in by the survivors' law firm to evaluate the personal and social impact of the flood. He stressed the loss of community caused by the disaster and talked about the special importance of community to the people of Buffalo Creek:

> The community in general can be described as the focus for activities that are normally regarded as the exclusive property of the individuals. It is the community that cushions pain, the community that provides a context for intimacy, the community that represents morality and serves as the repository for old traditions.

Some 18 months after the flood, 615 survivors were interviewed by psychiatrists; more than 90% were found to be emotionally disturbed, suffering from confusion, despair, and hopelessness. Crime, alcoholism, and the use of drugs increased after the flood; many people lost their morale, mental health, and respect for the law. For the survivors, the disaster showed that everything and everybody was unreliable. Erikson concluded that this would be a very difficult base from which to build a new community. Erikson's research was of primary use to the survivors' insurance company, but also would be of help to those who work with the survivors of natural disasters and to community planners.

Black Participation in Georgia Local Electoral Politics

Clinical sociologist Brian Sherman (1982) was a consultant with the Voting Rights Study Group in Atlanta (see Chapter 2). On behalf of the Study Group he designed and conducted research that documented the continuing problems of minority access to government that still exists in Georgia.

Sherman (1982:3) collected data from 60 counties for this study. The county was the unit of analysis because it is the "most important level for local political activity in Georgia" and because the county is the arena in which most residents can see for themselves their impact on, or exclusion from, the political process that affects their everyday lives.

Despite the abolition of the white primary, literacy tests, and the poll tax, Sherman found many barriers that still prevent blacks from participating fully in the political process. Among these practices were the manipulation of absentee ballots, voting by noneligible whites, voting by the deceased, purging of voter lists, switching to at-large representation, uncooperativeness on the part of white registrars, and a refusal to appoint black poll watchers. In this situation, the whites in power avoid blatant and overt racial intimidation and excessive legal violations; covert tactics are used and what is done is explained as being in the interest of "good government."

Sherman noted that whites have not tried to reach an accommodation with the black community for joint political action. He concluded that it was very important, then, for blacks to develop the experience, organization, contacts, and expertise for full political participation. As a start in this direction, Sherman recommended that a clearinghouse for information be established as an aid for black candidates in election campaigns and for use in voting rights court cases.

Sherman (1982:34) thinks that the Voting Rights Act has had a tremendous impact in Georgia:

> Blacks do register, vote, run for office and occasionally win an election. Without the Voting Rights Act, they would not have been able to do this in Georgia. As the details of this survey have demonstrated, white resistance is still both strong and successful. The continuation of the Voting Rights Act is necessary if blacks are to maintain their achievements and make future political gains.

Sherman was invited to testify before a U.S. congressional committee about the results of his study, and now is research director for the Voter Education Project in Atlanta. After every national census count, lines between voting districts are redrawn to reflect population shifts. Sherman's present job allows him to consult with black groups in southern states about local reapportionment plans. If a black group feels that the white power structure in the community has developed a discriminatory reapportionment plan, Sherman will investigate and contact the U.S. Department of Justice. He points out the defects of the plan and gives an analysis of the community situation showing possible reasons for the development of a discriminatory plan.

Sherman's research in particular is a good example of *action research*—it calls for attention, recognition, and action. It is the kind of work that can transform public consciousness if it is done well, is supported by other studies, and catches the attention of the public and policy makers. This is work of the kind C. Wright Mills, author of *The Sociological Imagination* and *The Power Elite,* would have liked. Mills encouraged his students to take on important research topics—the kind that would provide analysis but also influence the world.

Community Consultation

A *consultant,* according to community clinical psychologists O'Neill and Trickett (1982), is *someone who intervenes, who works with a system focus rather than an individual focus and whose advice may be accepted or rejected as the client chooses.* According to this definition, the consultant is a resource and has no permanent role in the system to which he or she acts as an adviser.

Consultation has become a professional activity for members of every social and behavioral discipline and other fields such as business, education, and nursing. Probably the most complete listing of the characteristics of a good consultant is that developed by Ronald Lippitt and Gordon Lippitt (1978). They identify three areas of competence:

1. *Knowledge,* including a thorough grounding in the behavioral sciences; knowledge of systems, human personality, and oneself; and an understanding of philosophical systems as foundations for value systems.
2. *Skill areas,* including communication, teaching, counseling; ability to form relationships and work with groups in planning and implementing change, and ability to conduct research and diagnose problems.
3. *Attitude areas,* including open-mindedness, courage, and the possession of a humanistic value system.

Professional consultants work in many different kinds of settings and use different models of consultation. These models can generally be linked to one of two perspectives — *social control* or *influence.* Gamson (1968), in discussing these perspectives, shows how each deals with conflict. The social-control perspective emphasizes the continuity and functioning of the system and sees conflict as disruptive and requiring control. The social-influence perspective sees conflict as a useful condition that allows change to occur.

Consultants' work should be viewed in relation to these perspectives. If one employs a social-control perspective, the powerful may maintain control through the assistance of the consultant. On the other hand, the powerless can benefit when an influence perspective is used.

Conflict Intervention

One major form of community-level consultation is *conflict intervention.* Since the 1960s a growing body of professionals — social scientists, group facilitators, lawyers, and labor leaders — has been refining and applying strategies to deal with problems such as racial struggles, housing-project disputes, and school controversies. Consultants who work in this growing field of community conflict intervention certainly are concerned with questions of social control and influence.

Conflict intervention is generally viewed as a process in which a *third party* (an outsider) enters into a conflict in order to influence its outcome in what is felt to be a desirable direction. According to clinical sociologist

James Laue (1981b:3), who has been working in this field for 20 years: "Because intervention always alters the power configuration of the conflict, all interveners are advocates—for either a specific party, a particular outcome or a preferred process of conflict intervention."

There has been increasing use of the four major techniques of conflict intervention—negotiation, conciliation, mediation, and arbitration—in this country and Europe, and to a more limited extent in Asia, Latin America, Africa, and the Pacific basin. The areas of application include family and neighborhood disputes, consumer disputes, intraorganizational and interorganizational relations, racial and other intergroup conflicts, federal–state–local relations, environmental disputes, and international conflict (Laue 1981b:7).

In order to understand the work of a community consultant better, we take a look at James Laue's work as a mediator. A *mediator* is an impartial individual who is acceptable at some level to all the disputants. The mediator assists the parties in reaching mutually satisfactory solutions to their differences and does this without having any formal power and without being able to impose penalties.

Laue, Director of the Center for Metropolitan Studies at the University of Missouri–St. Louis, was invited to be the mediator for the development of a Negotiated Investment Strategy (NIS) for the test city of Gary, Indiana. NIS is an experimental approach to getting government and private groups to work together on setting priorities for a community. NIS assumes that there are legitimate differences among these groups and attempts to negotiate agreements.

The NIS model has six essential parts (Berry, Kunde, and Moore 1982:44):

1. An impartial mediator
2. Three negotiating teams representing the public and private sectors of the city, the state, and the federal government, each of which is small initially but is subject to later expansion to assure representation of important interests
3. An opportunity of informal exchange of information before formal proposals are written
4. Formal face-to-face negotiating sessions with all teams present
5. A written agreement containing mutual commitments
6. A public review and adoption of the agreement with monitoring of subsequent performance by each party and by the mediator

The NIS model is distinct from other intergovernmental reform efforts in its use of an impartial "outside" mediator. James Laue facilitated an 8-month process in Gary, Indiana, that involved the mayor, the governor, and U.S. Steel, Gary's major employer and taxpayer. In his role as mediator, Laue provided structure and discipline for the entire process. As an outside mediator, he was expected to encourage new behavior from participants, several of whom had strained relations before entering the process.

The results of the long negotiations were striking (Berry, Kunde, and Moore 1982:53):

> The final agreement contained commitments from each of the three levels of government (and, in some cases, the private sector) on some 33 specific objectives in six major areas: downtown development, transportation, recreation, housing, industrial/commercial development, and health care. A seventh area — crime and public safety — was identified for future work.

A year after the agreement was signed, Laue and his mediating staff gave a progress report indicating which objectives had been met and on which only some or no action had been taken. The mediators have continued to monitor implementation and have been working with the Chicago Federal Regional Council in reviewing the status of the Gary Agreement for future action.

The most significant achievement in the Gary negotiation process was the improved relationship between the city, state, and U.S. Steel. A framework for cooperation was establised that should prove helpful to all parties in the future.

The Sociologist in the Community

In addition to these well-established roles of action researcher and consultant, the sociologist may take skills and knowledge out into the community to organize the community's resources to meet the needs of its people. An exemplary case of a clinical sociologist pursuing this option is that of Veronica Maz. A sociology professor at Georgetown University in Washington, D.C., she left teaching 15 years ago to work with the hungry and homeless of the nation's capitol.

In 1969, along with the late Reverend Horace B. McKenna, a Jesuit priest, and other community members, Maz co-founded an organization known as SOME (So Others Might Eat) to provide free food, counseling, and health care. Operating the soup kitchen, she gradually became aware of the numbers of destitute women in the city and the lack of services for them. In 1976 she decided to do something about it.

She started the House of Ruth by putting down a $1 deposit to rent an old roominghouse for women who were destitute or homeless. Eight women who had been sheltered in a nearby park became its first residents.

By 1978 the original 35-bed House of Ruth had expanded to include an annex for 30 battered women and two thrift shops. Dr. Maz, now with a $30,000 grant from the Cafritz Foundtion, also established two "second stage" shelters to which women from the main house could move and pay rent while still living in a situation of mutual support. She had, as well, convinced the District of Columbia to fund her Madison Center, a 65-bed facility for homeless women. All of this was accomplished through donations, contributions, and the efforts of Dr. Maz and her volunteers. A newspaper editorial that year saluted her work and said that she stood as a working definition of courage.

By 1982 Veronica Maz was in the news again. In September of that year, McKenna's Wagon—a truck that brings food to the destitute of the city—rolled onto the streets of Washington, D.C. The wagon was the newest project of Dr. Maz's soup kitchen for children, Martha's Table. The soup kitchen, which runs a lunch line for adults in addition to the children's facility, provides daily meals for about 100 destitute and homeless persons.

Some of the food on the wagon is purchased for five cents a pound from the Capital Area Community Food Bank in northeast Washington. Much of the food comes from donations—church members give sandwiches, pastries are donated by a bakery, and individuals working on Capitol Hill and living in the community give food regularly. Amazingly, McKenna's Wagon operates on a budget of just over $100 a week. This money comes from donations to Martha's Table by area residents, churches, and community groups.

The House of Ruth (or Friends of Ruth) is now established in 35 states; Dr. Maz hopes to expand McKenna's Wagon and the children's center in the same way. Her most recent accomplishment is the establishment of the National Institute, part of Martha's Table, which conducts one-day workshops around the country showing community activists how they can start a soup kitchen or a shelter. Maz also has gotten the Washington Redskins to endorse Martha's Table; the football players visit the center and hold events where items are sold and the proceeds given to the program.

What Veronica Maz has done is to take her knowledge and skills as a clinical sociologist out into the community to create new community-based institutions that meet people's needs. Her work stands as a fine example of the possibilities for clinical sociologists in the community.

Conclusion

There has been a surge of interest in developing effective community organizations on the part of citizens, foundations, and the government. Community scholars seem to agree that, in the next decade, neighborhood organizations will increase in number and importance. There will be many more block organizations, tenant groups, neighborhood councils, suburban civic associations, and local beautification, restoration, and ecology groups. The decentralization of municipal government also is expected to continue. All of which means that private and public neighborhood groups will probably gain political power.

This power will not be equally distributed. The growth of effective neighborhood organizations is expected to take place mainly in middle-class areas. Unless there is governmental commitment and funding, organizational efforts among the poor will not keep pace.

All these developments spell expanded opportunities for sociologists working at the community level. During this period, the role of clinical sociologists is expected to continue to grow in both community research and community consultation. Among other activities, sociologists will help communities explore alternative economic institutions, such as worker and consumer cooperatives, food-buying clubs, or neighborhood credit unions, and will help them develop new mechanisms for dispute resolution.

Review Questions and Exercises

1. Analyze the community in which you participate as a college student. What different groups and interests are represented? What are the problems of this community? How might these problems be resolved?

2. Select a troubled community discussed in a newspaper, news magazine, or recent journal article. Then do either of the following:

   a. Describe how one or more of the community intervention approaches described in this chapter are being applied to that case.

   b. Discuss how one or more of these clinical strategies could be applied to that particular case.

3. For this exercise, you should work with from two to five other students, preferably from diverse backgrounds. Complete these three steps:

   a. Each student should first consider Wellman's three points of view regarding "loss of community" and how these do or not relate to your hometown.

   b. Once you have done this on your own, get together as a group and discuss your findings.

   c. Complete the exercise by writing a brief group report comparing and contrasting your hometown communities and examining what might account for similarities and differences between them.

Readings and References

Berry, Daniel, James Kunde, and Carl Moore. "Negotiated Investment Strategy: Improving Intergovernmental Effectiveness by Improving Intergroup Relations" *Journal of Intergroup Relations* 10, no. 2 (Summer 1982): 42–57).

Biklen, Douglas P. *Community Organizing Theory and Practice.* Englewood Cliffs, N.J.: Prentice-Hall, 1983.

Christenson, James A., and Jerry W. Robinson, Jr., eds. *Community Development in America.* Ames, Iowa: Iowa State University Press, 1980.

Community Jobs. "Working for More Than a Living." 6, no. 4 (May 1982): 3–5.

Cox, Fred M., John L. Erlich, Jack Rothman, and John E. Tropman, eds. *Tactics and Techniques of Community Practice.* Itasca, Ill.: Peacock, 1977.

Erikson, Kai J. *Everything in Its Path.* New York: Simon and Schuster, 1976.

Etzkowitz, Henry, and Gerald M. Schaflander. "A Manifesto for Sociologists: Institution-formation — A New Sociology." *Social Problems* 15, no. 4 (Spring 1968): 399–407.

Finsterbush, Kurt, and C. P. Wolf, eds. *Methodology of Social Impact Assessment.* Stroudsburg, Pa.: Dowden, Hutchinson and Ross, 1977.

Frederich, Carl J., ed. *Community.* New York: Liberal Arts Press, 1959.

Gamson, W. A. *Power and Discontent.* Homewood, Ill.: Dorsey Press, 1968.

Laue, James H. "Conflict Intervention." In Olsen and Micklin, eds., *Handbook of Applied Sociology,* 67–90. New York: Praeger, 1981.

———. "The Development of Community Conflict Intervention." *Journal of Intergroup Relations* 9 (Summer 1981): 3–11.

Laue, James H., ed. "Intervening in Community Conflicts — II." Special Issue. *Journal of Intergroup Relations* 10, no. 2 (Summer 1982).

Lindblom, Charles, and David Cohen. *Useable Knowledge: Social Science and Social Problem Solving.* New Haven: Yale University Press, 1979.

Lippett, Ronald, and Gordon Lippitt. *The Consulting Process in Action.* La Jolla, Calif.: University Associates, 1978.

Littrell, Donald W. *The Theory and Practice of Community Development.* Columbia, Mo.: University of Missouri–Columbia, 1976.

Milgram, Stanley. "The Idea of Community." Book review of *The Social Construction of Communities. Science* 178 (November 1972): 494–495.

Nelson, Lowrey, Charles E. Ramsey, and Coolie Verner. *Community Structure and Change.* New York: Macmillan, 1960.

O'Neill, Patrick, and Edison J. Trickett. *Community Consultation.* San Francisco: Jossey-Bass, 1982.

Poplin, Dennis E. *Communities: A Survey of Theories and Methods in Research.* 2ed. New York: Macmillan, 1979.

Park, Robert E., Ernest W. Burgess, and Robert D. Mackenzie, eds. *The City.* Chicago: University of Chicago Press, 1925.

Redekop, Calvin. "Communal Groups: Inside or Outside the Community?" In Jack Klinton, ed., *The American Community, Creation and Revival,* 135–161. Aurora, Ill.: Social Science and Sociological Resources, 1975.

Roberts, Hayden. *Community Development: Learning and Action.* Toronto: University of Toronto Press, 1979.

Sherman, Brian. *Half a Foot in the Door — Black Participation in Georgia Electoral Politics: Sixteen Years after the Voting Rights Act.* Atlanta, Ga.: Voting Rights Study Group, 1982.

Smelser, Neil J. *Theory of Collective Behavior.* New York: Free Press, 1962.

Spiegel, Hans B. C. "New Directions." In Christenson and Robinson, eds., *Community Development in America,* 220–233. Ames, Iowa: Iowa State University Press, 1980.

Suttles, Gerald D. *The Social Construction of Communities.* Chicago: University of Chicago Press, 1972.

Tönnies, Ferdinand. *Community and Society.* Translated by C. P. Loomis. New York: Harper & Row, 1963. (Originally published 1887.)

UN Ad Hoc Group of Experts on Community Development. *Community Development and National Development.* New York: United Nations, 1963.

U.S. Bureau of the Census. *Statistical Abstract of the United States: 1980.* 101st ed. Washington D.C.: U.S. Government Printing Office, 1980.

Wellman, Barry. "The Community Question: The Intimate Network of East Yorkers." *American Journal of Sociology* 84 (1979): 1201–1231.

Wirth, Louis. "Urbanism as a Way of Life." *American Journal of Sociology* 44 (July 1938): 1–24.

Chapter **9**   AMERICAN PUBLIC POLICY
FORMATION AND IMPLEMENTATION
Thomas J. Rice

As American society moves deeper into the 1980s, it becomes increasingly clear that our social problems are worsening. Urban decay, unemployment, health care, pollution, education, crime – to name but a few obvious problem areas – are all in a state of crisis (Skolnick and Currie 1982). At the risk of getting depressed, we could add world (and domestic) hunger, nuclear terror, minority relations, natural resources, and human rights as arenas of enormous challenge to our problem-solving capacities. Such an inventory, however partial, raises several issues of direct relevance to our topic: American public policy.

Consider this. The solution to most social problems involves the allocation of resources – usually money – to targeted areas. This is the basic task of public policy. Since such resources are always scarce, choices have to be made. Priorities must be set. Which problems should be given highest priority? Should they be: poverty? crime? unemployment? Who decides? And by which criteria?

Sociologists have no snappy one-liners to make these hard questions go away. We do have the tools by which an educated public and professional policy makers can unravel some of their complexities and make rational assessments of the available options. In this chapter we examine how the sociological perspective can contribute to the formulation and implementation of public policy to deal effectively with the large-scale problems of U.S. society.

What Is Public Policy?

At this point in your study of sociology, it should be clear that definitions are not chipped in stone as holy writ. They are human inventions based on a particular perspective, some of which are more coherent and convincing than others. The ultimate test of any definition is its usefulness in bringing clarity and precision to a piece of analysis.

Policy is an example of a word everybody uses, but whose definition is ambiguous. We are often told we cannot do something because it is "company policy": not to take checks, not to accept returned merchandise without the sales receipt, not to allow sick leave for pregnancy. On the

153

positive side, it may be "policy" to be an equal opportunity employer, to pay the minimum wage, or to please the customer. It is safe to assume that these "policies" reflect basic goals of the organization, goals that may never be achieved in any literal sense.

Such is the case with many of our national policies. The Federal Employment Act of 1946 was defined as a "full employment" policy, meaning job opportunities for all those willing and able to work. With unemployment rates in the area of 8–10% over the past few years, it is clear that there is a major discrepancy betwen policy and social reality.

We have public policies on housing, poverty, racial and ethnic and gender discrimination, education, and the quality of the physical environment. All promise something of a utopia; none has come close to full implementation. In fact, the gap between our policy goals and the social reality is widening every year (Harrington and Rodgers 1981:15).

How, then, are we to understand the concept of "policy"? One way is to identify a number of distinctive features that all public policies have in common.

First, *policy is a political, not a scientific process.* Contrary to the naive though popular perception that policies emerge full-blown from the minds of scientific analysts, policy is always the outcome of a political process (Wildavsky 1974). Policies reflect the net outcome of a transaction between parties to the negotiation.

This implies that, second, *policy is a statement of power relations.* In the history of the U.S. Constitution, we have seen the addition of 26 amendments as steps toward greater social justice. Each came at exactly the moment advocates gained enough political power to force the issue (Harrington and Rodgers 1981:10). If we conceive of *political power* as a set of structured relationships, based on control over scarce resources, then there must be a shift in such structural relationships before policy can be affected. Only at the moment of a shift in the balance of power have specific social policies, framed by the U.S. Constitution, emerged as formal goals.

The 1982 defeat of an Equal Rights Amendment is an illustration of this "policy as power" thesis. Though women constitute 52% of the U.S. population (Sherman and Wood 1979:175–79), they have not been able to convert their numbers into political power. But power relations never exist in a social vacuum; they usually have the force of *ideology* (i.e., a system of beliefs supporting and justifying some particular social arrangement) behind them. The "natural inferiority of women" seems to be the ideological hangover behind the failure of the ERA.

Third, then, *policy reflects ideology.* In a mass society such as the present-day United States, the manipulation of opinion is a major industry (Young 1979). Public relations firms, advertising agencies, consumer psychologists, media consultants — all known as "communicators" — make billions of dollars selling images to the masses. Images are a necessity where substance is lacking; hence the need for Madison Avenue strategies to sell everything from breakfast cereals to presidential candidates. The image is everything once it is tailored to the ideological predispositions of the target population, the "consumer."

Such predispositions are rarely the result of rational judgment. They are more likely to be based on cultural bias, personal prejudice, or misinformation (Marger 1981, Chapter 12). There is absolutely no scientific basis for the stereotype of women as emotional, impulsive, or constitutionally fragile. Yet in a society whose ideology engenders this image, one is likely to find public policies that protect women but not their rights.

Ideology and policy formation also do not exist in a vacuum. Instead, in societies like our own, they occur within the framework of the *class system*. By this we mean the division of society into a hierarchy of classes separated by economic position. In such a system, some few are born to worlds of privilege; the vast majority, as Lillian Rubin (1976) puts it, to worlds of pain.

Policy reflects the class system. Both conservatives (Anderson 1978) and radicals recognize that those in the "higher circles" enjoy more wealth, status, and political power than those below them (Domhoff 1970). Comparative data on industrial democracies consistently show the United States to be extreme in terms of class inequalities (Gilbert 1982). A single percent (1%) of the population owns 80% of all the publically held corporate stock, while 86% own no stocks at all. The same 1% hold almost 30% of the nation's cash (Anderson 1974). This translates into the fact that the top one-fifth of the adult population owns three-fourths of the national wealth, not even counting income. What does this have to do with policy? The short answer is: a great deal.

If public policy is a product of the political process at federal, state, and local levels, it seems reasonable to argue that "some are more equal than others" in what is clearly an arena of powerful contenders. Always at stake are scarce resources: public funding, public lands, legal exemptions, judicial priority.

Recall that we defined power as *control over resources* that expresses itself in stable and structured social arrangements. The class system of the United States is such an arrangement, complete with its own justifying ideology and supportive institutions — courts, police, schools, the military, church, and family. But these are only secondary. The main institutions in any capitalist society are political and economic, in that they make up the system of production without which the social arrangements would collapse.

Since those who control that system of production also control the resources of land, labor, and wealth, it becomes clear that their interests will normally get priority in any power struggle involving public policy. Again, we have a vast body of research to support our point that a *power elite* (some call it a "ruling class") prevails in the realm of most public policy (Mills 1956; Domhoff 1967).

Summarizing these characteristics, we can now define public policy as we know it in the United States today. *Public policy is a formal statement of desirable social goals derived from a political process normally dominated by elites in their class interests and justified by a dominant ideology.* Policy is rarely based on rational knowledge, except when this can be linked to powerful political support (Lineberry 1977). Even official adoption of a public policy, however, does not necessarily mean that a program can or will actually follow it through to implementation.

We cannot rest easy just because the president announces, with full Rose Garden fanfare, some major policy position. Without an appropriate program for action and the actual commitment of needed resources to get the job done, such announcements by government leaders remain purely symbolic. This may have political benefits, but without implementation, public policy has no impact on social problems.

Policy and Social Science

There is an inherent tension between the approach of policy makers and that of social scientists. This hinges on the fact that public policy is a response to the immediacy of popular emotion, whereas, by definition, social science is not. Policy makers need attractive, speedy answers to practical problems; valid social research takes time. Moreover, even when their findings support popular opinion, scientists are tentative and uncertain in their interpretation of the evidence. Politicians respond to the prejudices of their constituency with images of certainty; they play to their audience, for that is the nature of American politics.

All of this demands considerable accommodation between competing needs and orientations. At this point in history, the burden seems to rest on the social scientist to adapt—or else to be ignored in the process. The sociologist who wishes to be involved in the formulation and implementation of public policy, therefore, must be not only a competent professional but an astute communicator in the political arena.

What do sociologists have to offer? Why should any policy maker be interested? Our strengths lie in four major areas:

1. We offer an analysis of the social context.
2. We provide concepts, models, and theories to break down complex problems into understandable elements.
3. We collect data, both quantitative and qualitative, on the costs and benefits of particular courses of action.

4. We make connections between social problems and anticipate side effects that are easily overlooked by technical specialists.

There is one final area: We bring a humanistic emphasis to our work that stresses the value of human development as the primary rationale for solving social problems. Following Dolbeare's (1982) analysis, let me now show that, if our goal is appropriate and effective public policies, then our society cannot do without the knowledge, perspectives, and methods of the clinical sociologist in the policy arena.

The Social Context: External Factors

Throughout this book, you have seen that sociological analysis considers problems in their historic and contemporary contexts. This can be seen as a mapping procedure; just as one stands a better chance of planning a trip with a good road map, so it seems wise to know the cultural, economic, and social terrain when formulating public policy. Whatever the preferences of the policy maker, a host of external constraints simply must be acknowleged as "social facts."

First, there is the *structure of the American economy*. Its most significant feature is that a few giant corporations—themselves strongly controlled by a few major banks—increasingly dominate industry and commerce. In both size and concentration, the trend is mind-boggling.

Fortune magazine, which has been tracking the corporate behemoths since 1955, shows us in precise terms what these industrial leaders are doing. For example, the top 500 organizations controlled 66% of all industrial sales and made 75% of profits in 1980, compared to 40% and 25% respectively in 1955. By 1980 they employed 75% of the work force, and a single corporation, Exxon, was reporting $79 *billion* in sales—more than the entire gross national product of most European nations. Each industry is dominated by a few giants—this condition of control by a few being known as *oligopoly*—and these giants are largely controlled by a few major banks. The Chase Manhattan Bank held controlling interests in 39 of the top 200 corporations as of 1969 (Dolbeare 1977:72).

Another defining feature of our economy is its international character. The day of the *transnational corporation*—an industrial organization spreading production and sales across national boundaries—is already here. Since 1950, hundreds of billions of American investment dollars have gone abroad—the annual growth rate is 10%. Given relatively cheap labor, few government regulations, generous tax breaks, and growing markets in developing countries, we can expect this transnational pattern to intensify for the rest of the century.

No government can ignore corporate priorities in setting policy. With its almost unlimited resources, the corporate sector can count on favorable treatment. Even when political leaders are not necessarily "probusiness," they must ensure a healthy economy, which requires that corporate interests be served. Corporate and banking leaders have the power to send the economy into a tailspin if they do not cooperate with government policy; that means politicans will lose their jobs, hence the political necessity of "gaining business confidence."

A second set of constraints on policy are the *dominant values and ideologies* in American society. Our central value is that of *individualism* (Williams 1970). The individual and not the group is seen as the center of social life; all our institutions, social arrangements, and public policies revolve around the individual pursuit of the "inalienable rights" of life, liberty, and the acquisition of "property" (meaning, in its technical sense, those forms of wealth that produce more wealth, such as factories, commercial real estate, and other investments, not personal possessions).

Related to this central value are several ideologies. First, there is the belief in *hard work* as an end in itself. Second is *personal responsibility* for all life chances. Credit and blame are placed on the individual, regardless of the objective reasons for particular outcomes. If you have great wealth, high status, and power, you deserve respect and deference. If you cannot provide for yourself and your dependents, you must shoulder the blame, regardless of circumstances. This practice of "blaming the victim" (Ryan 1971) and crowning the victor is highly supportive of individualism.

Since only individuals exist, there can be only individual problems. Nothing is social or collective in nature. Win or lose, you stand alone; so goes the ideology supported by this ruling value.

Ideological principles, as we have said, set the stage for both the formulation and implementation of American public policy. Although, for example, it would be *rational* to have an energy policy in which the state plans for the supply of oil, the American creed of "free enterprise" creates a climate in which no such proposal is acceptable. It does not matter that the oil market is monopolized by a few giants and that the transnational corporation is only an "individual" by legal fiction. Values are never rational; nonetheless, they form the basis of most public policy. Any policy maker who ignores this fact will live to regret the oversight!

A final constraint on policy is the *nature* of contemporary social problems. As any industrial society increases in size and complexity, we can bet that its social problems will keep pace. In the mid-1980s, America stands at the forefront of developed societies in the grip of institutional crises.

Consider the tradeoff between "guns and butter." The state of the domestic and worldwide economy has driven U.S. unemployment as high as 10% in recent years. At a time when policy makers have increased "defense" spending to unprecedented levels, the only way they have been able to keep budgets within anything remotely resembling control has been to cut back social programs serving the needy—food stamps, welfare support, legal aid, school lunch programs, aid to the handicapped. Genuine hardships are being imposed upon those who most need help, for reasons widely perceived to be more ideological than real.

This only exacerbates existing social divisions and tensions. Minority relations have deteriorated since the dramatic progress of the 1960s. Women still make 59 cents for every man's dollar. Aging continues to be a traumatic experience for the great majority of Americans; most of the poor, in fact, are minority women and those over age 65, and their proportion is going to increase sharply with the general demographic shift toward an older society (Sherman and Wood 1979, Chapter 7).

These and other social problems too numerous to mention are all linked to the larger structural features of American society. For example, as transnational corporations seek optimum profits, they often close down marginally profitable domestic operations—which would have been kept going by community-based owners—in favor of more attractive opportunities overseas. This results in unemployment and, often, the ruin of an abandoned community. Unemployment breeds poverty, despair, and anti-social behaviors such as alcoholism, child abuse, spouse beating, crime, divorce, mental disorders, and suicide (Bluestone, Harrison, and Baker 1981). These problems occur at a time when social service agencies, police departments, courts, and prisons are faced with declining budgets.

Under such conditions, the need for enlightened public policy cannot be overemphasized. Yet, in approaching these problems, policy makers usually ignore the historic causes of the problems and the present structures that act as problem generators. Urban decay, for example, is clearly the result of decades of government and corporate policies that favored suburban over urban development. Subsidies for corporate agribusiness over labor-intensive family farms hastened the massive rural-to-urban migrations beginning in the 1940s. Massive federal highway projects and the Federal Housing Administration's mortgage guarantee program encouraged the "white flight" from city to suburb. Finally, the systematic neglect of efficient public transportation, which forced reliance on heavy energy users (trucks, automobiles, airplanes), added a fatal ingredient to the urban decline (Harrington 1980, Chapter 6). None of this was inevitable. It resulted from policy decisions mired in economic, political, and value structures more rationalizing than rational about the roots of social problems.

Concepts, Models, and Theories

One of the major strengths of the sociologist is the ability to comprehend the complexity of these constraints while shaping a rational response to their existence. Our approach is to understand their dynamics and help design programs with full appreciation of obstacles and pitfalls. Sociological concepts, models, and theories supplement the analysis of social context in unraveling some of these thorny problems. What, then, are the tools of the sociological profession?

One of the most powerful concepts in clinical sociology is that of *system,* as discussed in previous chapters. Basic to a systems analysis of public policy are the concepts of *causes,* or "inputs," that set the policy process in motion, the *process* by which policies and programs are formulated, and the *effects,* or "impacts," of that policy. The strength of a systems analysis is that it separates the independent variable of causes from the intervening variable of policy-making processes, and these from the dependent variables of the effects the resulting policy have on the actual situation.

For example, revolutions in the Third World bring public pressure for a foreign policy that clarifies the U.S. position; these inputs trigger a policy-making process. Do we send in the marines? advisers? food? Or do we refer it to the UN? In risky ventures, such as those in present-day Central America, few politicians or political parties want to be blamed for policy failures. Hence, a blue-ribbon commission may be appointed to satisfy bipartisan interests, accommodate a variety of perspectives, and share responsibility if things do not work out as desired (Domhoff 1974).

What counts, however, is the impact of the policy—its implementation—not the process by which policy is arrived at or even the policy eventually formulated. What was the program? Did we unleash our military might, or did we simply decide to stay away? How much and what kind of resources did we commit? And, ultimately, did conditions improve? If the answer to this latter inquiry is no, then the policy failed, regardless of explanation.

Clearly, a scientific approach is called for that can help predict the probable effects of a policy during its formulation and then locate actual impacts during subsequent evaluation. One of the major problems confronting policy makers and analysts is the assessment, not only of direct effects of programs, but also of their unanticipated consequences. After all, the systems approach tells us that the parts of society are themselves interconnected into systems of systems; how, for example, does a change in employment policy affect education or health care?

One tool employed by sociologists working at this policy level is the *policy matrix.* Described by Robert L. Lineberry (1977), this helps in specifying unanticipated policy side effects.

If we examine even the simplified matrix in Figure 9.1, we can readily see the systemic interdependence of policy effects. A change in employment policy should have the intended consequence of increasing the numbers or quality of jobs in a given sector. This planned outcome (manifest function) is called *impact* by clinical sociologists.

Figure 9.1. A Policy Matrix

Policy Impact Areas

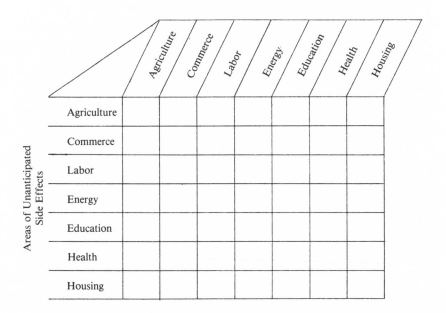

Invariably, there are spillover effects — sometimes benign, often not — which are termed *externalities*. In the case of employment policy, if job opportunities are expanded, this may reduce the rate of juvenile delinquency (which is high among unemployed teenagers), but it may also place new demands on educational institutions. This latent function may in turn alter residential patterns — and so on, with other unintended side effects.

Similarly, a vigorous environmental protection policy that leads to shutdowns of polluting industrial plants may be highly effective in cleaning up the air and water. But the externalities may be disastrous for employment in the locality. This in turn may have all the pernicious ripple effects previously mentioned, spilling over into health care, education, crime, housing, and so forth.

The policy matrix helps sensitize analysts to the latent functions and probable side effects of policy options. Because governments (and also corporations) are bureaucratically organized into specialized units, however, policy makers tend to think of policies as limited in effect to their intended sphere of impact. If administrators in the Department of Labor were to establish that new employment policy, whose job would it be to consider the effects on areas outside the agency's concern?

How are we to anticipate such pernicious side effects? Is it enough simply to inspect the policy matrix? No, it depends on the inspector. The policy matrix is essentially a *sensitizing* device. It does not predict or hypothesize anything about the interdependence of policy effects; for that, one needs sound theoretical training and a firm grasp of empirical findings in the areas under study.

Theory in any realm of science is used to explain why a certain phenomenon exists. By interrelating the known facts in its subject area, a coherent and concise explanation is constructed. Contrary to the notion that theorizing is pie-in-the-sky speculation, scientific theory is a complex and disciplined activity that depends on valid research findings for its construction.

When the Coleman Report was published in 1966, its findings demonstrated (again) that segregated schools were detrimental to minority students. The author, James Coleman, who is a competent sociologist, did not propose busing as a solution. This was a policy decision made in a theoretical vacuum. Even the most modest theoretical analysis would have revealed that busing would have negative side effects. Given the knowledge we had of racial attitudes and discrimination in the 1960s, it was safe to predict that many whites would flee to the suburbs, which would in turn reduce the urban tax base and trap lower-class minorities in the inner city, exacerbating problems of welfare, housing, health care, and, of course, education (Pettigrew and Green 1976).

Here a policy with principled and courageous intentions could reasonably have anticipated negative side effects. But to have done the analysis would have required a knowledge of race relations, how people behave under conditions of imposed policy, how a minority group (in this case, blacks) is treated by the dominant majority under conditions of stereotyping and prejudice, and so on.

A holistic systems approach drawing on empirical knowledge from previous sociological research might have resulted in a policy that worked. Certainly such an approach would be preferable to the contemporary tendency to consider each problem in isolation. One cannot anticipate and build strategies to mitigate all possible side effects; nonetheless, it simply is better to know than to be taken by surprise in the aftermath of what at first seemed to be a perfect policy option.

Clearly, then, in order to develop sound policy, one needs sound information. How many people are actually living in poverty in the United States? How accurate is the accepted figure of 30 million? Is it true that this number is increasing in both relative and absolute terms? Before we can even define the problem that a policy has to deal with, we need sound data on questions like these for each issue area.

Fortunately for those seeking rational information, the United States has a unique wealth of resources. The government gathers elaborate data on the economy and most areas of social life. Research institutes such as the National Opinion Research Center at the University of Chicago are available for more specialized information. Social service agencies, universities, and private organizations are all potential sources of data for the policy analyst. Erbschole's *Sources of Social Statistics* (1981) provides a useful listing of these resources.

These are all sources of *secondary data.* Where they do not suffice, *primary data* — those gathered specifically on the problem at hand — may be required. Whichever the case, the sociologist is inclined by training to rely heavily on data throughout the policy process. Research is a technically specialized area in each scientific field, and one that is essential to competent performance. Chapter 2 introduced some of the methods specifically employed by clinical sociologists to gather this kind of information.

Data never speak for themselves, however, even when they are unambiguous and consistent. Only humans speak; and when they do, it is from a particular set of assumptions about the good, the true, and the beautiful. Each person or administration has a vision of "how the world works," and people are not usually impressed by data to the contrary! The clinical sociologist acknowledges this reality while getting on with the business of advocating rational, humanistic problem solving. Whether as a teacher, researcher, consultant, or policy adviser, the practitioner must respond creatively to the facts as they are, rather than as one might wish them to be.

The Rational Problem-Solving Model

How, then, would the sociologist actually approach policy formulation and implementation? One of the most widely accepted strategies employed by social scientists (Lazarsfeld and Reitz 1975, Chapter 3) is an eight-step *rational problem-solving model* along the following lines.

Step 1, *problem identification,* is normally outside the sociologist's control. How is the existence of the problem established? Does it take some catastrophe, such as an airline crash? Perhaps someone "blows the whistle" on an organization, or an investigative reporter digs up information that results in a public outcry.

We may define a *social problem* as *a shared perception by a politically influential mass of people that something must be done to close the gap between what is and how people believe things ought to be.* As this definition suggests, problems are effectively defined by politicians responding to demands for action on the part of their constituency. However irrational the process leading to this first step, rational problem solving is possible when empirical research establishes the facts about existing conditions (what is), and when consensus can be reached regarding what ought to be, based on shared vision and values.

Step 2 is the *clear specification of goals.* Once the problem has been identified, the next task is to spell out policy goals in the clearest terms possible. There are two parts to this: establishing the criteria and then setting targets, ideally in measurable terms. Where quantification is impossible, qualitative judgments can be substituted, employing as many specific indicators as possible. How many people do you educate now, and at what level of quality? How many do you want to graduate next year? 10 years hence? Without such specification, evaluation of results will be vague and ineffectual.

Step 3 is the *rank ordering of goals.* It is rarely possible to attain all your goals; tradeoffs are the essence of policy decisions. Therefore, one needs to establish priorities. The sociologist can help the public and policy makers alike clarify the practical and conceptual issues relative to each goal. Since they can be based only on values and world views, the actual decisions are not up to the professional to make.

In educational policy, is quantity or quality more important? The United States has traditionally opted for quantity—educating as many as wish access. Other nations, such as France, have opted to educate only their elite, while keeping educational standards very high. The rank ordering of goals is a matter of values, in which the ordinary citizen knows as much as the "experts."

Step 4 is to *identify policy options.* One of the greatest errors consistently committed by policy makers is to limit their alternatives to familiar practices. There may be dozens or even hundreds of ways to solve any one problem; imagination is the only limitation. Once a problem is defined, goals established and prioritized, there are several methods of identifying and broadening the range of policy options (Lineberry 1977:28).

One method relies on *past policy experience.* Modest innovations on tried-and-true models is the rule here. This is, understandably, the most common approach.

An alternative, where the problem is new but its type has been dealt with previously, is to employ an *analogy.* That is, to view the case as similar to a previous one and borrow strategies that worked in the earlier case. If the problem is low morale in the schools, leading to high dropout rates, how have other organizations (e.g., corporations, the military, or churches) handled morale problems?

The *comparative* approach relies on straightforward imitation of policy models from other governments or regions. Most of our welfare policies, for example, are copied from Western Europe, especially Britain. Often, individual states, as well as the federal government, borrow successful programs developed by more innovative states, such as Oregon and California.

Social progress, however, requires *innovation,* in which prior experience is studied and then a new option is worked out, frequently in consultation with social and behavioral scientists and with input from the general public. For example, in 1974 California, under the leadership of the superintendent of public instruction, Wilson Riles, adopted a program comprehensively restructuring primary education through the third grade. This was based on the principle that parents would take an active part in planning, implementing, monitoring, evaluating, and modifying programs through volunteer Advisory Councils in every school and school district in the state (California Department of Education 1974).

However the policy options are conceived, it is essential to the rational process that many possibilities are considered initially. They can easily be discarded if they fail to "pass muster" in subsequent stages.

Step 5 is an *assessment process* in which proposed policy options are translated into data-gathering projects so that a cost–benefit analysis can be carried out. Economists, who have traditionally been considered the experts in such analyses, usually limit their calculations to that which is readily quantifiable in dollar-and-cents terms. The sociologist, however, seeks to broaden assessment to include qualitative considerations such as human safety and security, self-esteem, frustration, or stagnation.

The Occupational Safety and Health Administration (OSHA) illustrates this contrast. The agency adopted a policy to disallow qualitative assessments in workplace safety—with the result that there were more deaths in mining during 1981 than in the five previous years combined (*In These Times* 1981). Under the present system, deaths are not considered a "cost," whereas the considerable savings from reduced inspections and safety precautions are counted as positive "benefits" from such policies!

Step 6 is *matrix analysis,* in which the sociologist sets up a policy matrix (as in Figure 9.1) and searches for latent functions. As with all other steps, this calls for both data and theoretical insights based on the principle of interdependent systems. What, for example, is the relationship between a policy of military intervention in foreign countries and educational policy at home? Do we plan on conscripting young men (and, possibly, young women)? What kind of draft policy should we choose? Who do we draft? Who don't we draft? How will each option affect planning for postsecondary education? The point is that each policy option has the potential for widespread ripple affects, which should be anticipated as far as possible.

Step 7 involves *recommendations and implementation.* There is always a gap between the knowledge available to policy makers and the need for action on a given problem (Lazarsfeld and Reitz 1975:55). This is a major point of tension between social scientists and politicians, as already discussed. Where the time pressure is great, the sociologist must use whatever secondary sources are available, though they may be inexact; some data are better than none at all. The trained observations of experienced consultants can often generate solid information in a very short time. Often a set of recommendations must be formulated on what is, essentially, an impressionistic data base. In such cases, experienced judgments matter greatly.

Once top-level policy makers accept the sociologist's recommendations, it is common practice for the latter to drop out of the picture. Consistent with our position that implementation is the key to change, however, we argue that the clinical sociologist has a responsibility to convert recommendations into practical field operations.

Once we have worked from problem identification to implementation, it might seem that the process is complete. But without a review of progress toward the specified goals, the cycle remains incomplete; an *evaluation* stage is required for rational planning. It is essential to follow through by finding out how it is done, by whom, when, at what cost, and by which standards. Detailed records must be kept on each phase of the project so that breakdowns or oversights in the original conception of the problem can be pinpointed. Without such records, no improvements can be made, and the same errors may be repeated over and over (Lazarsfeld and Reitz 1975:61).

One can look at this rational problem-solving model as a systems theory of policy-as-process, in and of itself. Problem identification is the causal, or "input," phase. Steps 2 through 6 represent the "process" stages, while Step 7 is the effective, or "output," phase of policy process. Finally, the evaluation stage provides the necessary feedback allowing policy makers to learn from their mistakes and develop ever-more-effective program strategies. When any of the steps are not carried out in some way, one is almost guaranteed an irrational policy that is bound to fail.

Application: Race Relations

In this closing section, we demonstrate the application of clinical sociology to one of the most powerful arenas of conflict in American life. Throughout this chapter we have argued that public policy is a political process. Before we can evaluate any public policy in terms of its potential impact on social problems, we must understand the social context of our actions. We have already discussed the major features of the American social context in detail. Now let us show how it applies to race relations.

On May 17, 1954, the U.S. Supreme Court handed down a ruling that was one of the most controversial in the nation's history. "Separate educational facilities are inherently unequal," announced Chief Justice Earl Warren for the unanimous Court. This turned over an 1896 precedent to the effect that "separate but equal" facilities for whites and blacks satisfied all constitutional requirements, and it instantly brought to public awareness the nature of the American social structure.

Throughout American history, the issue of race relations remained unresolved. Blacks stayed at the bottom of the social order, disenfranchised, discriminated against, and segregated. Even the armed forces remained segregated before President Truman's Executive Order 9981 in 1948.

World War II had a major impact on race relations in America. Several related sociological factors accounted for this. The main ones were (*a)* an increasing awareness among blacks that their rights were being systematically violated; (*b)* a growing reform movement among white liberals for racial equality; and (*c)* a massive migration of southern blacks to northern cities, giving them increasing importance in regional politics.

In spite of these trends, as of 1954, 21 states and the District of Columbia either permitted or required separate school systems for black children and white children (Horowitz and Katz 1975:128). It came as no surprise that the Court's decision was greeted with howls of outrage, especially since the decision was based, not on legal precedent, but on sociological evidence presented to the Court by Kenneth B. Clark (1955), showing that separate school systems were damaging to black children.

There followed a period of intensive villification of sociology and social science as legitimate sources of evidence. Clark's integrity was impugned, since he was associated with the National Association for the Advancement of Colored People (NAACP). As these tactics failed, the opposition began to use its own version of social science to refute the findings used by the Court.

The consequence for sociology was simply to legitimate its use in the courtroom. It is now a commonplace of courtroom practice to use sociological evidence as the basis for legal decisions. This would never have happened without the political controversy. Unless some powerful political group finds such evidence supportive of its cause, however, the impact of social science remains minimal. The obvious implication for sociologists is that they must gain visibility for their work if it is to have an impact. This suggests the acquisition of more political skills than most practitioners now possess or perceive the need for.

Brown v. *Board of Education* effectively established a new policy of racial justice in the United States, but it was more than a decade before it was carried to any degree of implementation, supported by the Voting Registration Act of 1965. This resulted only after the emergence of the civil rights movement under the leadership of the Reverend Martin Luther King, Jr. Pursuing a philosophy of nonviolent confrontation modeled after that of Mahatma Gandhi, Dr. King launched a campaign for social justice within the legal boundaries of the Constitution. Recognizing that rigid institutions do not change without massive pressure, he based his tactics both on sociological knowledge of public attitudes, political trends, intersystems linkages, etc., and on his charismatic leadership.

The essence of Dr. King's strategy was that "if Negroes could vote, there would be no more oppressive poverty directed against Negroes, our children would not be crippled by segregated schools, and the whole community might live together in harmony." In other words, political equality would bring economic access, educational opportunity, and community solidarity.

When Dr. King said this, in 1965, it was a *theoretical* claim based on an analogy with other ethnic experience. It was not a simple vision, but one based on solid inference from empirical knowledge about U.S. society and how one gains full citizenship in it. His strategy, relying as it did on the sociological imagination, worked; in the mid-1980s, Dr. King's basic policy goal has been achieved, although its de facto implementation is still a long way off (for greater detail regarding the material in this section, see Horowitz and Katz 1975, on which much of the foregoing has been based).

In fact, the evidence seems to be that the position of black Americans has begun to slip downward from the earlier gains. Racial justice is not, evidently, a high priority for the individualism-oriented New Right. Perhaps it awaits another social movement, at which time the tools of clinical sociology may find even more direct use at the cutting edge of social change.

Summary

This chapter explored the usefulness of sociology in affecting public policy in the United States. Beginning with an extended definition of public policy, we emphasized its political nature, its relationship to power and social-class relations, and finally, the role ideology plays in the process. Critical to understanding policy is an appreciation that it is not an event or a document. Instead, it is a political process that can be understood only in a particular social context.

We examined the American social context in considerable detail. Three aspects of this context were selected for elaboration: (*a*) the structure of the American economy; (*b*) values and ideologies; and (*c*) the nature of contemporary social problems. Particular attention was given to the transnational corporation, the international nature of our economy, and the impact of these features on all aspects of American life. Individualism was described as the central value, and supporting ideologies of the work ethic, personal responsibility, private property, and free enterprise were explored. Contemporary social problems of national security, unemployment, the poor and minorities were discussed briefly as a framework of contraints within which public policy must be formulated and implemented.

We then raised the question, What does sociology have to contribute? In addition to an understanding of the social context, we presented a working sample of concepts, models, and research skills as part of the clinical repertoire. The concept of system was presented and the logic of cause-and-effect reasoning briefly discussed. The policy matrix as a way to anticipate unintended side effects was discussed in detail. We linked this to theory and data gathering as essential research tools. Finally, we presented a rational problem-solving model and discussed each of the eight steps in the process. Emphasis was placed on the nonlinear nature of problem solving and the need to adapt the model creatively to specific situations and contexts.

Finally, we offered a brief discussion of an application of clinical sociology in the 1954 landmark Supreme Court decision, *Brown* v. *Board of Education*. The work of Kenneth B. Clark was highlighted; he provided the expert-witness testimony from his own clinical research on segregation. Then the contribution of the Reverend Martin Luther King, Jr., was discussed, showing how he applied the sociological imagination to getting the resultant policies implemented in practice.

Policy studies represents a macrosociological form of sociological practice in which the sociologist works toward progressive, humanistic change at the level of the social structure itself. This is the scale of practice with which such exemplars as Kenneth B. Clark, C. Wright Mills, and Alfred McClung Lee have concerned their careers. But the utilization of sociology for effective social change is not restricted to the professional social scientist. This is the essence of the clinical sociological perspective — rigorous, humane, and effective. In both perspective and skill it can be a powerful tool of policy makers and citizens who wish to improve the world we live in.

Review Questions and Exercises

1. What are the major contributions of clinical sociology in policy formulation and implementation?

2. Discuss the main constraints on policy making suggested by the author. Critique the selections and offer others that may be equally relevant.

3. Working individually or with a group, and using the policy matrix, give several examples of potential externalities resulting from policy decisions in the following areas:

   a. energy
   b. employment
   c. education
   d. foreign policy

Preferably select real examples of policies from current newspapers or magazines to discuss.

Readings and References

Anderson, Charles. *The Political Economy of Social Class.* Englewood Cliffs, N.J.: Prentice-Hall, 1979.

Anderson, Martin. *Welfare: The Political Economy of Welfare Reform in the United States.* Palo Alto, Calif.: Hoover Institution, 1979.

Barnet, Richard. *The Lean Years.* New York: Simon and Schuster, 1980.

Bluestone, Barry, Bennett Harrison, and Lawrence Baker. *Corporate Flight: the Causes and Consequences of Economic Dislocation.* Washington, D.C.: Progressive Alliance, 1981.

Bowles, Samuel, David M. Gordon, and Thomas E. Weisskopf. *Beyond the Wasteland: A Democratic Alternative to Economic Decline.* New York: Doubleday/Anchor, 1983.

California State Department of Education. *Instructions for Comprehensive Program Planning.* Sacramento, Calif.: Office of State Printing, 1974.

Clark, Kenneth B. *Dark Ghetto: Dilemmas of Social Power.* New York: Harper & Row, 1965.

_____. *Prejudice and Your Child.* Boston: Beacon Press, 1955.

Dolbeare, Kenneth M. *American Public Policy: A Citizen's Guide.* New York: McGraw-Hill, 1982.

Domhoff, G. William. *The Higher Circles: The Governing Class in America.* Englewood Cliffs, N.J.: Prentice-Hall, 1970.

_____. "State and Ruling Class in Corporate America." *Insurgent Sociologist* 4 (1974): 3–16.

Erbschole, Michael. *Sources of Social Statistics.* Washington, D.C.: Pintail Press, 1981.

Free, Lloyd A., and Hadley Cantril. *The Political Beliefs of Americans.* Princeton University Press, 1967.

Gilbert, Dennis, and Joseph A. Kahl. *The American Class Structure: A New Synthesis.* Homewood, Ill.: Dorsey Press, 1982.

Harrington, Michael. *Decade of Decision: The Crisis of the American System.* New York: Simon and Schuster, 1980.

_____. and Harrell Rodgers. *Unfinished Democracy: The American Political System.* Glenview, Ill.: Scott, Foresman, 1981.

Horowitz, Irving Louis, and James Everett Katz. *Social Science and Public Policy in the United States.* New York: Praeger, 1975.

In These Times, August 10, 1981:7.

Lazarsfeld, Paul F., and Jeffrey G. Reitz. *An Introduction to Applied Sociology.* New York: Elsevier, 1975.

Lineberry, Robert L. *American Public Policy: What Government Does and What Difference It Makes.* New York: Harper & Row, 1977.

Marger, Martin N. *Elites and Masses: An Introduction to Political Sociology.* New York: Van Nostrand, 1981.

Mills, C. Wright. *The Power Elite.* New York: Oxford University Press, 1956.

Pettigrew, Thomas F., and Robert C. Green. "School Desegregation in Large Cities: A Critique of Coleman's 'White Flight' Thesis." *Harvard Educational Review* 4, no. 1 (1976): 1–53.

Piven, Frances Fox, and Richard H. Cloward. *Regulating the Poor.* New York: Simon and Schuster, 1971.

Rubin, Lillian B. *Worlds of Pain: Life in the Working Class Family.* New York: Basic Books, 1976.

Ryan, William. *Blaming the Victim.* New York: Random House, 1971.

Schiller, Bradley R. *The Economics of Poverty and Discrimination.* 3d ed. Englewood Cliffs, N.J.: Prentice-Hall, 1979.

Sherman, Howard J., and James L. Wood. *Sociology: Traditional and Radical Perspectives.* New York: Harper & Row, 1979.

Skolnick, Jerome H., and Elliott Currie. *Crisis in American Institutions.* 5th ed. Boston: Little, Brown, 1982.

Wildavsky, Aaron. *The Politics of the Budgetary Process.* 2d ed. Boston: Little, Brown, 1974.

Williams, Robin M., Jr. *American Society: A Sociological Interpretation.* 3d edition. New York: Knopf, 1970.

Young, T. R. "The Public Sphere and the State in Capitalist Society." *Red Feather Institute,* no. 50, Transforming Sociology Series, December 1979.

Chapter **10** HOW CAN WE ALL SURVIVE?
MANAGING SOCIAL CHANGE
Arthur B. Shostak

Sociology's origins lay in the attempt to understand and do something about the social problems of modernization. Its nineteenth-century founders believed that the method of science could be turned to the solution of difficulties and dislocations caused by the new industrial technology. That is, it was conceived as a way of managing social change and helping humankind stay in charge of events.

This same basic theme was taken up again, in the United States, when Chicago School sociologists turned their attention to the problems of urbanization in America after World War I. Some involved themselves with juvenile delinquency, others with race relations, others with the ecological problems of the emerging industrial city. Their approach came to be identified as *clinical sociology* and was first described by Louis Wirth in 1931.

Over the next several decades, as sociology became increasingly concerned with establishing itself in the mainstream of American social science, the clinical perspective was all but forgotten. Although many sociologists retained an interest in the problems of social change, all but a few (such as Alfred McClung Lee) shifted their focus to the *study* of problems harmful to the existing social system, rather than to the actual *solution* of problems caused by the system's inability to adapt institutions to social change.

This can be seen in the emergence of "applied sociology" as a subfield dedicated to using social science methodology to "keep the system working." Increasingly, this was equated with using sophisticated quantitative methods to help government and industry *rationalize* (i.e., streamline and increase cost effectiveness within) administration, production, or delivery of services. At most, the applied sociologist's role was seen to end with making policy recommendations to bureaucrats or government leaders, who are notably selective in the kinds of suggestions they are willing to accept, even from the experts they themselves have hired (see, e.g., Freeman *et al.,* 1983).

Beginning in the mid-1950s with "critical theorists" such as C. Wright Mills, and gaining increasing momentum throughout the next two decades, more and more sociologists began to question this status quo orientation. For one thing, the problems of social change were not going away; they were getting worse. By the 1980s, few (if any) Americans could ignore the crises of pollution, crime, and above all, the threat of nuclear war.

172

By 1978 the clinical sociological tradition reemerged. A new generation of sociologists, with the guidance of Lee and other elder statesmen,
formed the Clinical Sociology Association. Since then, a steady stream of
books, journals, and articles have been published carrying the message that
the sociologist can do more than merely *study* or blindly *support* society; he
or she can be an *agent of positive social change.*

Can clinical sociology really make a difference? Can it make a planned
and desirable difference that cannot be secured by a more conventional
social science approach?

Throughout this book you have seen how sociologists are using sociology both to understand and to do something about the problems of social
life. Glassner and Freedman, in their pioneering textbook (1979:403) define
the clinical sociologist as "a person who treats the destructive processes involving structures and interactions of human groups and societies."

In the same volume they point out that the existence of nuclear
weapons is the single greatest crisis of our times. A recent survey of 2892
representative adults conducted by the Values and Lifestyles Program of
the Stanford Research Institute shows that the American people are aware
of this; peace is their single biggest concern (Elias 1983).

You have already seen how clinical sociologists deal with crime; problems in the family, the community, and the workplace; and other consequences of rapid change in today's society. You have learned how the
sociologist can contribute to rational problem solving and the formulation
of efffective and humane public policy. But unless something is done about
the nuclear threat, everything else that we do may become meaningless.

How, then, might the sociologist use his or her knowledge and skills to
help secure global peace? How might a sociologist help Americans acquire
Mill's *sociological imagination* where nuclear dangers are concerned? That
is, acquire the ability to see the vital connection between political issues
relating to the social structure and the individual's private problems and
personal concerns? Above all, how might the clinical sociologist make a
truly distinctive contribution, one that helps Americans achieve more than
survival for survival's sake, one that helps push the peace-seeking process to
new heights?

Getting Started

Given the dilemmas of national security and the dangers obvious in the
global nuclear arms race, where might we begin? What are we to do? Even
more to the point, do you need a Ph.D. in the field before you can do
anything, or can you already get started as a "student clinical sociologist"?

Let us consider five possibilities, five tools that combine to empower
one who is exploring the role of clinical sociologist in a very special way.

Once we have done this, we can pass directly to some more specifically war-and-peace issues.

To begin with, you will want to stay alert to *reversal ideas,* those that prescribe a novel and desirable role for groups or individuals we rarely think about in this way. Harold Willen's 1984 volume, *The Trimtab Factor: How Business Executives Can Help Solve the Nuclear Weapons Crisis,* is a splendid example of this.

Willens examines our nuclear policy as a case study in corporate mismanagement. He strives to inform American business executives that the nuclear race not only absorbs their profits but is reversible, if only we apply sound business practices: "Freed from the devastating burden that robs us *and* the Soviet Union of vital productivity, both sides could address common problems and still compete in the marketplace. *It is a competition we can win.* And the business community—the trimtab factor—*must* lead the way" (1984:4).

A successful businessman, Willens offers a plan to allow nations to break the momentum of the arms race without endangering their security, even as he casts American business in the unheard-of role of pro-peace leadership. Clinical sociologists are well prepared to aid this sort of role redefinition; the kind of scenario Willens proposes is an exhilarating possibility to explore.

A second, especially relevant tool involves *irreverent ideas,* especially those reminding us to look for value and input from *every* quarter of society, not just from those—such as captains of industry—already in a position of deference and respect. The work of hard-boiled Chicago novelist Nelson Algren is a case in point.

Algren specialized in depicting seedy urban types that many sheltered readers flinched at—unattractive small-time boxers, pimps, whores, and petty thieves. Asked once to explain his irreverent viewpoint, he said he wrote out of "a kind of irritability that the people on top should be so contented, so absolutely unaware of these other people, and so sure their values are the right ones. There's a certain satisfaction in recording the people underneath, whose values are as sound as theirs, and a lot funnier, and a lot truer, in a way" (quoted in Drew 1984).

Wild ideas are another indispensable part of our intellectual tool kit. It is mind stretching and healthy, for example, to ponder sociologist Richard Sennett's advocacy of more disorder and less planned control in American cities. Sennett (1970) argues that an excess of order, rather than disorder, threatens our society. If we reduce the paternalism of municipal authorites and, for example, require urbanites to settle their disputes without reliance on the city police, people will gain finer control over themselves and become more sensitive to one another.

Compelled by such newly allowed disorder to deal affirmatively with one another, city dwellers might invent community forums for resolving their conflicts. These forums, in which people could honestly face others as concrete beings and learn how to "work it out," would be a fine training ground for peace movement membership or, at least, empathy.

If Sennett's prescription for what he calls the "anarchic city," and his call on planners to end their godlike presumptions about other people's lives, are not wild enough for you, try the mind-boggling "terraforming" ideas of NASA mission flight controller James Oberg. Considered in the light of the clinical social science principle that "unhealthy" systems can be changed by getting members to do something other than that which maintains the system, his ideas fit out specifications beautifully.

In his 1983 book Oberg calmly and factually explains how we can convert Mars, Venus, and other planets into second homes for earthlings. He does not see terraforming as a means of absorbing Earth's increasing population so much as a much-needed challenge to human ingenuity. Wild ideas of this sort — commonly found in modern science-fiction novels and stories — can help a clinical sociologist prepare for the inevitable question, "If we didn't spend 40% of our new wealth annually on the military, what might we substitute as a drive wheel for the economy?"

A fourth mental tool for peace-promoting sociologists involves *encapsulating ideas,* those efforts at condensation that try to encompass much of importance in memorably little. Guided by the sage notion that less can be more, certain social scientists strive to create numeric measures that can encapsulate, in "hard data" form, such subjective phenomena as "quality of life," "modernization," "risk of war," and "peacekeeping resolve."

Given the seemingly close connection between global war jitters and global numeric trends (as in life span, infant mortality, acreage under cultivation per capita), clinical sociologists welcome the unprecedented appearance in 1984 of what is to be an annual State of the World report. Prepared by Worldwatch Institute, this report is to update and assess developments in population growth, energy usage, natural resource depletion, military expenditures, and so on. The report will serve as a kind of report card, aggregating (adding up) different indices to provide numeric "shorthand" of use in understanding how things are really going on a worldwide basis, and how persistent hardships elsewhere heighten the risks of nuclear Armageddon everywhere.

Finally, in addition to reversal, irreverent, wild, and encapsulating ideas, it is advisable to ponder and utilize *anticipatory notions.* Expert forecasts of things-to-come provide invaluable tools for the sociologist interested in managing large-scale social change.

Typical is financier Felix G. Rohatyn's 1984 forecast that our national debt will climb to $2 trillion and Third World indebtedness will reach $1 trillion; our present social, economic, and budgetary difficulties will get totally out of control. "At that point, something will have to change." He urges the creation—and soon—of national and international mechanisms for getting governments, business, and labor to work in concert with one another. It is essential, he stresses, that these problems be dealt with, whether or not his particular suggestions are eventually followed.

Similarly, former Kennedy aide Theodore C. Sorensen forecasts that national affairs will continue to suffer from a costly gridlock in Washington policy making that is traceable to extreme factionalism among competing interest groups in and out of government. Sociologists may be intrigued by Sorensen's controversial 1984 reform recommendation for the adoption of a coalition government from 1985 to 1988 in which the new president would select his vice-president, half of his cabinet, and some of his staff from the other party—therefore enabling government to draw simultaneously on the finest talent in both major parties.

The law professor Arthur S. Miller (1983) joins the fray, going beyond Rohatyn's call for national industrial policy and Sorensen's consensus design to offer his blueprint for radical constitutional change. If the American government is to adjust to slower economic growth, more expensive and diminishing natural resources, and growing civil unease, it may have to switch to a parliamentary system, a unicameral (one-house) Congress of 100 members, consolidation of the 50 states into 10 or 12 geographically contiguous regions, and other such changes. "As Americans approach the 200th anniversary of the constitutional convention of 1787, there is no more important question confronting them than modernizing the ancient document, so as to adapt it to the new reality."

As with the ideas of Rohatyn and Sorensen, Miller's specific recommendations are nowhere as important as the ability of his anticipatory vision to spark interest and debate. This task is well worth a boost from clinical sociologists who grasp the intimate connection between America's financial and political gridlock *and* the problem of global peace. Strengthened by a lifelong interest in bold and controversial ideas that cast new roles for key players, that find something of worth in all players, that upset the commonplace, that try to get down to the essence, and that then peer over the horizon with verve and style, the clinical sociologist is especially likely to make a positive and honorable contribution to the peacekeeping effort.

How the Sociologist Can Make a Difference

Given our distinctive orientation and craft as sociological therapists, there seem to be five roles in particular that clinical sociologists can take to make a desirable, peace-aiding difference. You also can help to the degree that you perform these roles as a concerned student of sociology. But above all, remember: Once started, keep going! Without action, there is no change.

The role of *cultural translator,* for one, seems made to order. Many of us already practice on a regular basis the arcane art of moving between mutually suspicious persons, factions, or communities, attempting to lessen misperceptions and build new bridges of trust and empathy. Clinical sociologists could make extended and repeated visits to East European nations and the Soviet Union to locate counterparts and explore with them joint efforts to reduce xenophobia, strident nationalism, and other mass delusions that threaten world peace.

A second role we might play with merit is that of *publicist* for the cause of peace. Today, a stronger-than-ever case must be made for the legitimacy of arms-reducing efforts. The writer and educator Norman Cousins (quoted in Mapes 1984) warns that "the number one problem of our times is the real probability of nuclear annihilation; the number two problem is that our best minds are not focusing on the number one problem." Clinical sociologists seek contact and influence at every level of society. We might, thereby, nurture sustained interest in tension-reducing options across the social spectrum, the better to maintain the critical mass of participants that every social movement requires for success.

A third role would involve us as *assessors* of novel and perplexing ideas. For example, given our special interest in linking states of personal mental health to states of society's well-being, we could help other specialists and laypersons assess the new "bomb-is-good" notion of influential McLuhanites.

In characteristically bold and invigorating fashion, the disciples of Marshall McLuhan have begun to conceptualize "nuclear weaponing" as an information medium. They see it as a modern myth holding a power over the culture's thinking previously held only by religion. The bomb is now thought to bind people together in a way they have not known since the Middle Ages—albeit on the brink of collective suicide.

The nuclear threat and the geopolitical certainty of continuing to hang on the precipice is thought necessary for the cultural "rewiring" of people's brains in favor of preserving the peace. The Doomsday Bomb, as the ultimate information medium, may force a new mental environment on humanity and compel creation of an antibomb attitude ensuring that we never use it—provided, that is, we are not lulled by military propaganda about the efficiency of "limited nuclear warfare" into trying that fatal option.

Holders of this breathtaking redefinition of our post-Hiroshima reality dismiss the worldwide disarmament campaign as unnecessary and ill-fated. Some go so far as to welcome the further spread of nuclear weaponry to every corner of the globe! Critics recoil in horror and dismay, convinced that the

McLuhanites have gone off the deep end. Between these overstated positions, however, room exists for clinical sociologists to explore the matter sensitively and imaginatively, especially the notion that a new Bomb Culture is "rewiring" our minds in a peace-protecting way.

A fourth role would have clinical sociologists contribute as *defenders of the language,* as champions of truth-in-concepts and unyielding opponents of militaristic "newspeak." Especially frightening nowadays is the relentless effort some are making to sanitize the terms of warfare, to employ high-tech lingo as a valueless, emotion-free medium to enable otherwise value-holding, feeling, human beings to discuss a thermonuclear Armageddon.

As explained by the journalism professor Caryl Rivers (1984), "today, the more gruesome, the more grotesque the weapon of destruction, the more sanitized the terminology by which it is described." As language *is* politics — a lesson George Orwell taught us well (1948) — high-tech language such as "multiple independently targetable re-entry vehicles" tends to foster one of the most dangerous myths of modern geopolitics: that if we just deploy the right missles with the right initials, such as MIRV, everything will work out just fine.

Some politicians have taken this one step further — and brought us that much closer to the world of Orwell's *1984.* Realizing, perhaps, that Americans are indeed deeply and emotionally concerned with the threat of war, those who would devote our nation's resources to building up our arsenal of destruction (in the name, of course, of "defense") have begun to soothe public opinion with out-and-out "doublethink." For example, the MX missile has been affectionately nicknamed "Peacemaker."

Clinical sociologists can help rout this razzle-dazzle mystification of dreadful fact by spotlighting its two historic sources — the costly deification of both Science and the Omnipotent Male. We can help the public appreciate the limitations of science along with the mad absurdity of expecting males always to appear in control. We can and must, additionally, help change the related cultural myth that macho force and toughness can solve any problem.

In addition, then, to our potential contribution as cultural translators, publicists, assessors, and language monitors, certain of us could also serve as *thoughtful advocates,* possibly of a new world view and a new science. For example, Carolyn Merchant, a historian of science, advises us (1980) to "reexamine the formation of a worldview and a science which, by reconceptualizing reality as a machine rather than a living organism, sanctioned the domination of both nature and women."

A fine start in this direction would have knowledgeable clinical sociologists help rebut technocrats who champion the illusion of an impenetrable high-tech self-defense. At issue here is the seductive appeal of the

"Star Wars" scheme. This would create a protective arsenal in outer space to shoot missiles out of our sky. Such an option only misleads, with its suggestion that war is the business of technicians, a question, merely, of finding the right hardware.

Clinical sociologists could draw on their grasp of conflict resolution (as described in Chapter 8) to help citizens see through the fantasy of pinning our hopes on hardware. As the columnist Ellen Goodman warns (1984), the "Star Wars" scenario deceives with its naive suggestion that we do not really have to negotiate with the Soviets, that we can become invulnerable without giving up a single advantage. She urges us to shake off the fantasy that we can have our "Star Wars" high-tech ventures *and* authentic security at the same time: "The reality is that we are stuck here on Earth with the most human of problems—how to save ourselves. Our only weapon is that familiar and flawed software called the human mind."

Especially promising in this regard is the possibility that America may soon rectify a striking imbalance that has us supporting four military academies and five war colleges with no comparable mind-enriching program in the art of peacemaking and peacekeeping. Steady support grows for the establishment by Congress of a U.S. Peace Academy, much like West Point or Annapolis, but dedicated to changing radically the way our society deals with conflict. As such, one backer explains (Mapes 1984), the Peace Academy could prove "the key institution that shapes our society's future, and influences the decision as to whether or not there will even be such a future."

Clinical sociologists could make a distinct contribution to the Peace Academy's research into conflict-resolution techniques. Some could offer both short- and long-term courses to help train people from government, private enterprises, and other organizations in peacemaking skills. Many could visit and lecture at the Academy about their own search for nonviolent means of dealing with conflict, at many different levels of reality. Professors and college students alike could draw on Academy publications to bring war-and-peace topics into their college curricula, while off-campus clinical sociologists could invent ways to help their clients grasp the range of nonviolent options actually available to disputants.

Should sociologists soon join concerned others in a patient and persistent campaign to win passage of enabling legislation, they will be helping America make a long-overdue institutional commitment to peacemaking. A founding father of our discipline, William Graham Sumner, generally considered the first great American sociologist, advised over 80 years ago that, in the long run, a nation is likely to get what it has prepared for; this orientation becomes a self-fulfilling prophecy.

America now makes unstinting preparation only for violent responses to domestic and international disputes. A new Peace Academy could help widen the choice of actions acceptable to leaders and public alike, and could help move the whole future in a healthier direction than ever before.

Finally, and above all, as *peace scholars,* clinical sociologists must delve deeply into the considerable relevant intellectual work already on the library bookshelf. While sadly underutilized in the average college curriculum, the literature in peace studies is diverse, data rich, and generally mind stretching. Students and professionals alike owe it to themselves to check it out and give it relevance in their lives.

Exemplary resources such as the *Journal of Conflict Resolution,* when used with such volumes as Seymour Melman's 1983 book, *Profits Without Production,* and experimental techniques such as those of sociologist Jack Nusan Porter's Harvard Negotiation Project Approach, empower the concerned user much as demanded by this complex and fast-changing subject. Guided to outstanding offerings by various branches of the peace movement, the clinical sociologist who would "make a difference" must *first* undertake a thorough, exacting, and open-minded study of the bookshelf contribution others have made.

Using Sociology for a World without War

If as a sociologist — or even a student of sociology — you would promote gains across the board where global peacekeeping efforts are concerned, you might want to cultivate new ideas about role reversals, loser merits, off-the-wall possibilities, "bottom-line" summations, and over-the-horizon prescriptions. (That is, you might want to use clinical skills to help enlist fresh allies, such as America's business community, in the peace campaign.)

You might also want to "walk on the wild side," as Algren puts it, and explore the relevant feelings and ideas of society's "have-nots." You might want to take note of seemingly wild-eyed notions, the better to wring every possible gain from them, if and when their time arrives. You might want to study how others reduce complexity to manageable proportions, as in the new State of the World report. And you might want to note and store certain forecasts of farsighted social critics, the better to help the peace effort anticipate and help shape developments of major significance.

As for the primary task itself, if you would make a distincitive, sociological contribution, you can choose from the roles of cultural translator, publicist, assessor, defender of language, thoughtful advocate, or peace scholar — to cite only a few of the many roles likely to occur to you as you get involved. And that option — to get involved — is the indispensable first step, one that this entire exploration of *our* potential contribution to the peace-promotion campaign has sought to stimulate.

Beginning as students, and continuing throughout our lives and careers, clinical sociologists have a very special part to play in securing, enlarging, and enriching the peace, a part that beckons to all of us, all of the time. After all, unless we, as a species and as a society, survive, sociology will be of no use to anybody anymore. The greatest challenge of all, therefore, lies before us: How can we use this necessary science — sociology — to help manage social change on behalf of a world without nuclear war?

Review Questions and Exercises

1. Considering the threat of nuclear war, make up at least one reversal idea, one irreverent idea, one wild idea, one encapsulating idea, and one anticipatory notion — however fantastic, unrealistic, or off-the-wall — that would be relevant to dealing with this problem. Do not be afraid to use satire or other forms of humor, as these can be very potent facilitators of change in perspective.

2. What is the responsibility of the sociologist (or sociology student) with regard to oppressive, unjust, or destructive structural features, processes, or trends observed in the society? What, in your opinion, is the single most negative feature, process, or trend in our own society? What do you feel you can or should do about it?

3. Advocates of the "nuclear freeze" and others associated with the contemporary peace movement have been accused of being "unpatriotic" and of "playing into the hands of the Russians." Do some library research into the issues involved and what peace activists have been doing either nationally or in your own region. Then evaluate these charges in the light of your knowledge of sociology.

If you are working in a group, members might be randomly divided into two sides, one taking the position that the peace movement is indeed detrimental to our national interests and the other defending the antinuclear movement. The two sides should then have a debate or discussion, each trying to convince the other of the correctness of their position. For this exercise, it does not matter what you, personally, believe or how difficult it is to make a good argument for your "side."

Readings and References

Anderson, Marian. *The Empty Pork Barrel: Unemployment and the Pentagon Budget.* Lansing, Mich.: Employment Research Associates, 1982 edition.

Cox, Arthur Macy. *Russian Roulette: The Superpower Game.* New York: Times Books, 1982.

Drew, Bettina. "Record-keeper of Urban Life.": *In These Times,* February 1–7, 1984, 13.

Elias, Marylyn. "Our Big Concerns: Peace, Health." *USA Today,* November 11, 1983, 1B.

Freeman, H.E., R. Dynes, P. H. Rossi, and W. F. Whyte, eds., *Applied Sociology.* San Francisco: Jossey-Bass, 1983.

Glassner, Barry, and Jonathan A. Freedman. *Clinical Sociology.* New York: Longman, 1979.

Goodman, Ellen. "Nuclear Hardware Versus Human Software." *Philadelphia Inquirer,* February 7, 1984, 11A.

Ground Zero. *What About the Russians—and Nuclear War?* New York: Pocket Books, 1983.

Lee, Alfred McClung. *Sociology for Whom?* New York: Oxford University Press, 1978.

Mapes, Milton, C., Jr. "A Peace Academy to Build the Channels." *National Forum,* Winter 1984.

Markey, Cong, ed. *Nuclear Peril: The Politics of Proliferation.* New York: Ballinger, 1982.

Merchant, Carolyn. *The Death of Nature: Women, Ecology, and the Scientific Revolution.* New York: Harper & Row, 1980.

Melman, Seymour. *Profits Without Production.* New York: Knopf, 1983.

Miller, Arthur S. "The End of a 400-Year Boom." *Technological Forecasting and Social Change,* November 1983, 255–268.

Mills, C. Wright. *The Sociological Imagination.* New York: Oxford University Press, 1959.

Oberg, James. *New Earths: Restructuring Earth and Other Planets.* New York: New American Library, 1983.

Orwell, George. *1984.* New York: Signet, 1984. (Originally published in 1949.)

Perucci, Robert, and Mark Pilisuk, eds. *The Triple Revolution Emerging: Social Problems in Depth.* Boston: Little Brown, 1971.

Rivers, Caryl. "Armageddon Lingo." *New York Times,* February 2, 1984, A19.

Rohatyn, Felix G. *The Twenty-Year Century: Essays in Economics and Public Finance.* New York: Random House, 1984.

Scheer, Robert. *With Enough Shovels.* New York: Random House, 1982.

Schell, Jonathan. *The Fate of the Earth.* New York: Avon, 1983.

Sennett, Richard. *The Uses of Disorder: Personal Identity and City Life.* New York: Vintage, 1970.

Sorensen, Theodore C. *A Different Kind of Presidency: A Proposal for Breaking the Political Deadlock.* New York: Harper & Row, 1984.

Willens, Harold. *The Trimtab Factor.* New York: Morrow, 1984.

Wirth, Louis. "Clinical Sociology." *American Journal of Sociology* 37, no. 1 (1931): 49–66.

GLOSSARY

It is extremely important that you do not go past words you do not understand. The following glossary contains the vast majority of italicized technical terms used in this book; terms specific to the discussion in a single chapter or that require large portions of the chapter to explain are not listed. Words italicized in the glossary can themselves be found elsewhere in the glossary. Words not listed here or explained in the chapters can be found in any good dictionary.

Action Research A form of research activity designed to produce a change rather than just ascertain and report on the facts.

Actor A person viewed from the sociological perspective as an active participant in and doer of social life. More technically, *social actor.*

Arbitration A technique in which an "arbitrator" settles a dispute by imposing sanctions or decisions upon the parties involved — as opposed to a negotiated settlement or joint agreement.

Authority The accepted right to exercise *power* within a *social structure.*

Autonomy The ability of a person to choose to follow or to reject cultural styles and norms.

Available Data Term used in Chapter 2 for data that are already there and do not have to be generated by some use of research methods; similar to *secondary data.*

Battered Spouse Syndrome A pattern of spouse beating that continues over a period of time and may produce psychological problems (usage normally restricted to women victims).

Bureaucracy An organizational form in which activities are divided up among a *hierarchy* of specialized *positions* defined by formal rules and procedures.

Capitalism The form of social and economic organization emphasizing the private ownership of the means of production in which wealth is obtained by profits paid to owners, wages or salaries paid to workers.

Causal Analysis Method of explanation accounting for one social fact as the "effect" (or *dependent variable,* which see) of another social fact (or *independent variable,* which see) which is held to be the "cause" of that "effect." Causal analysis is the central focus of *quantitative methods* (which see).

Central Tendency Statistical concept that is a more precise way of saying "average."

Chicago School A group of sociologists associated with the University of Chicago in the early part of the twentieth century who developed, among other things, the conduct paradigm, urban sociology, clinical sociology, and *qualitative analysis.* Also refers to their general approach.

Clinical Sociology A historical tradition within the larger discipline based on the premise that sociological knowledge, perspective, and method can and should be used to guide and facilitate interventions for positive change at any or all levels of social life.

183

Cohort   The group (in the sense of "a collection") of individuals born within a given time span, typically 5 years.

Collective Behavior   The actions of temporary, unstructured groups of people focused on and reacting to the same event, rumor, person, custom, or situation.

Community   A collection of people within a geographic area among whom there is some degree of mutual identification, interdependence, loyalty, and social organization of activities.

Community Development   A group of people in a *community* reaching a decision to initiate a planned intervention to change their economic, social, cultural, or environmental situation.

Complementarity   The scientific principle that there can be more than one valid (albeit partial) explanation for the same phenomenon and that a complete description may require fitting these seemingly contradictory alternatives together into a complex picture of the whole.

Compulsory School Attendance   Laws mandating that juveniles under a certain age attend school.

Concilation   A technique involving a combination of fact finding, negotiation assistance, community organizing, and other activities aimed at finding constructive forums and methods for conflicting parties to use in settling their differences.

Conduct   Human behavior; that is, behavior patterned by *culture* and directed toward *socioculturally* defined goals.

Confidence   Statistical concept referring to how accurate one's inferences will be; usually given as "confidence intervals" or "limits," such as "plus or minus 4%."

Conflict Intervention   A process in which a third party enters into a conflict in order to influence its outcome in what he or she judges is a desirable direction.

Consultant   Someone who intervenes, who works with a *systems* (rather than individual) focus and whose advice may be accepted or rejected as the client chooses.

Control Group   In a *controlled experiment* the group of subjects not being exposed to manipulation of the *independent variable.* Contrast with *experimental group.*

Controlled Experiment   A form of experiment in which the researcher seeks to "control" (hold constant) all other factors in order to determine the effect of a suspected *independent variable* upon a *dependent variable.*

Corporation   An organization owned by stockholders and which is treated as if it were an individual under the law.

Correlation   Statistical concept referring to the existence of a relationship between two or more *variables.*

Cost–Benefit Analysis   A method of policy analysis, usually quantitative, which evaluates each policy alternative by the ratio of projected costs to projected benefits.

Cultural Norm   See *norms.*

Cultural Relativity   The social scientific principle that *cultures* vary and can be understood only in terms of their own values, and in their own contexts rather than by the standards of another culture.

Culture   The complex whole of learned, patterned ways of thinking, having, and doing common in a society; this includes technology and its artifacts *(material culture)* as well as language, symbols, norms and values *(symbolic culture.)*

Debunk   To explode a myth or show the lie in something; an important clinical function of sociology.

Definition of the Situation   What a person believes, feels, takes for granted, or imagines to be so; the actions of the actors participating in a situation effectively define that situation for all involved.

Delinquent   A juvenile who commits a criminal act but is deemed not responsible by virtue of his or her age.

Dependent Variable   A *variable* or social fact whose state, existence, or value (quantity, amount, kind) is determined by the state of something else (the *independent variable);* that which you are trying to explain or account for.

Depersonalization   The process through which a person becomes a social object; a stripping away of the personality in social interaction. Depersonalization often occurs in total institutions (hospitals, asylums, jails, etc.)

Descriptive Statistics   Procedures used to give an accurate picture of quantitative data.

Deviant Behavior   Ideas or attributes that some, though not necessarily all, people in society find wrong, bad, crazy, disgusting, strange, immoral, or otherwise objectionable.

Disease   A physical dysfunction in which the body and/or mind is not working or responding appropriately, the kind and nature of which is determined by medical diagnosis. Contrast with *illness.*

Dis-ease   Sometimes used to refer to a condition of mind–body stress often associated with *illness* or *disease.*

Distribution   A set of observed scores, frequencies, or measurements used in quantitative analysis.

Division of Labor   The breaking down of work and other social activities into smaller, discrete units or roles.

Dramaturgical Analysis   A form of sociological description employing the language and concepts of the drama, based on the idea that life is (or can be looked upon as) theater.

Ecology   The scientific study of the relationships among living organisms and between them and the physical environment.

Electoral Process   The process by which candidates are elected to office, including voting and voter registration.

Equifinality   The principle in systems theory stating that different systems may arrive at the same end state from differing initial conditions by different routes of development. See *system.*

Ethnic Group   A group of people sharing a distinct history and subculture who consider themselves "a people"; *ethnicity* refers to participation or membership in an ethnic group.

Ethnocentrism   Judging others' behavior, values, or life style from the perspective of your own cultural standards. Contrast with *cultural relativity.*

Evaluation   Considering facts; leading to understanding, evaluation is based on formal or informal research. Contrast with *value judging.*

Evaluation Research   Methods used to determine the effectiveness of programs, agencies, organizations, or interventions.

Exchange   Transaction between people or groups in which one party gives something symbolic or real to the other party; a theory based on the concept that society is a system of exchanges between groups or individuals.

Experiment   Research method in which one varies one or more variables to determine causal relationships and/or test *hypotheses.*

Experimental Group   That group of subjects in a *controlled experiment* exposed to manipulation of the *independent variable.* Contrast with *control group.*

Exploratory Survey   Term used in Chapter 2 referring to an informal survey where the goal is to discover the important facts about a field or situation rather than generalize from a *sample* to a *population.*

Externalities   Unintended or unanticipated side effects (*latent functions*) of a policy or program.

Feedback   The process by which change in one element of a system brings about compensatory changes in other elements so as to maintain the pattern of the whole. See *system.*

Field   Any setting in which social activity takes place in everyday life; *field work* refers to research strategies involving the study of social life in its natural settings.

Frequency   The number of times a single observation or score occurs in quantitative research.

Function   What a social fact, process, element or unit of organization does; its consequences or role, especially with regard to the whole system or subsystem of which it is a part.

Functional Analysis   A basic form of social scientific explanation looking at elements of social life from the perspective of "What need [function] does this serve in the scheme of things?" or, more simply, "What does it do?"

Gemeinschaft   A German term used by Tönnies to describe traditional *communities* characterized by strong *primary relationships,* a sense of tradition, and common belonging.

Gender   *Sociocultural* definition of a person's sex; that is, not biological sex per se but "maleness" or "femaleness," which may or may not have anything to do with biological reality.

Gesellschaft   A German term used by Tönnies to describe modern communities characterized by secondary relationships, competition, and high division of labor.

Grand Theory   Term for theories framed at an extremely high level of abstraction to explain the entirety of social life.

Group   Also known as *Social Group.* A collection of individuals organized into an interdependent whole *(human system)* characterized by more or less stable *roles* and *role relationships* and functioning as a social entity in its own right.

Health-Care Policy   The system of decisions, values, and attitudes that de-determines the distribution of health-care resources and the access to those resources in a given society.

Hierarchy   A form of social organization composed of positions (or *statuses)* like a ladder, so that each "rung" is in some way "higher" than the one below.

Humanist   Term used to describe a people-centered value orientation viewing the proper goal of science as to actively serve human needs.

Human System   Any collection of interdependent human beings or groups connected by more or less stable patterns of role relationships, communication, or other exchanges into a particular configuration identified as the *system.* Also known as a *social system.*

Hypothesis   An educated guess about the relationships between two or more *variables.*

Ideology   A system of beliefs held by a *social group* or society that rationalizes and defends particular social arrangements while repudiating alternatives.

Illness   The subjective response to a bodily or mental dysfunction or *disease;* the problem as experienced by the individual and/or the person's social environment. Often referred to as *sickness.*

Independent Variable   A *variable* or social fact whose existence or value (quantity, amount, type) determines the existence, value, or change in value of another element, known as the *dependent variable.*

Inferential Statistics   Quantitative methods used to generalize from descriptive statistics to a larger group or population.

Institution   A social institution is a widely accepted, relatively stable cluster of *roles, statuses,* and *groups* that develop around the basic needs of a society (e.g., family, politics, economy, education, and religion); sometimes used to refer to similar *social structures* developing within lesser *social systems.*

Institutionalization   The process by which new ideas, meanings, roles, and other sociocultural elements are incorporated into the framework or culture of a *social structure.*

Internalization   The process by which concepts, ideas, *roles, norms,* and other elements of *culture* and social organization become part of an individual or group's *definition of the situation,* character, and habitual conduct. See *socialization.*

Interview   A method of gathering information by talking directly with an individual, usually in question-and-answer form.

188   USING SOCIOLOGY

Jurisdiction   In political sociology, a political entity such as a city, county, or state.

Label   The identification of a given characteristic of importance. When a person is labeled, all his or her behaviors are interpreted in terms of the label.

Latent Function   The nonapparent but important *function* a given event or process plays in a system, often with unanticipated and/or long-term consequences. Contrast with *manifest function.*

Laws   The written and codified standards used to define offensive behavior, ideas, or attributes of individuals referred to as "crime."

Life Chances   The probability that a person in a given social *status* or stratum will attain or fail to attain valued goals or experiences ranging from fulfillment of basic needs to opportunities for power, status, and privileges.

Life Style   The way of life of a group or individual—how people live; what sort of possessions, interests, customs, habits, and preferences they display.

Looking-glass Self   One's self-concept based on how one believes others evaluate one's appearance and behavior.

Macrosocial   Level of sociological analysis explaining elements of social life in terms of the whole social order; a focus on the larger structures of society. Contrast with *microsocial.*

Manifest Function   The obvious, intended, or purposeful *function* of a social behavior or process; what it is supposed to do. Contrast with *latent function.*

Material Culture   Technology and the products of technology, such as roads, buildings, clothing, utensils, appliances, and other "artifacts." Contrast with *symbolic culture.*

Mean   A measure of *central tendency* equivalent to arithmetic average (sum divided by number of cases).

Median   A measure of *central tendency* stating where the middle of the *distribution* lies, halfway between the highest and lowest observations; typically used in government statistics.

Mediation   Technique of conflict resolution involving a third party (or "neutral") acceptable to all disputants and whose role is to help the negotiation process work, with the ultimate goal of helping parties reach a mutually satisfactory solution to their differences.

Megalopolis   A continuous belt of urban, suburban, and industrial development spreading betwen *urban areas.*

Metropolitan Area   Counties or groups of counties with one or more central cities of at least 50,000 population, a density of at least 1000 people per square mile, and outlying areas dependent on the central cities.

Microsocial   Level of sociological analysis viewing both society and *social structure* as emerging from discrete acts of individuals or groups; a focus on concrete social interaction as opposed to the larger social order. Contrast with *macrosocial.*

Mode   A measure of *central tendency,* the most frequent observation in a *distribution.*

Multicausal Explanation A sociological explanation for a phenomenon or *variable* in terms of more than one causal or "explanatory" factor.

Natural Area Part of a city forming a single ecological unit or *community*.

Negotiation Technique in which advocates selected by the parties represent their interests in a more or less formalized discussion setting, engaging in give and take in an attempt to get the best settlement of the disputed issues.

Network A group of people linked together more or less informally by common interests or activities. *Social support networks* are coming to replace families and other traditional *primary groups* for an increasing number of people as a source of *primary relationships. See social support.*

Norms Rules or standards governing acceptable and unacceptable social behavior; shared expectations about how individuals in given roles and statuses will behave, and thus the cultural standard of normalcy. Technically, *social norms,* to be distinguished from *statistical norms,* the "average" as determined by counting or measuring a population or sample.

Oligopoly The effective control and domination of a market or industry by a few powerful firms or individuals.

Open Experiment Form of experiment based on trying different arrangements to find out what happens.

Organization A complex *secondary group* deliberately established to fulfill defined purposes; a kind of complex, goal-directed *human system;* also termed *formal organization.*

Paradigm A set of assumptions about the nature of a phenomenon or class of phenomena, accepted as true by its adherents, which guides their thinking and conduct of scientific research.

Participant Observation A form of social research in which the investigator studies a social phenomenon from the perspective of the people involved in it by becoming part of their everyday life.

Pathology A harmful, diseased, or aberrant condition of an organism or part of an organism; also used by extension to refer to *social systems, culture,* etc.

Pathology of Normalcy Those ways of life considered normal by many people because so many people do it, but which may lead to various unpleasant or undesirable consequences.

Percentile A quantitative measure stating what percentage of a *distribution* lies below a given observation or score.

Population In statistics, the entire group or category from which a *sample* has been drawn.

Position A discrete location within a *social system* associated with a task, *role,* or function determined by the structure and goals of that particular system. Also known as a *status.*

Power The ability to advance one's interests over those of others, to influence the behavior of others and/or the outcome of events, typically by maintaining control over scarce resources.

Power Elite   A cohesive set of political, economic, and military groups holding the power in a society.

Prejudice   An attitude toward any category or group of people that prejudges and *stereotypes* their characteristics.

Pretest   Test run of a *questionnaire* or study of subjects done before experimenting to establish a basis against which to evaluate changes.

Primary Data   Material gathered firsthand by the researcher; contrast with *secondary data.*

Primary Groups   Small groups whose members have intimate personal ties with one another in intense emotional relationships ("primary relationships"). Contrast with *secondary groups.*

Projection   Pinning one's anger, pain, troubles, or behavior on someone else, who is blamed and seen at fault; positive feelings can be projected also, but in either case it is a matter of attributing cause over one's own feelings to another person or seeing one's own feelings in that person.

Property   In its technical sense, those forms of wealth that produce more wealth, such as factories, commercial real estate, and other investments, not personal possessions.

Qualitative Methods   Strategies of research and analysis focusing on the kind, nature, meaning, emergence, relationships between, and interpretation of categories, conditions, and processes in social life.

Quantitative Methods   Strategies of research and analysis based upon measuring or counting pehnomena, reducing them or their qualities to numbers, and then determining their empirical relationships through statistical or other mathematical procedures; goes hand in hand with *causal analysis, descriptive* and *inferential statistics.*

Questionnaire   A list of items (questions) used to gather social scientific information from a large number of *respondents.*

Race   An *ethnic group* believed to be genetically distinct from other groups (e.g., "the Negro race," the white race") and thus treated differently from other groups.

Random Sample   Statistical concept of a *sample* drawn at random from a *population.*

Rationalize   In technical usage, to streamline, increase cost effectiveness and efficiency by following rules of "scientific" analysis; rationalization is the process of rationalizing societies or organizations; used also in an entirely different sense of "to justify something" to oneself or others.

Reapportionment   The process by which voting districts are rearranged, at least supposedly to ensure equal representation for all voters.

Reciprocity   The concept (central to *exchange* theory) that social transactions should be balanced (i.e., "reciprocal").

Relativity   The concept that "the facts," even physical facts, can vary depending on the viewpoint of the observer and the method of observation.

Respondent   Term used by social scientists to refer to those whom one interviews, surveys, etc.; often abbreviated "R."

Role   Expected behavior patterns, obligations, and privileges attached to a particular *status* in a *social system;* sometimes employed in the theatrical sense of the part the person plays in social life.

Role Relationship   The expected pattern of behavior, obligation, differential *status,* and privilege holding between *roles* in a group or other *social structure.*

Sample   A number of groups or cases drawn from a larger *population.*

Score   In statistics, a number used to express results of some kind of test, responses to certain kinds of questions, or *frequency* of observation on a particular *variable.*

Secondary Analysis   Analysis based on *secondary data.*

Secondary Data   Another term for *available data* referring, in particular, to statistics already gathered and compiled by agencies or other researchers, such as census data; contrast with *primary data.*

Secondary Groups   Larger, less intimate groups involving relationships with few strong emotional bonds and with interaction between members only in the context of specific roles ("secondary relationships"). Contrast with *primary groups.*

Segregation   Formal or informal practice of keeping people with different social characteristics apart, as in separate schools and residential areas for blacks and whites.

Self   The person as known to himself or herself; the self-conception or self-image arising primarily in social interaction as a result of how the person perceives others respond to his or her actions.

Self-fulfilling Prophecy   A social process through which predictions about the nature of individuals, groups, processes, or things come true because people accept them as *definitions of the situation.*

Sickness   The definition that someone with a *disease* is unable to fulfill normal role obligations. Sometimes used as a synonym for *illness.*

Sick Role   The complex of behaviors expected of someone who is socially defined as sick or ill. This includes being temporarily relieved of normal role obligations until normal functioning is restored through medical treatment.

Significance   A statistical concept referring to certainty that a statistical relationship is not merely due to chance; scientists most typically accept a relationship to be "significant" if they can be 95% certain that this is the case. Contrast with *confidence.*

Situational Analysis   How a person characteristically or habitually interprets the meaning or nature of situations. See *Thomas Theorem.*

Significant Other   A person with whom one has an intense relationship and whose thoughts, feelings, opinions, and actions are most important to one's own self-concept.

Social Class   A group sharing the same level of wealth and/or economic power and opportunities in society.

Social Group   See *group.*

Social Interaction   Interpersonal behavior typical of humans in which each actor responds to the actions of the other in terms of their meanings to him or her, thus fitting together a joint line of conduct.

Socialization   The process by which a person learns to *internalize* the rules and expectations for behavior of the society or social group to which she or he belongs.

Social Organization   Term for how activities, interactions, or systems are arranged or the concept that they are arranged in terms of *sociocultural* factors.

Social Support   A set of exchanges which provide the individual with primary relationships, material and physical assistance, and a sense of *Gemeinschaft*.

Social Structure   More or less stable patterns of personal and interpersonal action and relationships that serve as the organizing framework of social life. Often used to refer to the organization of the whole society.

Social Support Network   See *network*.

Social System   Often refers to how a society is set up, to *formal organizations,* or used as a synonym for *human system*.

Social World   A collection of people, groups, and *human systems* sharing a *subculture;* often used similarly to *community* but without reference to geographic proximity.

Society   A group of people who are more or less self sufficient and who share a common territory and culture.

Sociocultural   A term referring to the *social-structural* (organizational) and *cultural* (symbolic) aspects of social life simultaneously.

Socioeconomic Status   A measure combining a person's or group's education, income, and occupation as an index of position in the *stratification* system; abbreviated SES.

Status   A specific *position* in a *social structure* along with the rights and obligations that go with it; also used to refer to the evaluation of a person's social location in terms of the prestige, privileges, and life style it carries (e.g. "high" vs. "low" status).

Status Offender   A juvenile who is defined as acting in an illegal manner because of his or her age ("status").

Stereotype   A cluster of beliefs and attitudes used to characterize a whole category or group of people without regard for individual differences.

Stigma   Negative stereotyping that evaluates a person with "different" characteristics as "bad," "undesirable," "unclean," etc. Also refers to the characteristics themselves.

Stratification   Structured inequality; a hierarchical arrangement of groups or categories of people in a society creating different layers, or "strata" unequal in terms of power, privilege, prestige, and access to valued resources.

Structural Functionalism   A theory of society based on the concept that the *social system* is maintained by carrying out necessary functions and that *social structure* is created in the process of meeting society's functional needs.

Subculture   Portion of the total *culture* sharing the larger culture but also sharing meanings, norms, beliefs, life styles, etc., differing from those of the larger culture; ethnic, occupational, and age groups frequently possess their own subcultures.

Succession   The replacement over time of one group of inhabitants of a natural area by another.

Survey   A research procedure in which one interviews or gives questionnaires to a large number of people.

Symbol   Anything that stands for ("means") the qualities of something else; language, for example, is our species' single most important symbol system.

Symbolic Culture   Those elements of a *culture* based on shared meanings, interpretations, or understandings, including language, music, dancing, values, norms, and other patterns of conduct. Contrast with *material culture.*

Symbolic Interactionism   Theoretical school within the conduct paradigm stressing the exchange of meanings in social interaction as the key to understanding social life.

System   Any set of mutually interdependent elements organized into a whole; systems are characterized by the patterns of interconnectedness between these parts and are maintained by *feedback.*

Theory   An idea, statement, image, or formal proposition seeking to explain the relationship between two or more things or to make sense out of things.

Thomas Theorem   The concept, set forth by William I. and Dorothy Swain Thomas, that whatever a person or group defines to be real is real in its consequences; often referred to as *the definition of the situation.*

Total Institution   An organization that regulates all aspects of a person's life under a single bureaucratic authority and within which the person lives on a 24-hour-a-day basis (e.g., a hospital or a prison).

Urban Area   A city of at least 2500 inhabitants.

Urbanism   Louis Wirth's concept that there is a unique *subculture* and *life style* associated with city life.

Value Judging   Jumping to conclusions on flimsy evidence, ideas based on limited past experiences, prejudice, or lack of full awareness.

Values   Shared beliefs about what is good, right, proper, desirable (or their opposites) common to a *social group.*

Variable   In a theory or research project, any element, factor, social fact, or condition that can vary in some observable way (e.g., educational level, sex, age, *social class).*

Verstehen   A German word used in sociology to mean "deep understanding"; the tactic of seeking to understand the conduct of a social actor by seeing it from his or her viewpoint.

Voting Rights Act (1965)   An act of Congress specifying certain conditions in states and counties that, if found to exist, will trigger federal intervention in both voter registration and elections; greatly, increasing the registration of both blacks and lower-class whites in the southern United States.

Wholeness   General systems concept that the properties of the system cannot be predicated from its parts and that the whole system functions as an entity in its own right.

Work Group   The functional unit of an organization, the group or team that actually works together to get a job done.

Workplace   The setting within which work takes place, referring to both social organizational and physical contexts.

X   Statistical label often used interchangeably with *independent variable;* that which explains something else.

Y   Statistical label often used interchangeably with *dependent variable;* that which is explained by something else.

ABOUT THE AUTHORS

Harry Cohen, Ph.D., is a Professor of Sociology at Iowa State University, Ames, Iowa. A transplanted native of Brooklyn, New York, he lives in Iowa for the academic year and in San Francisco during summers. He is the author of *The Demonics of Bureaucracy* (1965) and *Connections: Understanding Social Relations* (1981), both published by Iowa State University Press.

Jan Fritz, Ph.D., is Assistant Professor of Sociology at Georgetown University in Washington, D.C., where she directs the Sociology Department's community internship program. Past-president of the Clinical Sociology Association, she has served as a consultant in educational institutions, companies, and crisis-intervention organizations, and conducts training workshops for clinical sociologists in conflict intervention and other professional skills. She is author of *The Clinical Sociology Handbook* (Garland, 1984).

John F. Glass, Ph.D., teaches part-time at Antioch University and other colleges and universities in the Los Angeles area, where he lives. First President of the Clinical Sociology Association, he practices as a clinical sociologist doing human relations training, organizational consulting, clinical supervision, and marriage and family counseling. A consulting editor of the *Journal of Applied Behavioral Science,* he is co-editor of *Humanistic Society: Today's Challenge to Sociology,* published by Goodyear in 1972.

William M. Hall, Ph.D., is Instructor in the Criminal Justice Program at Alfred University. His research interests include the juvenile justice system and police decision making. He also works as a part-time police officer in an upstate New York police department.

David J. Kallen, Ph.D., is Professor, Department of Pediatrics/Human Development, at Michigan State University, East Lansing, Michigan. A sociological social psychologist and author of numerous professional papers, he was Vice-President of the Clinical Sociology Association, 1982–1984.

Christopher A. Pack, Ph.D., is Associate Director of Medical Education at Bon Secours Hospital in Grosse Point, Michigan. He is a UCLA-trained sociologist.

Thomas J. Rice, Ph.D., teaches at Georgetown University in Washington, D.C., and is also External Examiner for the National University of

Ireland. An experienced consultant to government, industry, and educators seeking to humanize work environments, he is National Treasurer of the Association for Workplace Democracy and Vice-President of the Association for Humanist Sociology.

Patricia See, Ph.D., is Chairperson of the Sociology Department at Chapman College, Orange, California. She also maintains a small private practice and seeks to educate the broader Southern California community through public symposia and media coverage in such areas as prevention, problem solving, stress reduction, and conflict resolution. A native of Vermont, she has lived extensively in south Florida, Mississippi, and, now, Southern California.

Brian Sherman, Ph.D., is Research Director of the Voter Education Project and has been Research Analyst for the Southern Regional Council, an action research civil rights organization. He is co-founder of Sociologists on Call, a network of sociologists who donate their expertise to progressive social change groups. He is founder of the Available Resources Band, and is Public Service Director of WRFG, community radio in Atlanta.

Arthur B. Shostak, Ph.D., has been a clinical sociologist since 1961, first at the University of Pennsylvania and, since 1967, at Drexel University in Philadelphia. In addition to publishing 13 books and over 120 articles, he has lectured in Canada, England, and Israel and has consulted with government agencies, major unions, and companies like Proctor & Gamble, Johnson & Johnson, and Polaroid. A founding member of the World Future Society and past-president (1976–1977) of the Pennsylvania Sociological Society, his latest book is *Men and Abortion: Lessons, Losses, and Love* (Praeger, 1984).

Roger A. Straus, Ph.D., is Assistant Professor of Sociology at Alfred University in Alfred, New York. He previously engaged in private practice as a clinical sociologist and worked as a marketing executive. Founding editor of the *Clinical Sociology Newsletter,* he currently edits the *Annual Review of Hypnosis* for the International Society for Professional Hypnosis. Author of numerous professional papers, his first book for the general public, *Strategic Self-Hypnosis,* was published by Prentice-Hall in 1982.

Index